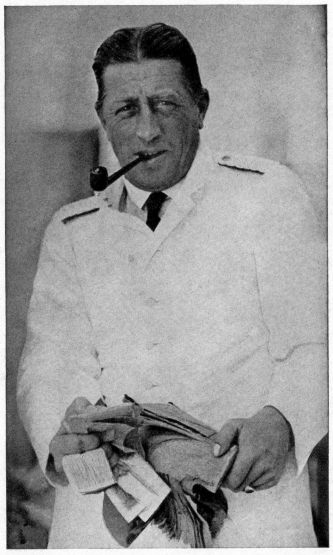
Count Felix Von Luckner, the most romantic and mysterious figure of the World War, with powerful hands tears a telephone book into four parts.

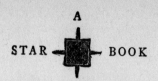

A STAR BOOK

COUNT LUCKNER, THE SEA DEVIL

By LOWELL THOMAS

*ILLUSTRATIONS
FROM PHOTOGRAPHS*

GARDEN CITY PUBLISHING COMPANY, INC.
GARDEN CITY, NEW YORK

CONTENTS

COUNT LUCKNER,
THE SEA DEVIL

COUNT LUCKNER
THE SEA DEVIL

I

WE MEET A FLYING BUCCANEER

IT WAS on a flying field in Central Europe that I first saw the "Sea Devil." We were on our way from London to Moscow by air, and had come as far as Stuttgart with stops at Paris and Basle. While waiting for the mechanics to tune up the big Fokker monoplane in which we were to cover the next stage to Berlin, we lunched in the little tea room on the edge of the flying field, kept by the widow of a German pilot killed in the war. Suddenly, through an open window, from off to the east in the direction of Munich and Ulm, we heard a familiar drone, and a moment later a silvery monoplane darted from a billowy cloud bank, the rays of the afternoon sun glistening now from one wing and now from the other. In a series of sliding swoops, with motor off and noiseless except for the whistle of the propeller, it dropped gently on to the turf and sped across the field.

Uniformed aërodrome attendants ran over, leaned their spidery metal ladder against the glistening duraluminum fuselage, and opened the cabin door. Two passengers descended, a giant of a man and a

dainty slip of a woman. The former, who climbed down first, was tall, of massive frame, with huge shoulders, and altogether one of the most powerful-looking men I had ever seen. After him came the little blonde, who looked for all the world like a fairy who had arrived on a sunbeam. Putting her slipper to the top rung of the ladder she jumped into her escort's arms.

What a voice that man had! It boomed across the flying field like a foghorn or the skipper of a Yankee whaler ordering his men aloft.

As they came toward us, he walked with a rolling seaman's gait. In his mouth was a nautical-looking pipe, and his jovial weather-beaten countenance suggested one who goes down to the sea. He wore a naval cap cocked over one eye, and a rakish light brown chinchilla coat, called a "British Warm."

Every pilot and mechanic on the field stopped work and saluted the couple. The mariner who had dropped from the sky saluted in all directions after the cheery but somewhat perfunctory manner of the Prince of Wales. One could see that he was accustomed to doing it, and presumably was someone of more than local fame. He even saluted us, as they passed into the little restaurant, although he had never set eyes on us before and we had not saluted him. But the newcomer seemed to take the whole world, including strangers, into the compass of his rollicking friendliness. We were still sitting on the veranda when they came out and drove off for Lake Constance. He called, or rather bellowed, "*Wiedersehen, wiedersehen,*" to everybody, as he squeezed into the door, and the frame of the limousine bent under his weight. The man simply radiated personality, and turning to the commandant of the Stuttgart Flug Platz, who stood near me, I said:

"Who is that?"

"That? Why that's the Sea Devil."

"And who may the Sea Devil be?"

"Why, the Sea Devil is Count Luckner, who commanded the raider *Seeadler*. The young lady is his countess."

I remembered the *Seeadler* vaguely as a sailing ship that had broken through the British blockade and played havoc with Allied shipping in the Atlantic and Pacific during the latter part of the war. Certainly, this Sea Devil looked the part of a rollicking buccaneer. I thought the age of pirates had vanished with the passing of Captain Kidd and the Barbary Corsairs, but here was one of the good old "Yo-ho, and a bottle of rum" type.

My wife and I continued our aërial jaunt across Europe, via Berlin, Königsberg, and Smolensk, to the capital of the Bolsheviks, but later on, while flying back and forth across Germany on our way from Constantinople to Copenhagen and from Finland to Spain, whenever we dropped down out of the skies in Germany we heard more of this Sea Devil. That first encounter with this modern buccaneer had aroused my curiosity, and each new yarn that I heard made me keen to see more of him. Incidentally, we found that he and his dainty countess were doing almost as much flying as we were, although entirely within the borders of Germany and Austria. Cities were declaring half holidays in his honour, and apparently this Sea Devil was more of a popular hero than even the great Von Hindenburg. As for the youth of Germany, they fairly idolized him, and crowds of boys met him at every aërodrome.

There were other German sea-raiders during the World War that most of us remember far more vividly than we recollect the *Seeadler*. They were the

Emden, the *Moewe* and the *Wolf*. But these three were either modern warships or fast auxiliary cruisers, while this giant count with the foghorn voice and the sea legs had run the blockade in a prehistoric old-fashioned sailing ship. That, together with an almost unbelievably adventurous personal story, made romance complete. Added to which we discovered that he had the unique and enviable reputation of disrupting Allied shipping without ever having taken a human life or so much as drowning a ship's cat.

Upon returning home from his buccaneering cruise the Count of course received a score of decorations, and his own government signally honoured him in a way that has rarely happened in German history. He was presented with a cross that places him outside the scope of German law. Like the kings of old, he "can do no wrong"—at any rate, not in his own country. He was even called to Rome and decorated by the Pope as "a great humanitarian."

When we encountered him at Stuttgart, he was on a sort of triumphal tour of Germany, exhorting the youth to prove worthy of their inheritance, and in cheery seaman's language he was telling the boys and girls to keep up their courage, "stay with the pumps, and not abandon the ship." They in turn seemed to look upon him as a modern Drake or John Paul Jones.

Upon our return from Moscow, we learned more and more of this Count Felix von Luckner: that he was a member of an old and famous military family, a descendant of a Marshal of France, who had run away to sea as a boy, and then served for seven years before the mast, roaming the wide world o'er under an assumed name as a common jack-tar, suffering the beatings, starvation, shipwreck, and other hardships that the sea visits upon its children. We heard how during his turns ashore he had even joined the Sal-

vation Army in Australia, had become a kangaroo
hunter, a prize-fighter, a wrestler, a beach-comber
and a Mexican soldier, standing on guard before the
door of Porfirio Diaz's presidential palace. Long
since given up as dead, he had been listed by the
Almanach de Gotha as missing.

Then, one day, after he had fought his way up
from a common seaman to the rank of an officer of
the German Navy, he returned to his family. A series of life-saving exploits had brought him fame,
with the result that he became the protégé of the
Kaiser. As an officer aboard the *Kron Prinz* the finest ship in the Imperial Navy, he had survived the
Battle of Jutland.

Then came his golden chance. Shortly after Jutland, he was commissioned to perform the audacious
feat of taking a sailing ship through the British blockade in order to raid Allied shipping.

The *Seeadler* maintained a destructive career for
months, ranging the South Atlantic and Pacific,
dodging cruisers and sinking merchant vessels. She
scuttled twenty-five million dollars' worth of shipping, and wrought incalculable damage by delaying
hundreds of cargo vessels from venturing out of port,
and raising the rates of marine insurance. After a
cruise as full of excitement and thrills as the voyages
of Captain Kidd and Sir Francis Drake, the Count's
raider was wrecked on the coral reefs of a South Sea
isle. From then on, the Sea Devil and his crew adven-
tured from atoll to atoll in the far-off Southern ocean,
passing from one surf-beaten shore to another in
open boats or in ships they contrived to capture.

We were sitting in the lobby of the Hotel Adlon
in Berlin, one evening, when again I saw that magnificent nautical figure. A mutual friend introduced us,
and that evening my wife and I listened to great

stories of the sea, told with a manner of inimitable vigour, sailor-like jollity, and dramatic inflection. After that, we met often, sometimes on board his trim schooner the *Vaterland*, on which he was setting out to sail round the world, and again at my home near New York, where the Sea Devil and his countess came. On these occasions, I got the complete story of his life and his buccaneering experiences on the most adventurous cruise of our time.

The Count is a born actor; in fact, I verily believe him to be the finest actor I have ever seen. If he had not run away to sea, what a career he might have had on the stage! But his inborn flair for pantomime was only to be heightened by life at sea. Sailors are vigorously expressive men, full of mimicry, and blustery actors of parts. You seldom see a sailor with the phlegmatic stolidity that you find in lumpish landlubbers. When the Count tells you he raised a marlinespike, he jumps to the fireplace, seizes a pair of tongs, and illustrates with it. When he tells how he knocked a man cold in Fiji for spitting in a sailor's face, he acts out the whole affair.

As a sailor, he had spent long years before the mast under the Union Jack and the Stars and Stripes. So he told his tale to me in racy sailor's English. He has one amusing peculiarity of speech. Nearly every other word is the expletive, "By Joe!" In explaining this, he remarked that the language of the sea consists principally of a blistering string of oaths. He said these oaths had become so much a part of him after seven years before the mast that for a long time afterward he was unable to express himself without using sulphury profanities. Of course, this caused him much embarrassment and trouble when he returned from his long voyages and attempted to qualify as a naval officer. It caused particular consternation

when, after his years at sea, he returned to the
bosom of his stately and highly respectable family.
In fact, he had to submit himself to a long and rig-
orous course of self-discipline to extract the blazing
nautical oaths from his common speech. He achieved
this in his English diction by a resort to the expression, "By Joe." Whenever one of these hair-raising
oceanic apostrophes came leaping on to his tongue,
he had trained himself so well that it automatically
changed itself into "By Joe." This habit still clings
to him as a salty reminder of fo'c'sle days.

At the time when Count Luckner was raiding the
seas, I had been thrown in contact with the most
picturesque adventurer that the World War had
brought forth—Lawrence of Arabia. Here, in the Sea
Devil, was his naval counterpart. They were the two
great adventurers of the two respective sides during
the World War. While Colonel Lawrence, mounted
on a ship of the desert, led raids across the sands of
Araby, Felix von Luckner scoured the seas in a windjammer. Lawrence led Bedouins on fleet Arabian
horses and racing camels, romantic people travelling
in the most romantic way known to land. The Sea
Devil commanded sailors before the mast on a sailing
ship, romantic people travelling in the most romantic
way known to the sea. In each, adventure climbed
close to its highest summit.

Lawrence was a man slight and frail, diffident, silent, and soft-spoken, who might have been taken
offhand for the most bashful of youths, a most eru-
dite scholar, an archæologist whom the war caught
practising his profession among the antiquities of
Assyria and Babylon. War and its forays must seem
the last degree removed from this studious and utterly cerebral spirit. One could find no greater contrast to him than in this brawny sea rover with the

booming voice and blustery manner, who raided the
seas from Skagerrak and Iceland to Fiji and the
Marquesas.

The ex-Kaiser, the ex-Crown Prince, Hindenburg,
Ludendorff, Von Tirpitz, and sundry others of our
late enemies, have given us their personal accounts of
the part they played in the World War. But none had
a tale to tell like Count Felix von Luckner. With
me the story lies close as a companion piece to the
story of Lawrence of Arabia, and I pass it on to you
in the words of the Sea Devil and, I hope, with something of the tang of the sea.*

---

*The reader will notice that in Count von Luckner's narrative, the
precise chronological order of events is occasionally not observed. The
map used as lining paper in this book shows the route of the *Seeadler*
and the names and dates of ships sunk, and other events in their chronological sequence.

II

FELIX RUNS OFF TO SEA

Take a windjammer out as a cruiser? Sneak through the blockade and go buccaneering on the high seas?

"By Joe!" I thought, "that's something."

It was a romantic thing all right in this day and age, when the sailing ship is getting to be something of a relic of the fine old times, the heroic age of the sea. But it wasn't because I had read a lot of sea stories and had become fascinated with the old world of rigging and canvas. I had been there myself, had been there good and proper.

The reason I was assigned to the command of the *Seeadler* was because I was the only officer in the German Navy who had had actual experience with sail. I was born Graf Felix von Luckner and was now a lieutenant commander, in the Imperial Service, but I had spent seven years of my early life as a common jack-tar before the mast. The fo'c'sle was as familiar to me as charts are to an admiral. That was why this windjammer cruise of war meant so deuced much to me, why it hit so close and was so personal.

I cannot make that part of it clear without telling you something of my early life at sea, a thing or two about the old days when sailing before the mast was all they say—and more. It's a yarn about shipwreck, storm, and cantankerous captains. So, sit yourself down there, by Joe, while I light my pipe and weigh anchor.

My first mental picture of life at sea dates away
back to the time when I was a little fellow living in
quiet, charming old Dresden. I saw a bill of fare
from the liner, *Fuerst Bismarck*. By Joe, there were
fine delicacies on it. I read it until my jaws began to
move. So that was how people feasted at sea? Ah,
then, how wonderful it must be to be a sailor. Perhaps, some day, I might become the captain of a
great steamer where they had meals like that. The
more I thought of it, the better I liked the idea, and
from then on I had my mind set on going to sea. I
read of the voyages of the wily Odysseus and of Sind-
bad the Sailor. On the river near our home I built a
boat of an old box and christened it the *Pirate*.

"Oceans, straits, and gulfs are all very fine, but
of what concern are they to a Von Luckner?" asked
my father. "You are to be a cavalryman."

You see, my great-grandfather had started the
cavalry tradition among us Von Luckners. They had
tried to make a monk of him, and had put him in a
monastery. But he didn't like that job, and among
his fellows at the monastery he was called "Luckner
libertinus." When he was thirteen years old, he ran
away and joined the army of the Turks, in a war
against the Austrians. In those days, the cavalrymen
all had boys to feed and look after the horses, carry
munitions, and clean rifles. So, while still a mere
lad, my great-grandfather became a professional
soldier, a soldier of fortune. After he had learned a
lot about the Turks, he left them and joined the Austrians. That was when he was fifteen years old. Later
on, he joined the Prussian Army, as a lieutenant of
cavalry, under Frederick the Great.

Finally, he formed his own regiment, which became
famous throughout all Europe as "Count Luckner's
Hussars." They had their own specially designed

On board the *Cæsarea*, the skinflint captain and part of his crew, Phelax Leudige standing fifth from the left.

The wreck of the *Cæsarea*.

The runaway sailor came home at last, but not until he had worn the Kaiser's uniform with honour. He dropped the name "Phelax Leudige," and after completing his studies and examinations saved five lives, became famous, and was promoted to the rank of Lieutenant-Commander in the Imperial Navy.

brown uniforms, and as mercenaries they fought in any war that came along. In those days, it was the custom for soldiers to fight for whoever could afford to pay them. The King of Hanover was in the habit of buying regiments, and my great-grandfather sold him his on the condition that it was still to be known as "Count Luckner's Hussars." The King broke his word. So my warlike ancestor went to the King's castle, boldly charged him with treachery, then took off his mantle and tunic covered with the decorations that the King had given him and threw them into the open fire.

"Henceforth I will fight against you," he shouted.

Shortly after this, he joined forces with the King of France, and then, during the French Revolution, he continued to serve the new French government as the commander of the Army of the Rhine. When the *Marseillaise* was written, it was dedicated to him because he happened to be the commanding general in the region where this immortal song was composed. After winning a number of important victories in Belgium, he was made a Marshal of France.

When the campaign was over, he led his army to the outskirts of Paris, and then, accompanied only by his aides, he went into the city to demand the back pay that was due to his soldiers. But instead of getting it, he was treacherously seized and sent to the guillotine. You see, it was cheaper to kill him than pay him. Although always a Royalist at heart, he was above all a soldier, and fought faithfully and valiantly for any monarch or government willing to hire his famous regiment. All our histories tell of him and his gallant deeds.

From then on, all Luckners became cavalrymen. It seemed to be in the blood. My grandfather, an officer, was accidentally killed while on a hunting expe-

dition. My father fought in all the wars from 1848 down to the World War. In 1914, when he was ninety, he wanted to join up again. He insisted that he was still able to do patrol duty, because his eyesight was unimpaired and he was still a horseman. When the general staff refused his request on the ground that he was too old, he was very angry.

"It is because I am so old that they *should* take me," he said. "Let me serve as an example to the younger soldiers. I have fought in many wars, and will be living proof to them that the surest way to live a long and healthy life is to be a soldier."

Ships, harbours, the seven seas had nothing to do with a Von Luckner. My father scoffed at my talk of becoming a sailor, so I never spoke to him any further about it. He tried to tell me what a fine cavalryman I would make, and asked me to promise that I would wear the Emperor's uniform with honour.

Now, in Germany, unless you had a good education, there was no hope of your ever becoming an officer. And the courses were stiff. Instead of studying, I preferred to read your American Indian stories, especially those of James Fenimore Cooper. I knew the names of many of your famous Indian chiefs, and as a youngster I dreamed of voyaging to America to hunt buffalo.

My father hired a tutor to cram me with book knowledge, but after six months that worthy went to him in despair and said:

"It is no use; the boy doesn't learn. There is a devil in him."

Next they put me in a private school in the country, thinking that association with other boys would fill me with ambition to learn. Instead, I learned how to fight. Although only ten years old, I was a husky

young devil, fond of sports, and ready for anything that would provide a thrill. My father thought the teacher was too soft for me, so he sent me off to another school, where the teacher was a strong man and something of a ruffian himself. By Joe, how that man used to pound me! My father also gave me many lickings, and I considered he was entitled to do so. But this other man? Well, I stood it from him just once. Then, when the second beating came, I ran away. For eight days nobody knew where I was. I lived in the fields like an animal, eating apples and other fruits. Then they found me. My poor father was ready to give me up as hopeless, but I still had a true friend, my grandmother. She told my father he had been far too stern with me, and said to him:

"Give me the boy, Henry. A little kindness may still make a good lad of him."

"You are welcome to try," responded my father, "but you will only spoil him the more."

Well, Grandmother had the right idea. She made a bargain with me. There were thirty-four boys in my class at school, and in my studies I always stood thirty-fourth.

"My lad," she said, "study conscientiously and I will give you fifty pennies every time you advance a place. I will continue doing this until you are at the head of the class!"

I couldn't figure right then how much I stood to make. I never was much at arithmetic. But I guessed it would be considerable, and I considered Grandmother a good fairy.

I studied with all my might. The next examination came, and others were ahead, but not I. I was in despair. My grandmother encouraged me, and I studied still harder. Another examination came, and I moved up four seats! She gave me two hundred

pennies, and I felt like a millionaire. But at the following examination I dropped back two seats. She was not discouraged with me and said she hardly expected me to go ahead without a few rebuffs. I was afraid she would demand a rebate for the places I had lost, but she did not. I now saw myself clear of all financial difficulties. By going ahead with an occasional dropping back, my income would be endless.

I turned into quite a despicable swindler, but it was not out of pure avarice. I had formed the idea of breeding rabbits and had set my eye on a fine rabbit sire that would cost me several marks. To get the sum needed I would have to be promoted several seats which, I reasoned, could be easily done, especially with occasional slidings back. But I had bad luck and got no more promotions. What was to be done? I needed the money. So I told Grandmother that I had been promoted two places. I got the pennies. Another week I told her I had gone ahead three places; another week one; and still another week four. The intricacies of finance and greed led me to a series of fake promotions that soon landed me at the head of the class. I had the cheek to put on that I had gained that honour.

Of course, Grandmother was happy and very proud of the success of her policy of kindness with me. One day, she happened to meet my school superintendent and could not resist expressing her elation.

"And what do you think of our Felix? Here he has progressed to the first place in his class by that simple method of mine of giving him fifty pennies for every form he moves up. I tell you, there is nothing like kindness. It takes a grandmother to handle a boy."

In utter astonishment, the superintendent replied:
"What, Felix in first place? That's some mis-
understanding. So far as I know, Felix is in thirty-
fourth place."

My grandmother rushed home and began to over-
whelm me with reproaches. It happened that she had
two bulldogs, one thirteen and the other fourteen
years old. They suffered from asthma. The wheezing
dogs started a commotion in the next room. That di-
verted her attention from me, and she bustled out
to see what was the matter. When she returned, her
flare of temper had subsided, and she merely said
laconically and finally that she was through with me.
"In you there is a devil," she cried.

She did not tell my father of the adventure, for
fear it would make her ridiculous. All he knew was
that, when Easter came, I was promoted on probation, with the accompanying suggestion that it would
be best if I left school. So he sent me to a school in
Halle, a city of Prussian Saxony, and engaged a
private tutor to coach me in addition.

The end of my school days now came speedily.
My father, perhaps taking a leaf out of my grandmother's book, resorted to a promise. If I were
promoted, I would be allowed to visit my cousin, who
lived on an estate in the country, a thing that I
wanted very much to do. When the examinations
came, my father was away. He had left me with the
tutor, who was to permit me to depart for my cousin's
estate if I gained the promotion. As usual I flunked the
examination, and came home angry and sullen. The
tutor met me, eagerly asking whether I had been
promoted. I bit my lips and lied impudently. I said
I had been promoted, but that the superintendent was
away and had not been able to sign my report, which

would be mailed later. The tutor, delighted that his coaching had been so successful, gave me immediate permission to leave for my cousin's.

I took my father's big boots, his water boots, his little coat, his trousers, his sport shoes. I was big for my thirteen and a half years, and they would fit me. My brother and I each had a savings bank. I had eighty marks in mine. He had one hundred and ten marks in his. I took my savings and forty marks of his. I would repay him later.

I was away. Where? If I had a devil in me, surely it must be a sea devil, because I now dreamed of nothing but the sea. I had promised my father to wear the Emperor's uniform with honour. I would not return home until I wore the Emperor's naval uniform, and with honour. I was firm in my decision about this.

I was all excited when I stepped off the train in Hamburg. Here was the great seaport town, and here was I, a lad going to sea. In the railroad station I saw a large sign advertising the Concordia Hotel with the prices of accommodations listed, from fifty to seventy-five pfennigs a cot. That seemed a little high to me, but never mind. A porter took my baggage. I was well dressed, and he treated me with a good deal of respect. When I directed him to the Concordia, he looked at me.

"So you are one of those fellows driving out to sea?" He changed instantly from polite German to common, vulgar, Low German in addressing me.

I had stumbled on the sailors' favourite hotel, but sailors didn't seem to be held in much respect by porters.

When I got to the Concordia, I soon discovered that sailors do not frequent palatial hostelries. It was a "rear house," situated in a back yard. Here in

America you would call it a "sailors' flop." I asked the clerk for a cot, for seventy-five pfennigs. He showed me into a room where there were six cots. I remonstrated that, when I paid the highest rate, I didn't want to sleep in a room with five other people. He laughed and replied that if I was not satisfied with five companions he would give me a fifty-pfennig room with forty-nine companions. I chose the five.

My first evening I spent along the famous Hamburg water front, Sankt Pauli, known to sailors the world over. There was the gigantic "Vanity Fair," or White City with all its lights and excitement. Here I saw all manner of seafaring folk, from Malays to West Indians. In front of some of the amusement halls stood African Negroes in weird costumes.

At the shipyards, where I offered my services as a cabin boy, I was told that, since I was only thirteen and a half years old, they would have to have a written permission from my father before they could engage me. So I decided I had better address myself directly to captains aboard their ships. When I went to the part of the harbour where sailing ships rode at anchor, I found it an immense basin with a forest of masts, and the vessels moored at considerable distance offshore.

While gazing longingly at them and wondering what to do next, I came upon an old man and got into conversation with him. He was a salt-bitten tar. For thirty-five years he had sailed before the mast. Now, in his old age, he operated a little ferryboat. So I asked him to row me out to one of the ships. The old tar handled his jolly-boat with amazing skill. Never before had I seen anyone scull. As I gazed up at the lofty masts all around us, old Peter told me

that sailors had to climb these in storms when it was impossible for a greenhorn to hold on.

I went aboard several ships, but the captains also insisted on my showing them permission from my father. After I had been turned down, old Peter saw that my spirits were at low ebb. When I admitted to him that I had run away from home, it seemed to touch the sympathy of the old wanderer. But when I told him my father was a landowner and a count, he looked at me in awe.

"A count? Why, that ranks next to a king!"

He could hardly get over it—a count's son running away to become a sailor before the mast! The tragedy of it made him take such an interest in me that we instantly became warm friends, and he asked me to come and share his humble quarters. From then on, for a week, I spent most of my time with old Peter Boemer.

"For thirty-five years, for my whole life," he pleaded in his broad Hamburg dialect, "I was a sailor. What have I now? All I am is captain of this little rowboat, carrying people for a few pfennings a trip. Go back to the Count, your father, and when he gives you a licking for this, thank him for every lick."

I must go home. He was certain of that. He must persuade me to go home. But the idea of notifying my parents never occurred to him. That would be squealing, and squealing is not a virtue among sailors. I saw him every day for a week, and notwithstanding all of his unanswerable arguments, still I refused to go home. At last he saw that it was hopeless to plead with me any longer, so he agreed to help me get on a ship without having any papers.

He got me a post as cabin boy aboard the *Niobe*, a craft the memory of which grows more vivid with the

passing of the years. Then he insisted upon seeing to it that I was properly outfitted for the sea. Under his direction, I expended the last of my money for warm underclothing, oilskins, a sheath knife, tobacco, and a pipe. I was very proud of the pipe. He took me to his room high up in a dingy house on a dingy street. Suspended from the ceiling was a stuffed flying fish. On a wall hung the painting of a ship on sail canvas. I was filled with admiration when Peter told me he had painted it himself. In a cage was a parrot, as old and dishevelled as Peter. He had brought it from Brazil, and it spoke only Portuguese. On the bureau were Chinese curios and other souvenirs of long voyages.

"And this is my sea chest," he said, as he hauled forth an ancient weather-beaten but staunch box, and emptied out of it various examples of his own weaving and knitting.

"Every sailor needs a sea chest," he continued. "It is watertight and will float. For thirty-five years it travelled with me around the world. It is yours now, by Joe, and I hope it will serve you as well as it served me."

That old sea chest was destined to serve me well as long as I had it. I lost it when I ran away from the lighthouse at Cape Leeuwin, Australia.

He put me aboard the *Niobe*, that never-to-be-forgotten argosy, showed me to my bunk, and fixed my mattress and bolster.

"You are born a count"—he shook his head—"and you become a sailor. Count and sailor don't go together. It is like a Paris shoe on a Russian peasant's foot. You are Count Felix von Luckner no longer. You must change your name."

Then and there I rechristened myself, took the name of my mother's family, and called myself

Phelax Luedige. Under that name I sailed the seas for seven years.

My last gift from old Peter was a motto. Putting his hands on my shoulders he said:

"My boy, always remember, one hand for yourself, and one for the ship."

By this he meant that, when aloft, I must hold on with one hand and work with the other. But the motto had a wider meaning than that. In every channel, sea, or backwater of life—one hand for yourself and one for the ship.

I stood at the rail while the tug towed the *Niobe* out of the harbour. Old Peter, with his marvellously skilful stroke, sculled alongside the slowly moving vessel all the way out past the piers of Sankt Pauli.

"My boy, God speed you," he shouted. "This is as far as I can go. I will never see you again. It's hard on old Peter to see you go away."

I wanted to shout something in return, but tears were streaming down my cheeks.

Peter had carefully packed my sea chest, and when I opened it I found his picture right under the lid. Across the bottom he had scrawled, "Don't forget your old Peter."

The low coast gradually melted into the haze. Years were to pass before I should return to my homeland and to the friend who had helped me get to sea.

III

SAVED BY AN ALBATROSS

THE Russian full-rigged ship *Niobe*, bound for Fremantle, Australia, was an old craft, dirty and mean. I have seen many another like her, but she was a classic. Her captain, too, was something of a classic. When old Peter spoke to him about taking me, although I had no permission from my parents, he replied:

"I will take him provided he doesn't want any pay!"

I didn't want any pay, but should have preferred a more agreeable-looking shipmaster. He had a sour, sallow face with a long goatee, half Mephisto, half Napoleon III. He hated Germans.

I knew no Russian. The others knew no German, except the captain. He knew it brokenly, just enough to abuse me. The helmsman spoke a little English. I had learned a few words of English in school. I never did learn Russian. That language has always been a puzzle to me. During the long trip of eighty days on the *Niobe* I was among people whose talk between themselves, and nearly all of whose speech addressed to me, I couldn't understand.

I discovered the helmsman's knowledge of English the first day out. I was delighted to find that here was at least one sailor with whom I could converse. He asked me questions. What was my father?

"A farmer," I replied.

"Well, then," quoth he, "it will be just the right thing if I appoint you chief inspector."

That sounded important, and I walked a little stiffly as he led me down the deck. We came to a pig pen where there were half a dozen large and particularly filthy porkers. The chief inspector's office was that of cleaning the pig sty.

"And besides," the helmsman added cordially, "I will appoint you superintendent of the starboard and larboard pharmacies." I promptly discovered that in the language of the sea a pharmacy was a latrine.

In cleaning the sty, I was not allowed to let the pigs out. I had to go in there with them, and it was very narrow quarters. The unspeakably dirty animals rubbed against me constantly while I laboured with pail and brush. The sewage was so deep that it filled my shoes. I had only two pairs of trousers. Soap and water were not to be wasted. I grew filthier than the pigs. And then there were the "clinics."

Everyone kicked me because I looked like a pig and smelled like one. They called me "Pig." For food I had to go around and eat what the sailors left on their plates. They said that was the way pigs were fed. For breakfast, instead of coffee and rolls, there was vodka with stale bread to soak in it. I got the leavings of this. The salted meat, of which I got the scraps, was so strong that I could scarcely force it down my throat. I often thought of that bill of fare from the *Fuerst Bismarck*, which had lingered in my thoughts. I had made a mistake there, by Joe.

I was afraid of the masts. I dreaded the thought of going aloft. But I said to myself that I must get used to it. So I climbed desperately every day, a little higher, a little higher, always practising. Finally,

one day, I got to the crow's nest, halfway to the top. I thought that was fine. I felt so proud I called down for the others to see where I was.

"Any old sea cook can get that far," the helmsman shouted back scornfully.

That hurt me and made me all the more determined to learn how to go aloft as the sailors did. I kept trying, and I watched the other apprentices skipping nimbly high up in the rigging.

We had a storm rounding the Cape of Good Hope, followed by a heavy swell. All the sails had been reefed except the storm sail, and we were ready to set the main topsail. Eager to show how much I had learned about going aloft, I climbed up to help unfurl the canvas. I forgot old Peter's advice: one hand for the ship, the other for yourself. The sail, filled with a sudden gust of wind, blew out like a balloon. I fell. I grabbed hold of the gasket, the rope that holds the sail to the yard, but it burned through my hands. I dropped ninety feet on to the braces, the ropes that hold the yard. If I had struck the deck, I would have been killed. At that moment the ship heaved with a swelling wave, and I was thrown out into the sea.

The *Niobe* was tearing along with a speed of eight knots. I came up astern. The wash in her wake swirled me around, but I could see a sailor throwing me a life preserver. I couldn't find it. The waves were too high. I sank, and when I came up I saw the ship a long, long distance away, it seemed. I threw off my heavy oilskins and sea boots, although there seemed little use trying to save myself by swimming. Even if they did put out a lifeboat, they would never be able to find me in that heavy sea.

Above me hovered several albatross, those huge white birds that seem to think everything floating is

for them to eat. They swooped down upon me. I was ready to sink, but still had enough strength to fight at them, waving with one hand and then another. A great white form swooped down. A bird's talons seized a human hand. And I in turn clutched at it. A drowning man grasps a straw, even a bird. The albatross beat the air with its wings, frantically trying to rise. I still kept my grip on its claw. The huge bird was keeping me afloat. Then the albatross began to strike at my hand with its beak. It hurt and wounded me badly. I have the scars on my hand to this day. Still I held on.

"Phelax," I said to myself, "you will never get back to your ship, but maybe another ship will find you if you don't let go."

The other albatross were flying above, circling around, watching the strange proceedings

It seemed to me as though my hand had been torn away by the repeated striking of that beak. Then, all at once, a swell lifted me high above the other waves, and I saw a lifeboat coming. I let go of the albatross, and he was glad to get away, by Joe. He shot up into the air to join his companions. That bird had saved my life, and so had his friends. The sailors could never have found me had they not seen those birds hovering above me. They knew that I must be swimming there.

In the boat I said to myself that I supposed the captain would be happy to see me back again. When we came alongside, he stood up there above, pointing down at me.

"You, you ——! Come up here! I wish to —— you had stayed out there and that we were rid of you! Look, my sails are blown away, blown away."

In the commotion caused by my going overboard,

he had lost two sails. I sat down there in the little boat with the blood flowing out of my hand and trembling. The sea was high, and the lifeboat danced up and down while the sailors made vain efforts to swing it over the davits. In a wild toss the boat rose as high as the ship's gunwales. I was so excited that I made a crazy jump, hit the deck, and was knocked unconscious.

A moment later, the boat was smashed against the ship's side. The sailors were pitched into the water, nine of them. For a while, it seemed that some of them would drown, and it was only after a struggle that the last of them managed to catch a rope and clamber on deck.

I lay stunned. The captain leaned over me and shouted in my face.

"You German dogs like to guzzle. Wake up and take some of this!"

He put the neck of a vodka bottle in my mouth and let the liquid fire trickle down my throat. Next day I was too sick to stand on my feet. The captain ordered me out of my bunk and to work. I tried but couldn't get up. Then he beat me, saying I was a drunken loafer.

Later I learned that when I had fallen overboard the quartermaster immediately called for volunteers to man the lifeboat. The captain, who had never dreamed of sending help to me, shouted to him, shaking a harpoon:

"If you lower the boat, you will get this harpoon in your belly."

As a matter of fact, they were not obliged to send a boat for me. A captain need not attempt the rescue of a man overboard if it is liable to endanger the lives of others of his crew.

The quartermaster, however, calmly walked away, got his volunteers, lowered the boat, went after me, and left the captain in a towering rage.

The shock of that experience brought on a sort of nervous spasm which made my hands shake. I was like that for four years, and even to-day I sometimes have nightmares and dream of falling from a mast, of the albatross, of the captain and the vodka.

I lay in my bunk and thought it over. I had been Count Felix von Luckner, of a titled, landowning family, descendant of a long line of military officers and of an illustrious Marshal of France. Now I was a mere cleaner of the pig sties and the latrines, fed like a pig on scraps left by others, cursed and beaten and considered by the captain to be carrion not worth saving from the sea. I said to myself:

"You put yourself in this fix, by Joe, and you've got to take your humiliation and punishment like a man."

So this was the life at sea? Certainly, it was not what I had expected. I wondered if I had made a mistake. Well, mistake or no mistake, I had promised my father to wear the Emperor's uniform with honour, and I would not go home until I wore the Emperor's naval uniform with honour. But how far away from me now seemed epaulettes and gold braid.

The *Niobe* did not put in at a single port on our way out. After we passed through the English Channel, until we reached Western Australia, we saw nothing save sky and sea, the sky light or dark, the sea in quiet or in storm. In fact, we only came in sight of land once. This was when we sighted an island somewhere off the African coast. I could see palms, rows of palms, and white houses with red roofs and green shutters. I stood at the rail and gazed. What a joy it must be to walk and breathe on that green

island. It seemed an abode of all happy things. I was sure that living there must be a fairy princess. I was very much of a boy, and I had been reared on German stories. I was wretched, and yonder was a land so fair. It must be the haunt of a fairy princess. I stood with my elbows on the rail and my chin on my hands and dreamed of her.

Singular that I should have then thought of a fairy princess. A few years later, I visited that same isle. By then I had become a naval officer of the Kaiser. I wandered all through its palm groves, remembering how once I had sailed past it, the miserable cabin boy of the *Niobe*, and had had visions of a fairy. This time I did indeed find a fairy princess there, and promptly lost my heart to her. We became engaged, and a little later she became the guardian angel of the raider in which I sailed the seas. She was a visitor on the isle, and her name was Irma.

But my fairy princess was only a wild fancy as I stood at the rail of the *Niobe*. The dreamy bit of land with its graceful palms and pretty houses grew small in the distance as the wind bellied out the mainsail and swept us on toward Cape Verde. Finally, I was left gazing at a speck that vanished on the horizon. And still I remained motionless and in my trance, until a howl cracked my ears and a kick nearly split me in two.

"Get along there, you loafer," roared the captain.

But the latter part of the voyage was not so bad as the first. I was getting used to mistreatment, and was rapidly developing into a hardened seaman. The captain remained brutal, and so did most of the men, but there were several who grew kind toward me, among them the boatswain and the helmsman. So I began to experience some of that

comradeship of the sea for which a sailor will endure many a hardship.

Finally, after eighty days at sea without touching at a single port, we sailed into the harbour at Fremantle. I had always thought of Australia as a land of kangaroos, of black aborigines with bows and arrows, and of bushrangers. But Fremantle turned out to be as commonplace and bleak a port as you could hope to see. However, I met some sailors off a German ship, and the sound of my native language and association with my countrymen made me happy. They took me to the Hotel Royal. They went there to drink beer and I to share their company. But the proprietor had a daughter, and I transferred my interest to her. She was what you call a bonnie lassie, and she listened to my chatter. After I told her my story, she urged me to desert from my ship. She even talked to her father about me and got him to take me on as a dishwasher. That was all right. Dishwashing had been perhaps the most elegant of all the jobs assigned to me on the *Niobe*. But I could not abandon old Peter's sea chest. So the German sailors helped me to smuggle it off the ship. The *Niobe* sailed presently. Luckily, the captain did not ask the police to find me, as he had a right to do. Maybe he considered himself lucky to get rid of me.

IV

SALVATION, KANGAROOS, AND FAKIRS IN AUSTRALIA

ABOUT the only amusement I could find in Fremantle was listening to the Salvation Army band. They had a hall where they had preaching and where bums and sailors stood up and told lurid tales of their experiences. Then they all sang songs. It was the songs I liked. I couldn't tell much about the words, but the tunes were lively and the big drum fascinated me. This music was altogether different from the music back home in our churches at Dresden. But what interested me most of all was that this Salvation Army post had a gramophone. I had never seen one before. I had come to Australia expecting to find a wilderness of kangaroos and savages, and here was this marvellous product of civilization.

"By Joe, Felix," I said to myself, "everything in the world is different from what you thought."

I couldn't shake off the notion that this gramophone was a hoax. I thought somebody hidden must be talking into that horn. I could not get near enough to investigate. The place was always crowded, and only those who "got religion" were allowed up front. So I persuaded a friend of mine from a German boat to keep me company, and we went up at a big meeting and offered ourselves for salvation. We gave testimony of our past sins and told what bad sailor lads we had been, and then we signed a pledge never to touch strong drink.

The gramophone was O. K., I found, and that made the Salvation Army O. K. with me. I became enthusiastic, somehow, or other, with the songs and excitement. I actually "got religion." I joined up, and they gave me a job putting moth balls in clothing donated by charitable people. At any rate, I no longer had to wash dishes, and here was an army in which I might become a lieutenant. I remembered how my father had wanted me to become a lieutenant in the German Army. Why not become a lieutenant in the Salvation Army instead? I used to daydream and build castles in the air like this while placing those moth balls in the piles of old clothes.

Since I was converted and saved and stood on holy ground, I felt I should tell the whole truth. So, one night at a meeting, I got up and testified and told my fellow soldiers of the Salvation Army that my right name was Count Felix von Luckner. That made a sensation. They immediately used me for advertisement. "Halleluiah! We have saved a German count from perdition," they announced. "Before he came here he drank whisky like a fish. Now he is a teetotaller."

Well, by Joe, people came from all over town to see the reformed count.

They put me in a uniform and sent me out to sell the *War Cry*. I sold a lot. People didn't mind buying the *War Cry* from a count. I thought I could become a captain. It was no trouble to leave whisky alone, *because I had never tasted it in my life*. But I did like lemonade and ginger ale, especially ginger ale, which I thought contained alcohol because they offered it to me in the bars where I sold the *War Cry* and because it tasted so delicious. I thought I was putting something over. They got on to it in the saloons and had their joke with me.

"Count, have a ginger ale," they would call whenever they saw me, and I would wink and drink it down. I thought they were laughing because I had put one over, and I laughed too.

I got tired of it. I got tired of everything except the sea. I was a sailor, I reasoned, and the only lieutenant I could ever be was a naval lieutenant and the only kind of captain a ship captain. The Salvation Army people were very good to me. They said I was too young to be a sailor, but that they would get me a job somewhere near the sea. So they found me a job in a lighthouse. It was almost like being at sea, they told me. All day I could look out and see fair weather or storms with ships sailing at peace or rolling and heaving.

I became assistant to the lighthouse keeper of the Cape Leeuwin Beacon, which is south of Fremantle and the biggest light on the southwest Australian coast. "Assistant"—what a fine title! And "beacon," a word that meant everything to the ships driven by the fury of the storm. Wasn't I a sailor who knew all about that from experience? Well, they put me to cleaning the "windows"—that is, the lenses. The thousands of prisms of the reflector astonished me not a little. Each day I wound up the weights for the revolving apparatus. The rest of the time, when I was not sleeping, I kept watch. There were three other lighthouse keepers, who lived in little houses on the cliff. They passed the days playing cards and fishing. They had pushed all of their duties on to me. For doing their work I got ninepence a day!

The daughter of one of the lighthouse keepers was named Eva. She was pretty and very charming. One day I kissed her. It was an innocent kiss, but we were in a bad place, a room with a locked door,

but which was open on the side of the sea and looked down on the beach. One of the men was fishing there and saw us. He hurried to Eva's father. Soon there was a cursing and knocking at the locked door. We were terrified. The threats and banging grew more violent. I threw the door open, dashed out and away, frightened half out of my wits.

I left behind me all my belongings. That was how I lost the sea chest that old Peter had given me. It was too bad. Late that night I sneaked back and made off with one of the horses. It was worth about thirty shillings, which I figured was about the value of the luggage I had to abandon.

I rode to Port Augusta, and for a time worked in a sawmill. The work was frightfully hard. The pay seemed good, thirty shillings a day, but the cost of living was so high—one had even to pay for water —that it left only a few shillings out of a day's pay. The work was lucrative only for Chinese coolies, with their low standards of living. I was able to save sixty shillings and then couldn't stand it any longer.

One day I met a Norwegian hunter who had been shooting kangaroos and wallabies and selling their skins. I gave him my money, and my watch that I had brought from Germany, and he gave me his rifle. Then I went into the forest and became a hunter, or at least tried to. After a month, the solitude got on my nerves, and I left the kangaroos in full possession of their native bush.

In Port Augusta I watched a steamer discharge its passengers.

"Oh," I said, "what kind of a crowd is that?"

They were a troupe of Hindu fakirs. Unable to withhold my curiosity, I went up and talked to them. When they learned that I was a sailor, they said I

was exactly the man they needed for pitching their large tents, currying the horses, and distributing advertisements, and the like. They explained that their trade was similar to mine, since they were always on the move, only they travelled on land.

They had with them several dark-eyed Hindu girls who looked bewitching. I joined the fakirs.

We travelled from one end of Australia to the other. I pitched their tents and booths in public places. Handling the canvas did remind me a little of my work as a sailor. In Fremantle, when I went around passing out handbills, I heard on all sides:

"Hello, Count. No more Salvation Army, eh? Have a ginger ale."

I found the ginger ale as good as ever.

The fakirs made a mango tree grow before your very eyes. It is one of the classic tricks of India. It was my task after the show was over to clear the place where the tree had miraculously grown. I could never find any sign of preparation. A bowl of water would be brought in and shown to the spectators. The fakir would sit down in such a way as to hide it from the audience. In a little while he would step aside and the bowl would be filled with live goldfish. I could never discover any mechanism for this. A fakir would say to a spectator:

"That is a valuable ring you have on your finger. You must not lose it, But, look, you have lost it already. I have it on my finger."

And, indeed, he would have it on his finger.

There was a little Malayan girl with whom I flirted, thinking I could learn the secret of the tricks from her. At first she was very shy, but then became more friendly. She did tell me how some of the magic was done, but only some of the minor effects. I learned them quite well, and to this day can perform

them. The major spectacles, she, herself, thought were miracles. It seems to me impossible for any European ever to learn the more important secrets of these sorcerers. The old masters, accustomed to be worshipped as beings endowed with supernatural powers, hold themselves inaccessible. The two chief fakirs of our company, with their long beards and a poise made perfect by lifelong training of the will, made a sublime picture.

One Sunday morning I sat on the beach washing my clothes. Three men came up, stopped and gazed at me. They looked me over as though I were beef on the hoof. I have always been big-framed and powerfully muscled, with an arm like iron, and shoulders as wide as a barn door, bulging with sinews.

"How old are you, boy?"

I replied that I was nearly sixteen.

"How would you like to learn boxing?"

"Very much," I replied, "because if I knew how to spar, I would be less likely to get a thrashing."

They took me to a school of boxing, where I was submitted to another examination. They gave me six pounds sterling and agreed to train me for the prize ring. In return, I was to box for Queensland, exclusively.

That began a strenuous time for me. I was put to work with all kinds of gymnastic apparatus to harden my body, particularly chest and stomach, to resist blows. I went through three months of that kind of training before I was allowed to try a boxing pass. Then I practised sparring with an experienced boxer. I was told that, after I had progressed far enough, I would be sent to San Francisco for additional training and would make my début there as "the Prize Boxer of Queensland." It all looked very rosy. I liked boxing and do to this day.

An American craft was in port, the *Golden Shore* a four-masted schooner plying between Queensland and Honolulu. She was later put on the San Francisco–Vancouver–Honolulu run. They needed hands and offered to take me as an able-bodied seaman at the excellent pay of forty-five dollars a month. From cabin boy to able-bodied seaman in one jump—that was an inducement, by Joe. The usual line of succession is: cabin boy, yeoman, 'prentice seaman, able-bodied seaman. I guess I was made to be a sailor, because that promotion looked bigger than anything else in the world. I quit my boxing and shipped aboard the *Golden Shore*.

In Honolulu I came upon a mystery, a fantastic mystery. It sounds unbelievable. I, myself, cannot explain it. Someday I hope to meet someone who can. One of the cabin boys aboard the *Golden Shore* was a German named Nauke. He was a violin maker by trade who had lost all his money and put to sea. We became fast friends. At Honolulu, Nauke invited me to go ashore with him. He brought along a can of condensed milk, a delicacy he knew I liked. We went sightseeing, and one of the sights was that of royalty. We stood outside of the palace grounds and watched the Hawaiian potentate while he had tea. He sat in a reed chair, and a couple of his wives stood beside him. A well-dressed gentleman who seemed to be on a stroll came up to us and began to talk to us in English.

"Don't waste your time on anything like that," he said. "Why not see the hula-hula dance?"

Nauke and I said all right, because the hula-hula was just what we did want to see.

The gentleman asked whether we had any better clothes to wear, to which we responded that we had not.

"It doesn't matter," he said, "I will provide you with a suit each."

He took us to a carriage drawn by four mules, and we all got in. I remarked to Nauke that the gentleman seemed to be a man of means. The gentleman turned his head.

"You mustn't talk so much," he said in German.

We came to the sugar plantations outside the town. The carriage stopped. Our host led us to a field path, until finally we came to a European house that had an air of distinction. Young colts grazed within a fence. Through the large windows of the stately villa I saw a row of large black tables such as are used in Germany, in a lecture room. Our host told Nauke to wait outside, and got a piece of cake for him. I whispered to Nauke not to go away.

I felt very strange on entering the house. The man showed me into a room next to the hall with the many tables. He was about to lock the door. I asked him not to. In the room was a long black table like those I had seen in the other room. The man said he was going upstairs to get a measuring tape. While he was gone, I noticed that under the table were two long narrow boxes with heavy locks on both sides. What if I should end in one of those boxes! But I was confident. What had I learned boxing for?

The stranger returned with a tape. He measured my arm. Unlike a tailor, he measured from wrist to shoulder instead of from shoulder to wrist.

"Thirty," he announced, repeated it once, and muttered several other numbers between his teeth.

He pulled my coat halfway down my back, thus hindering my arms. He remarked that the light was poor, and turned me so that my back was toward the outer door. I could hear a creaking that told me someone was moving behind that door. I noticed on

the floor below the lower part of the table a disorderly pile of old clothes which looked as though they might be sailors' togs. The gentleman took off my belt and laid it on the table. Attached to the belt was my knife case. It was empty. I wondered where my knife might be. I remembered having it that morning. I had peeled potatoes with it. My blood froze as between empty bottles on the window sill I saw a chopped off human thumb with a long sinew attached. The gentleman was about to let down my trousers, which would have kept me from running.

I jerked my coat back into place, knocked the man down with a heavy blow, grabbed my empty knife case from the table, kicked open the nearest door to the open, and jumped out, shouting for Nauke. He appeared, still munching his piece of cake. We ran out into the plantation and threw ourselves down among the cane. There was the sound of a whistle and of galloping horses and running men. They were hunting for us along the roads. We groped our way among the fields, and, after losing our way several times, finally reached the beach.

We looked up an English-speaking policeman and told him our story. He shrugged his shoulders and said it would take a special force of detectives to discover how many sailors had mysteriously disappeared on the islands. Our captain merely remarked that we deserved a good thrashing for going ashore. We sailors on the ship laid a plan to take the plantation by storm on the following Sunday, and gathered our weapons for the raid. But on Friday a quarantine was proclaimed, due to some infectious disease that was spreading, and the raid was off. In later times, I often inquired about the strange circumstance, and heard tales of white sailors disappearing on the islands, but never a solution of the mystery.

On board the *Golden Shore* was a lad named August from Winsen on the Luhe, in Germany. He and I talked over the ever-beguiling idea of serving a master no longer, but of being our own masters. We knew that fishing was considered good on the western coast of North America, and we determined to go into business for ourselves as fishermen. The *Golden Shore* took her course to Seattle, and there we were informed that the fishing was best around Vancouver. At Vancouver we looked things over and came to the conclusion that the ideal thing would be to live in a boat and hunt and fish by turns. That would be a state of perfect independence. We used what money we had to buy a rifle. Now all we needed was a boat.

At the fishing village of Modeville, a number of sailboats were moored off shore. They belonged to Indians and half-breeds, whose camp fires we could see and whose savage dogs barked out fierce alarms. It was about dusk. Cautiously, we launched one of the canoes on the beach and paddled out to one of the sailboats that had taken our fancy. We got aboard quietly and cut the anchor rope. The boat was set lightly for drying. There was only a slight breeze, and we drifted very slowly. Somebody ashore saw the boat drifting. A canoe came paddling out in leisurely fashion. We gave the sail a hoist to get up more speed. The men in the canoe noticed this at once. They yelled and paddled hard. We were in a fix. But as we passed out of the lee of the high mountains, we got a windfall, the sail bellied out, and the boat scudded swiftly along. From the shore they fired at us with rifles, but we were away.

We sailed to Seattle, and there the sailors of a German boat gave us a supply of food and some white lead with which to paint our boat. We hunted and

fished and got along, and then grew tired of it. We were honest lads, and tried to return our boat secretly to Modeville. We were caught and haled before a Canadian judge. He was lenient and put us on probation for a few weeks.

That was my first adventure at piracy.

In Vancouver I signed on the four-masted English ship, the *Pinmore*, on which I was now to make the longest uninterrupted voyage of my life. It took us two hundred and eighty-five days to sail from San Francisco around the Horn to Liverpool. We had rations for a hundred and eighty days, and sea water got into our water tanks. We lay in calms for long periods on our way south, and then were held back by long-continued storms off Cape Horn.

It was as though that ship harboured a devil. We did not meet a single craft that we could ask for provisions. None of the rain clouds that went drifting past came near enough to provide us with water. Between the half rations and the brackish water in our tanks, six men died of scurvy and beri-beri, and the rest were so ill with these dread diseases that their abdomens and legs swelled up as though with dropsy. We used only the storm sails. None of us was able to climb into the rigging. When at length we sighted England off the Scillys, the last portion of peas had been distributed, and when the tug hove up to us in St. George's Channel we all cried, "Water, water!" We drank all the water that we could hold, and still we were thirsty. Our bodies were dried up. I was a fortnight in hospital.

I gave the *Pinmore* a willing farewell, hoping never to see her again. Strange how coincidence turns. I did see her again, a long time later, from the deck of my raider *Seeadler*.

WRESTLING CHAMPION OF SANKT PAULI

WHEN a German sailor came back from a cruise with a bit of money burning holes in his pockets, Hamburg and the bright lights of Sankt Pauli were his goal. When I left the *Pinmore*, I had a thousand marks in my jeans. This was a new thrill, and I had it all changed into silver, so that I could feast my eyes on it. Proudly I strutted down Sankt Pauli water front, a full-fledged sailor, back from his first cruise around the world. I swaggered like a veteran old salt. But my thoughts were not of the gay amusement parlours of Sankt Pauli. There was another mission that had brought me to Hamburg.

I went to the old house at the Brauerknechtergraben and climbed the creaking stairs. The name Peter Breumer was still on the door. A broken old woman answered my knock and ushered me in. From the roof hung the flying fish. On the wall was the painting of the ship. The ragged parrot was in its cage.

"Peter? He is dead. I live here now. I am his sister."

"Peter dead?"

"Yes, three years ago. And that's you, his boy, whom he helped to go to sea. How often he said: 'Where may the boy be now?' But Peter is gone."

I went to his grave at Ohlsdorf. It was shabby. I got a big iron anchor and had a brass plate fixed on

it with the engraving: "I did not forget you.—
Your boy." Then I placed it on Peter's grave, a
fitting monument for a sailor.

Since the raids of the *Seeadler* the grave of old
Peter has become a kind of shrine where people
visit, especially German children.

It was in December, and the festival called the
Hamburg Dom was being held. In Sankt Pauli were
many diversions and shows. In one show, Lipstulian
the wrestler held forth. Fifty marks were offered to
anyone who could throw him. My pals said:

"Go up there, Phelax. You can beat him."

I said no. I had no desire to make myself conspicu-
ous. On the platform the wrestler drew himself up
in his tights and taunted me.

"My lad, you had better bring along a bag in
which to carry home your bones."

I considered this an insult, and climbed on to the
stand. The barker outside shouted.

"Step inside, ladies and gentlemen. We have
found a sucker who is going to get his bones crushed."

Lipstulian paced the platform like a prize steer.
I gave my purse to our sailmaker to hold. Attendants
escorted me to a little booth, where they dressed me
in a red and white shirt and pants and a belt. When
I stepped on to the platform Lipstulian looked at
my bare arms and became pensive.

It was not real wrestling, but merely a test of raw
strength. Lipstulian tried to jerk me to him and tip
me over before the signal had been given. That made
me angry. I seized him, but could not lift him.
The sailors howled encouragement to me. One of
my shipmates offered me an additional fifty marks
if I downed him. On the third attempt I lifted him.
He tried to support his foot against a tent pole, but
slipped. I threw him to the floor.

The barker howled that I had not put the champion on his back. That found little favour with the audience. There was a tremendous din. The sailors were ready for trouble. The manager paid me in silver. He gave me, however, twenty instead of the promised fifty marks. I did not protest. I felt good-natured. My shipmates were hoisting me on their shoulders. They carried me to the nearest saloon, where, as the victor, I treated the crowd again and again.

My shipmates took me to a photographer, where they had a picture made of me in wrestling togs with the inscription on it—the Champion Wrestler of Sankt Pauli. By Joe, but I was proud of that picture. It was a visible indication that I had been somebody.

That night I sat looking at it. I had often wanted to write to my parents. They must think me dead by now. I was ashamed to have them hear from me as a nobody. But now . . . I looked at the picture again. On the back of that formidable representation of the Champion Wrestler of Sankt Pauli I wrote: "To my dear father for remembrance, from his faithful son Felix, 1902." I addressed an envelope.

Then my courage left me. The difference between that photograph and our life at home, between the "Champion Wrestler of Sankt Pauli" and the stately, severe Count Heinrich von Luckner, my father, came vividly upon me and made my heart sink. I put the picture back in my sea chest.

The remembrance came back to me how my father expected me to become an officer in the Imperial Service, and how I had vowed that I would never go back until I was a naval officer in the Imperial Service. Let them think me dead until I was able to go home clad in the Imperial naval uniform.

When I did return home as a naval officer, I jokingly showed my father the photograph of the Champion Wrestler of Sankt Pauli. He took it from me and for years carried it proudly in his wallet.

THE TRAGIC CRUISE OF THE *CÆSAREA*

BY JOE, I've got a real sea yarn to tell you now. Wait a minute till I light my pipe, and I'll tell you about the voyage of the *Cæsarea*.

She was my first German ship. With a cargo bound for Melbourne, we set sail from Hamburg. My friend Nauke was aboard, and again we were comrades. The captain was a clever sailor, but an old skinflint. The cook, who on German ships is called "Smutje"—smudgy, smutty—was a good fellow, but was keen to please the miserly captain. Together, they did wonders in skimping our food. On Monday we got peas, on Tuesday beans, on Wednesday, for a change, yellow peas, on Thursday brown beans, on Friday "blue Henry," which looked like coffee beans, but smaller, on Saturday corned beef (bully beef), and on Sunday, as a Sabbatical delicacy, we got a special dish called "plum and dumplings." The fare never changed, and we were always hungry. Very good, Smutje, you were an excellent fellow at heart, but that penny-squeezing captain made a son-of-a-gun of a sea cook out of you, and you are the hero of this tale.

One day I was sitting on a topyard. I could hear Smutje down in the galley whistling "My Heart Is Like a Beehive," which was a song hit of those days. I whistled along with him. My heart was like a bee-

hive, and girls were the bees and one of them was the queen bee. I could see her floating in front of me. Yes, it was the same fairy princess of my dreams whom I had seen in imagination from the deck of the *Niobe* on that first voyage when we sighted the Isle of Fuerteventura in the Canaries. My fairy princess lived on that distant tropic island of waving palms and white houses. So I whistled as loud as I could the same tune that Smutje was whistling, "My Heart Is Like a Beehive."

"What is that?"

I couldn't trust my eyes. I saw two arms thrust from the galley. They supported a big tray, which they thrust on to the skylight of the galley. The tray was heaped with a big stack of pancakes. What? A thousand miles out at sea, and pancakes fresh and warm?

I slid down the rope, and tiptoed to the galley. I took that stack of pancakes from the plate and slipped them inside my shirt, against my breast. Then I climbed to the yardarm again. Whew! By Joe, those pancakes were hot! They were burning into my flesh. When I was halfway up the mast I thought I should fall down, but I kept saying over and over, "Phelax, you are a sailor now, and a sailor never winces." When I was aloft I laid the pancakes on the yard, and ate them as fast as I could. There were fourteen of those pancakes.

Smutje was still whistling. "Ah, but just wait, you old sea cook, and see what kind of a beehive your heart is in a few minutes!"

Two arms were thrust out of the galley, and very carefully, so the flapjacks might not slide off, the empty platter was lowered. Next a long shrill whistle and then a smothered cry:

"My flapjacks!"

Smutje came climbing to the roof of the galley, thinking that perhaps with the rolling of the ship the flapjacks had slid off the plate. Then he roared, cursing:

"Damned pack of thieves."

I called down from aloft.

"Who is a thief, Smutje?"

"Not you," he replied, "because you are working up there. But did you see anybody take my flapjacks?"

"No, I haven't been looking that way, Smutje."

I slid down to talk with him, still amazed at the phenomenon of encountering fresh, hot—very hot—flapjacks on the high seas.

"What was that you were talking about, Smutje? Flapjacks, how can that be?"

"I will tell you. Phelax. You are the only honest fellow aboard."

"I know that, but go ahead."

"It is the captain's birthday to-day, Phelax. Nobody aboard can make him a present except me. I fixed fourteen flapjacks for him. Is that too much for the captain's birthday?"

"No, Smutje, it is not too much."

"And a delicious cranberry jelly to go with them."

"Cranberry jelly, Smutje?"

"Yes; a fine cranberry compote. Now, by Joe, Phelax, you know I am a good fellow. I would say nothing if some son-of-a-gun stole one flapjack, but, by Joe, I say the one who took the whole fourteen is a son-of-a-gun, by Joe."

"I agree with your opinion, Smutje, he is a son-of-a-gun, by Joe."

"You are an honest fellow, Phelax, and I always give you the best. That cranberry compote is no use to me now, anyway. You can eat it because you are

honest and because you will help me to find the thief."

The compote was just what I needed, what I had missed. It should have been spread between the pancakes, but still it was going to the same place.

"How can I catch the thief, Smutje?"

"Watch to-night, and see who eats the least peas."

"All right, Smutje, I will watch."

"Be sure to catch him, Phelax, and now, because you are honest, here is the cranberry compote."

It was delicious.

That night I reported to Smutje that each of the other men had eaten approximately an equal amount of peas. It was not part of the bargain to report that I had scarcely eaten any. I promised to continue the hunt for the culprit, and Smutje was confirmed in his opinion that I was the only honest man aboard.

The *Cæsarea* docked in Melbourne, and there an important event occurred. The captain invited the German consul to dinner, and then took counsel with Smutje.

"We must have something good when the consul comes."

Smutje immediately fell in with the suggestion and replied: "Yes, on such an occasion nothing is too good."

The captain restrained his enthusiasm.

"But there must not be too much expense."

"No, certainly not. Let us have ducks. That is something good and does not cost much around here."

I heard the captain inviting the first mate to his table.

"But don't forget to put on a white collar, Mate. It is the consul who is coming."

"Thank you, sir, thank you." And the first mate grinned all over his face.

Then the captain tackled the second mate.

"I invite you to supper to-night at eight bells. The consul is coming."

"Thank you, sir, thank you." The second mate wiped his mouth with the back of his hand.

It was on a Saturday. I sat near the porthole of the galley, patching my trousers and very busy at it. All the while I kept an eye on Smutje preparing the ducks. They were roasted, stuffed with prunes and apples, and I do love them that way. I was waiting for the moment when Smutje would go aft to get something.

I didn't see the captain. He was sitting on the bridge reading his newspaper, apparently. He had made a hole in the middle of the page, through which he looked down into the open door of the galley and kept his eye on the ducks. At first he did not see me. The mast was in the way. Then he happened to lean to one side, and caught sight of me near the porthole industriously mending my trousers.

Suddenly, a marlinespike came flying past me.

"You loafer, by Joe. What are you sniffing around the galley for? And so you brought your pants along for wrapping purposes!"

I promptly moved on.

At night the consul came. The captain and the mates were all dolled up. They had even cleaned their finger nails. In the cabin the consul was the only one who was given a napkin. On the skylight sat Nauke and I. We watched the ducks on the table. We had brought along a boat hook, waiting for the moment when the consul should leave.

The consul ate well, but the captain seemed to have very little appetite. He took only one small helping of the duck. The two mates held back out of

politeness. It would have been bad manners for them
to eat more than the captain.

When the duck course was done the captain would
not let the birds be taken away, but kept them in
his sight. When the consul left, the captain had to
escort him to the gangway, but he ushered the mates
out first, so that they would not have a chance
to snatch a drumstick, and, before he left the cabin,
he had Smutje take the ducks away to the pantry.
Nauke and I watched all this from the skylight.
There was no chance for us to use our boathook.

The pantry, however, could be reached from the
bull's-eye. We waited till Smutje had gone to his
bunk, and then stole our way to the bull's-eye. I
reached in. Good luck. The pantry was open. Smutje
must have forgotten to close it. The unfortunate part
of it, however, was that it was the *captain* who had
left the pantry door open. He had stolen down to
have his fill of ducks, and at this moment was sitting at a table with a bird before him. His back was
turned to the pantry.

I fished around and first got a big handful of plum
and apple stuffing, which I put in my pants pocket
for safe keeping. I was very quiet about it, and the
captain heard nothing. I felt around again, and found
a whole, fine bird. It must have been my excitement
and delight which caused me to make a slight noise.
The captain looked around and saw the magnificent
fowl suspended in midair and going away. With half
a drumstick in his mouth he yelled:

"My bird!"

Then he jumped, and grabbed my arm just as it
was disappearing.

"Let go that bird," he howled, twisting my arm.

I let the bird go, and kept silent in spite of the

pain, hoping that he would let me go without learning who I was. He reached for a rope and spliced my arm to the brass handle of the drawer. Nauke reached into my pants pocket and took out the stuffing to save it from destruction during the coming licking.

The captain came out.

"Oh, it's you, Phelax. You don't like ducks, do you? But you like the rope's end."

With that, he gave me an awful beating with a rope's end. I howled, by Joe.

Limping and sore, I went forward to get my share of the stuffing from Nauke. He had eaten it all. That made me so angry that, in spite of my soreness, I passed a good share of my licking on to him. Smutje shook his head and remarked sadly that the society of thieves had corrupted the only honest fellow aboard.

We took on a supply of sausages made out of pemmican that were to be sewn up in canvas and whitewashed so they would keep. For this work younger seamen are used, they being considered more honest and unspoiled than the older hands. I was not in line for the job. However, we slipped appropriate advice to the yeomen on the sly. Broomsticks were cut up in lengths a trifle shorter than the sausages. The two ends of sausages were cut off and spliced to the ends of the pieces of broomstick. The dummies were then tied up in sail cloth in such a way that the ends could be inspected. After this they were whitewashed. When the captain carefully counted the one hundred and sixty sausages and inspected the unmistakable sausage ends of each one, he said:

"Thank God, boys, that you are still honest."

Later on he stormed and raged when he had to revise this good opinion.

We contrived to swipe a number of hams out of

the galley. The captain accused Smutje, which made that honest sea cook so indignant that he deserted the ship at Newcastle. Now there was no cook, no Smutje. The captain asked for volunteers, but none came forward. Ships' cooks as a rule think themselves indispensable and irreplaceable, and make the sailors think so, when in fact they often cannot do more than cook pea soup and fry doughnuts.

"If nobody wants to be the cook," said the captain, "I shall have to commandeer one. Phelax, can you boil water?"

"Yes, sir."

"Into the galley, then, and beware if you burn the peas."

I did not know how long my new job would last, so I immediately began to eat until I was ready to burst. My first pea soup was a great success. I took care, and, to make myself popular, put in a hambone and half a bottle of the captain's red wine. The captain and the crew all said:

"What a soup, Phelax! You are a master cook."

The next day the bean soup burned. I had heard that in a case like that the thing to do was to put some soda in. I didn't know how much, so I tried two handfuls, and then added half a bottle of the captain's red wine. The soup still tasted good, and they said:

"Phelax, you are a born cook."

At six bells the soda had done its work, and I was fired from the galley. The captain was sick for three days. Nauke was ordered into the galley, and proceeded to do pretty well.

Four weeks after Smutje left us, we got him back. The harbour police found him in a hotel where he had been hired as a chef. He should have waited for deserting until the last day before sailing time,

as most men do when they clear out. There is less chance of recapture then.

After discharging cargo at Melbourne, we took on a shipload of Australian coal and set sail for Caleta Buena in Chile. I'll never forget that part of the voyage, because I managed to pass New Year's in a Chilean dungeon. After a spree ashore, I determined to go back to the ship in a certain particular direction. I went in that direction until I came to a wall. I climbed over it and fell into a pig sty. Hearing the grunts of the porkers, the owner of the place, a very dignified gentleman, came out. I told him I wanted to go to my ship.

"I will escort you to your ship," he offered with grave politeness.

With no less politeness, I accepted his kindness.

He led me to a house, in front of which stood a police guard. I was astonished, but he invited me to enter. I did.

"This thief has tried to steal my pigs," he told the police officers inside.

"I want to get back to my ship," I protested.

They threw me into a cell, where there were a number of others, sailors among them, who had been celebrating New Year's Eve too well. I fell asleep on a bench. I awakened. A woman was being hurled into the cell. I fell asleep, and when I became conscious again, I found that the new arrival had taken a place beside me, and fallen asleep with her head in my lap. I raised her from my lap, to place her on the bench. She yelled, "*Robadores!—caramba.*" The guard came in, and the señora, still shrieking, told him that I had beaten her. They seized me and threw me down a dark stairway into a dungeon. I fell over a mule harness into a pile of saltpetre dust. I put my head on the harness and fell asleep again.

"Phelax, it is the reward of your honesty. First for your honesty you get the compote of cranberries. Now you get two pain expellers instead of one—for your honesty."

Eleven years later, as an officer in the Imperial Navy, I went from Kiel to attend a dinner in Hamburg. At the Hamburg railway station, as I called for a taxi, I heard a voice quite close to me.

"Hello there, Phelax."

"Hello, Smutje."

"How have you changed, Phelax! Are you an officer in the Imperial Navy?"

"Yes, Smutje."

"How have you changed, Phelax! Do you still remember your old cookie?"

"You bet I remember you, Smutje."

"Well, how have you changed, Phelax!"

"By Joe, Smutje, I have an invitation to dinner, but I'd rather have dinner with you. Come along."

I took him in the taxi to Hotel Atlantic, the finest in Hamburg. Bellboys came to open the door and usher us in. Cookie looked around.

"This too, Phelax?"

"Yes, Smutje."

"How have you changed, Phelax!"

I ordered champagne and cigarettes brought to a private room. There Smutje and I sat talking over old times. The waiter brought the wine. Cookie looked at the waiter's evening clothes in awe and then looked at me.

"How have you changed, Phelax!"

He essayed to grow friendly with the waiter, and ventured a familiar, joking remark. But the pompous waiter disdained to talk to such a fellow, ignored him, and turned to me.

"Do you wish anything else, Count?"

"Hey, Phelax, did you hear what he called you? Count! Are you a count?"

"Yes, Smutje."

"How have you changed, Phelax!"

He thought for a while, and then gave me his two hands.

"You swiped my fourteen pancakes, Phelax. I haven't forgotten it. I shall be proud all my life that a count swiped my pancakes."

The *Cæsarea* took on a cargo for New York. It consisted chiefly of chalk packed in barrels. Abaft we had a load of arsenic, three hundred tons packed in small barrels, which, because of its great weight, took up little room. It was a badly stowed, ill-balanced load. Of our new crew, some were sent from Hamburg and some were signed in England. These latter were stokers and trimmers who had never been on a sailing ship before. They could neither steer nor set sails. They received higher wages than we, and yet we had to do all the work. As a consequence, we treated them pretty roughly. Even our Hamburg cabin boys, whose duty it was to clean the sailors' quarters, were loath to do this for the green hands who knew less than they.

The captain had hopes of a fast run to New York, which certainly seemed an easy jump after our trip through the latitudes of the hurricanes. But we had storm after storm from the first day out, and could make scarcely any headway at all. With our worthless crew, it was particularly miserable and trying. Christmas came, and with it the first fine weather and a fair wind. After a long time, we could set the topgallant sails again. It was fine to see the deck dry once more. The captain said:

"This is a sign from God. Let us celebrate Christmas properly."

So thankful was he that the old skinflint gave orders for Christmas cheer regardless of expense. In sailor fashion, we made a Christmas tree out of a broomstick and decorated it with coloured paper. The captain sent down a ham and a bowl of punch. When the candles were lit, a committee called on him to wish him a Merry Christmas and invite him to look at the tree. He accepted, and came down jovial and merry. Our new Smutje brought the flowing bowl, and we stood in line, each glass in hand, ready to toast the captain.

Then a white squall struck us.

A squall is called white when you have not seen it coming. It hit us square on the bow. The ship shivered from one end to the other, and was pushed sternwise. The foremast went overboard. Its yard smashed upon my bunk. The main topmast followed. Everything went to pieces. Only the lower masts remained. We tumbled on deck. The captain ran to the steering wheel, where the helmsman had been knocked down and could not get up. (He died two days later.) The combers were sweeping over the ship. With axes we cut away the wreckage. The sails on the lower yards, the only ones that were in place, had to be braced into the wind. In four hours we had the ship under control again. The green crew had hidden themselves below. We were so enraged with them now that they did not dare to show their faces.

The storm turned into a hurricane. It blew throughout Christmas night and the next day. On the second afternoon of the storm, at eight bells, the steerage deck broke under the heavy load of arsenic. That broke several rivets, and the ship began to leak. We hurried to shift the barrels. Several had burst. We did not realize our danger from the arsenic dust. It produced terrible inflammation, and after several

days most of us were badly swollen and bloated. Nevertheless, the arsenic was stowed again.

The ship started going down at the bow, and the carpenter reported three feet of water in the hold.

"Clear the pumps!"

We pumped, by Joe. The water in the hold grew deeper. We pumped until we grew weak. They gave us liquor to strengthen us. When we felt we could go on no longer, the cry went up:

"Grog ahoy!"

The grog made us pump again, although we doubted that we would win out.

A breaker came over the deck and swept away the galley. The cookie was making coffee for us and warming himself at the fire. He went overboard with his stove, pots, pans, and the coal box. He hung for a moment on the chimney, crying out for help at the top of his voice. There was no chance to save him. An old sailmaker next to me shouted:

"Smutje, you're all right. You've got plenty of coal for your trip to the devil."

That joke in the teeth of death made me shiver, since death was so close to us all

We worked at the pumps for forty-eight hours. The water in the hold rose higher and higher. We were at the end of our rope. The constant drink, too, had worn us out. We could pump no longer. The captain, harpoon in hand, threatened:

"The one who stops pumping, I'll harpoon him."

A voice from abaft sang out:

"Look out! Breaker!"

At the pumps we could not see the comber, but we heard it roaring. It broke over us. Six men were swept away from the pumps. Two were washed straight overboard. A third was thrown against the shrouds. His arm was smashed, and then he was

washed overboard. Another's skull was fractured. Still another was left on the deck in a heap with several broken bones. I was lucky. There were several timbers on the deck. I braced myself with one foot between two of them. The wave drove them together and pinned my foot. I fell, and my leg snapped. The timbers still held my foot, while the swirling water tugged and twisted me as though it were determined to carry me into the sea.

The mate released me with a crowbar, and the captain had me taken to his cabin. My leg was bent like an L.

"We have lost seven men," he said, "and we cannot afford to lose another. Carpenter!"

They tied me to one wall and fastened a block and tackle to the drawer of the sideboard. They hitched the tackle to the foot of my broken leg, and pulled slowly until the leg was straight and the bones in place. By Joe, it hurt. The carpenter measured me and made a pair of splints, which they fastened tightly to the leg. The splints were long enough to act as a wooden leg, and I could walk around, painfully, but enough to be of some use.

The *Cæsarea* was sinking now. We cleared the lifeboats. But first we poured out oil to calm the sea. The boats were swung overboard and lowered into the water with long ropes attached to them. A man tied a rope around his body, jumped overboard, and swam over to the boat and climbed in. The next one followed and was hauled in by the first one. They tied a rope to me and threw it to the men in a boat. Then they threw me overboard, and the men pulled me to the boat. One boat was under the command of the captain. The first mate had the other. We could make no headway rowing, so we simply held the boats against the heavy sea to keep them from overturning.

In spite of my broken leg, I did my share of the work.
The boats drifted apart. I was in the captain's boat.
The mate's boat was lost and never seen again.

The storm lasted for four days. We had a little
hardtack soaked with salt water, and a small supply
of fresh water. It was bitterly cold. What wood we
might have burned was soaking wet. It was almost
impossible to sleep. On the fourth day, we sighted a
steamer. Its course would take it some distance away
from us, but we were certain that we could hail it.
With great jubilation, we hoisted a pair of pants on a
mast as a signal. We were certain we saw the vessel
change its course. We were overjoyed. Nevertheless,
the steamer gradually disappeared.

All our food was gone now, and only a very little
water was left, which the captain, with an inflexible
will, doled out in minute quantities. The weather was
fair now, and we could sleep. Our thirst increased. We
sucked our hands to start the spittle in our mouths.
We wanted to drink sea water, knowing that it would
hasten our end. The captain encouraged us:

"Don't throw away your young lives. Look at me,
an old man. I won't give up."

On the sixth day, we decided to draw lots to deter-
mine which one should be sacrificed so the others
might drink his blood. No one proposed a start of
the drawing of lots, each afraid that he would draw
the fatal number. The authority of the captain still
preserved a remnant of drinking water to be doled
out. Late in the afternoon, we defied him, seized the
water, and drank the last drop.

The next morning we sighted a steamer. We waved
feebly, and she bore down upon us.

At that moment our last strength left us. We were
delirious with joy, but we could not move. We lay
slumped in our boat. The ship, the Italian steamer

Maracaibo, came alongside, and dropped rope lad-
ders. We were as if asleep. The *Maracaibo* had to get
its cranes out and hoist us aboard like pieces of
freight. Afterward, we were unable to remember how
we had reached the steamer's deck. We slept for
sixteen hours. When we awakened, all the doctor
would give us was a little milk. Three of our men
died. In New York, where we arrived the next day,
they went ashore and gorged on ham and eggs. It
killed them.

I was taken to the German hospital. My leg was in
such condition that at first they thought they would
have to amputate it, but finally the head surgeon
decided that he might be able to save it, and he did
save it. After eight weeks I left the hospital and was
ready to go to sea again.

VII

THE BEACH COMBER'S ADVENTURE
WITH THE *PANTHER*

THE leg I had broken aboard the *Cæsarea* was scarcely well knit when I broke the other leg. This was after I had shipped on the *Flying Fish*. But let me jump ahead a few years and tell you this tale exactly as I related it to the Emperor. That was after I had realized my boyhood ambition and become a lieutenant commander in the Imperial Navy.

H. M. S. *Kaiser* was one of the proudest ships of the German Navy. She was always kept spick and span. You can bet that she was shining now. His Majesty was aboard for a visit. We sat in the saloon after dinner, smoking, drinking, talking. For several days the Kaiser had amused himself by having me tell stories of my adventures before the mast. To-night the Emperor said to me:

"Luckner, what was your worst experience?"

I thought of the fight with the albatross, the scurvy and beri-beri aboard the *Pinmore*, the flogging at the rope's end aboard the *Cæsarea*, the three days in the dungeon in Chile, the setting of my broken leg with block and tackle, the plan to draw lots and see whose blood would be drunk in the drifting lifeboat.

"My worst time, Your Majesty? It was aboard Your Majesty's ship, the *Panther*."

The *Panther* was a small ship but a memorable one

in the German Navy. You will recall that it was the part she played in the Tangier dispute of 1908 that nearly brought on a world war at that time.

Von Plessen, the stately old courtier, glared at me. An admiral across from me scowled. The Emperor smiled.

"By thunder, you must tell me about it."

I told my story.

I had sailed on the Canadian schooner, *Flying Fish*, bound from Novia Scotia to Jamaica with a cargo of lumber. We had already entered the harbour of Kingston when the wind left us. While we were becalmed, we made ready for discharging the cargo. The ship lurched with a slight but unexpected roll. A beam slipped and fell against my leg. The bone snapped just above the ankle. They took me to a hospital ashore. On German ships, the owner is responsible for all accidents aboard, but on Canadian ships, you pay your own hospital bills.

"How much money have you?" they asked me at the hospital.

I replied that I had six pounds coming to me from the ship, which, according to regulations, the captain would deposit for me with the German consul, together with whatever articles of property I had on the ship. The hospital was not expensive, and the surgeon said the money would be enough.

Three weeks after I entered the hospital, they sent to the German Consulate for my money. Only three pounds was to my credit there. The captain of the *Flying Fish* had sailed away, taking half of my money with him. None of my belongings were at the Consulate either. He hadn't even bothered to leave them for me. At the hospital, they called me a liar and threw me out into the street. The plaster cast was still on my leg and foot. For clothing I had only what

I had worn to the hospital, trousers, jacket, and one boot.

I could not walk unaided, but I dragged myself to a stick of bamboo, which I broke into a length that I could use as a cane. With this support I could limp along.

"Phelax," I said to myself, "you must go to the ocean. It is your element. You must go to the beach."

I went to the sandy shore and lay there. When night came, I buried myself in the sand and slept all night, slept well. In the morning, I was half starved. I found some cocoanuts. Although terrible food for an empty stomach, I tried to eat them. While sitting there wondering what would become of me, a steamer arrived.

"Phelax," I said, "you are a sailor and there is a ship."

I took my stick and hobbled along the beach and down the long pier. The ship was a British collier, and they were making ready to unload coal. I went to the mate, told him what had happened to me, and asked him for a chance. The plaster cast was still on, and below my trouser leg my huge white foot looked like a club. In the hospital, I hadn't had a haircut or a shave. My hair was long and matted. My beard was half grown. My face was burned red from lying in the sun. The mate eyed me up and down.

"You look like a bum, by Joe. Clear out, by Joe, get out."

So they kicked me out, kicked me off a dirty collier, by Joe.

The collier discharged its coal in bags, and I found an empty bag. I was glad to have any new possession, even a gunny bag. I washed it out on the beach, and at night used it for a pillow. I still had my sheath

knife, and a Negro helped me cut the plaster cast from my leg and foot. Half of the skin went with it. The tropical sun burned the raw flesh until it swelled and ached dreadfully. The coal sack did me good service now. I stepped into it and wrapped the rest of it around my leg. It was a stocking and a shoe for me.

I saw a Negro cutting bamboo and gave him a hand. He took me to his hut and handed me sixpence and some maize to eat. It was cooked and warm. For days I had had only cocoanuts to eat. It was delicious. Rain began to fall, a heavy, tropical rain. It would not be good sleeping on the beach that night. I asked him to give me shelter in his hut. He looked at me just like the mate of that collier had done. Although he wouldn't have me in his hut, he said I might sleep in an old shanty covered with palm leaves where he kept his tools. It was dry, but all night I could hear cockroaches running around, on the walls, on the palm leaves, and big rats chasing them. Whenever I fell off to sleep, they ran over my face. Next morning the Negro gave me cooked maize again, and then we went out to cut bamboo.

Over the bay I saw a white boat, a wonderful white boat. It looked like a yacht. Oh, by Joe, if I could only get a chance on a beautiful boat like that. I hobbled down to the pier. The boat was coming in. It was a warship. Then I recognized the flag, the German flag. It was the *Panther*, the first German warship I had ever seen. It was so white and clean, oh, home, so white and clean! I was miserable and hungry, and there were my countrymen, a warship of my country. I felt my tangled beard and my long tangled hair. I looked down at my tattered clothes and the coal sack on my foot. Could I go to my country's ship looking as I did? I only stood and watched. Four officers in white uniforms came down

the gangway and down the pier. I went toward them
to hear the sound of German, and when I heard it I
was never so ashamed of myself. They passed near
me, but did not look at me.

"Phelax," I said, "that was what you might have
been if you had stayed at home and studied those
lessons."

I felt I could not look at the *Panther* any longer,
and went wandering miserably around the town. It
was dark. Three or four sailors came down the
street. They were talking and laughing. One of them,
a gigantic fellow, spoke in broad Saxon. When I heard
my native dialect, I thought to myself: "In the darkness nobody can see how you look. It would be good
to talk a few words in Saxon."

"Hello, *Landsmann*," I sang out, and I never let
myself go so broadly in the Saxon dialect as I did
then.

He stopped and talked with me. He was a stoker
on the *Panther* and hailed from Zwickau in Saxony.

Those fellows made me tell them about my plight.
Could they spare me a piece of bread? I asked.

"Sure," replied the Saxon. "Meet me at the end
of the pier at six bells. I have no more time now. I
must go back on board."

I was at the end of the pier fifteen minutes ahead
of time. The Saxon came off the ship and gave me a
great loaf of rye bread.

"Come to-morrow at the same time," he said,
"and there will be another loaf for you."

I did not sleep that night, but passed the hours on
the beach eating that bread. I nibbled it in slow bites
so that I might not lose any of the delight.

The Saxon gave me a loaf of bread every night,
and finally said:

"To-morrow is Sunday, and on Sunday we have

coffee and cakes aboard. Come aboard the *Panther* at half-past three to-morrow, and have coffee and cakes."

"By Joe, mate, can I come aboard a German warship like this?"

"Never mind, boy, we'll receive you." And he persuaded me to do what I wanted to do more than anything else.

When the sun rose the next morning, I started to make my toilet. The beach was my dressing room. The ocean was both mirror and wash basin. I scrubbed my hands and face with sand and water. I ran my fingers through my hair and beard, trying to comb them. I tried to smoothe the wrinkles out of my coat and trousers. I tucked the coal bag around my leg and foot fifty times, to make it look its best. I sneaked on board like a criminal. The sailors gave me a good reception. Everybody sat on benches, and had coffee and cake. There was a cannon under a tarpaulin. I tried to get a glimpse of it. I was bashful and ill at ease. I felt as though I was among rich people in a mansion.

The young officer of the watch passed and saw me. The sailors jumped up, and stood at attention. I stood up, putting the foot with the coal sack behind the other one to hide it. The officer called the boatswain.

"In the future," he said, "I want you to see that no such tramps get aboard. Throw this unspeakable creature off.

"Get out of here," yelled the boatswain.

I slunk across the deck to the gangplank like a beaten dog. I had seen this beautiful ship. I had seen a German warship for the first time. Poor castaway that I was, the sailors had welcomed me aboard. Holy feelings had been aroused in me. And now . . .

I heard the sailors mutter. One of them said quietly to me:

"Don't worry, Phelax. We will get you fine clothes. The lieutenant, we will take his pants. The boatswain, we will take his shirt. We will give you a coat, shoes, and a cap. The barber will be there too. At eight bells on the pier."

At eight bells on the pier they brought me the boatswain's blue shirt, the lieutenant's white trousers, and the remainder of a highly presentable outfit. The barber was along. He took me to the edge of the pier and cut my hair. My long hair fell down into the water. Then he shaved me. I could scarcely wait till morning to dress. Every article of my new clothes that I put on made me feel more like a millionaire, and when I threw away my coal bag and put on those fine shoes, I walked like the finest dandy in Berlin.

I went to the captain in charge of the piers. My smart clothes got for me an excellent post as dock inspector. After a month I went to sea again. With my dock inspector's recommendation, I got a good berth on the *Nova Scotia*, running between the West Indian islands.

The Kaiser listened to the story attentively, and when I had finished he looked queerly at the other officers. There was a twinkle in his eye.

"It would be appropriate and poetic," he said, "if Luckner went back to the *Panther* now."

So, a few months later, by order of the Emperor, I was transferred to the *Panther*, which was stationed in the Cameroons. I went down to Africa, and the moment I boarded the *Panther* I went to the fo'c'sle. None of the men I had seen there before were on the ship. It was the custom to transfer officers and crews every three years. I looked around, half expecting to see poor tattered Phelax sitting there somewhere. I

sat down where I sat before. Although an officer now in a trim, white uniform with gold braid, in reality I was that miserable beach comber Phelax, again. I dreamed I had the coal bag on my foot once more. I reached down and felt smooth hose and a smart shoe. I leaned back and dreamed of the coal bag.

VIII

PITFALLS FOR THE SAILOR, AND THE CANARY
THAT SPOKE LOW DEUTSCH

That's a sailor's life, glorious one day, miserable the next. I went on month after month drinking down in deep draughts the experience of the sea. A heady drink it is.

The sea is the sailor's power, yet he is always eager to get to port. There are two places that are ever in his mind: his home, if he has any, and the port where he will be paid off. For months Jack Tar handles no money. He dreams of the wad of bank bills that will be placed in his hands and of ways to spend it. Aboard, no magazine or newspaper, no matter how old, is left unread. Old fashion plates go from hand to hand. An evening suit with a waistcoat cut as low as possible so as to show a vast expanse of festive shirt front arouses a general discussion.

"Hans, my boy, look at that rig. What would your sweetheart in Düsseldorf say if she saw you in that?"

Mail-order catalogues are thoroughly thumbed.

"What! a gramophone like that for forty marks? I must have it, and all the latest songs."

They plan trips into the interior of the Fatherland.

"We will go to Munich in Bavaria. They say you can see the Alps from there."

The homegoings are anticipated with elaborate talk.

"Won't the old woman be glad to see me, parti-

cularly when I unwrap that silk dress I bought for
her in Singapore."

The most disagreeable thing that can happen
aboard a sailing vessel is to be becalmed on the
homeward voyage, and the nearer the home port the
more irritating it is. The captain begins to look for a
Jonah. The first unfortunate for him to vent his rage
upon is the helmsman. Nothing he does is right.
The skipper is certain that as long as that hoodoo is
at the wheel there will never be any wind. He is
driving it away. Taking the helm himself, however,
seems to do no good. He calls the youngest cabin boy
and orders him to scratch the mainmast, which is
supposed to bring wind. When this does not help,
he gives the boy a broom and chases him to the top
of the mainmast, to sweep the sky. Then he takes
either an old pair of pants or an old boot and throws
it overboard. Wind must certainly come now. He
stamps down to his cabin and sits and smokes for a
while awaiting the wind. When he returns to the deck,
the calm is still unbroken. He starts in with the helmsman again, angered by the leering grin on the face of
the Jonah.

"Here, Jan, you are such a fine fellow. You take the
helm, by Joe, and see if you cannot get some wind up.
You are good luck. You are an old friend of St. Peter."

Presently, indeed, far away on the horizon you can
see a slight curling of the water. A slight breeze is
coming.

"Jan, what did I tell you? You shall have half a
pound of tobacco."

The other sailors watch these manœuvres with pro-
found sympathy.

On shore everything is different from what Jack
Tar expected. He has had the experience a hundred
times, but he always has it again. The crowds do not

give companionship. Everything is too much in a hurry. What people talk about does not interest him. He is out of touch with things. Besides, people do not sit and talk except for a little while. Someone always interrupts, or people grow impatient and go away, too much in a hurry. Jack Tar misses the usual hour for intimate conversation, on watch at night. The sea heaves slowly. The stars are bright above. The ship follows her course. Conversation is never interrupted by outsiders, and you can talk as long as the watch lasts.

Jack Tar is ever a mark for thieves. Aboard ship the comradeship of man with man will not tolerate dishonesty. A theft between shipmates is the worst of crimes. No sea chest is ever locked. On land Jack Tar likes bright lights and gaieties, and there, for some reason, a great abundance of swindlers are found to take him in. You go about Sankt Pauli, all sails set. You join a group and find that a horse has fallen down and broken its leg. You hear a groan. You turn around, and somebody says:

"Please, young man, can't you tell me the shortest way to a pawn shop?"

"A pawn shop? I don't know of any."

"That is too bad. I am forced to pawn the last heirloom from my dear mother."

"What is it?"

"A diamond ring."

He takes the ring from his finger, kisses it, and hands it to me. While I look at it, a well-dressed man sidles up and addresses me.

"I beg your pardon for having been curious enough to listen to your conversation. It is luck for you that I happen to be a jeweller. I should not like to see you taken advantage of. Real diamond rings are seldom offered in the streets."

The first fellow gets mad:

"Do you think I would try to cheat anyone with the ring that belonged to my sainted mother?"

"I have nothing to do with you. I am trying to protect this young man."

The jeweller examines the ring through a glass, and then whispers to me.

"Ask him how much he wants for it."

I ask, and receive the reply.

"Ten marks at least."

"He must have stolen it," the jeweller whispers again. "It is valuable. Give him twenty marks for it to get it quickly. Then follow me to my store, and I will give you a hundred."

Delighted at the opportunity to make some money on land, I give the man twenty marks for the ring. He hurries away. I look for the jeweller, whom I am to follow. He has disappeared. At a bona fide jeweller's I am told:

"It is a rhinestone, not a bad value for three marks."

Tedje and I take in the Hamburg Dom. From the rows of booths come promises of unparalleled sights. The sights we see in strange lands don't interest us, but at carnivals ashore it is different.

"Step in, step in," a barker howls, "and see what nobody ever saw or ate."

"What is it?" Tedje demands cautiously.

"Step in, and you will hear a canary bird talking Plattdeutsch, Low German. Five hundred marks reward if the bird does not talk Plattdeutsch."

We have never heard a canary bird talking any language, least of all Plattdeutsch. We join the crowd going in.

A canary bird in a cage is brought on to the platform. An elegantly dressed gentleman announces:

"Permit me to introduce this bird to you. His name is Hans."

"Never mind," shouts a sailor, "we want to hear him talk Deutsch."

"You will hear him, gentlemen. Hans—" and now he speaks in the Plattdeutsch dialect—"Hans, tell me what I should smoke, a cigar or a pipe." He pronounces the word pipe as "peep," in Plattdeutsch fashion.

In response the canary bird twitters:

"Peep."

"There, you see, gentlemen, the bird has talked Plattdeutsch."

There is loud laughter, and we all go out and tell the other suckers that the bird talked Deutsch. Why should we be the only fools?

Perhaps Jack Tar gets engaged to be married to the daughter of a "crimp." That costs him all his money. Or he gets drunk and everything is taken away from him.

Hein and Tedje meet back on their ship.

"Well, Tedje, how did Munich strike you?"

Tedje, who did not get away from the Hamburg water front, merely asks in turn:

"Did you get your gramophone?"

Although the North Sea may not be exactly the sailor's friend, the disillusioned tars are glad when sail is raised and they see water all around them once more.

At sea the sailor is on terms of intimacy with nature. He is friendly with the stars. He understands the clouds, and upon them he relies to tell him about the weather. He knows most of the fishes he encounters, although there are very few kinds that can be caught with hook and line from deck. When a school of porpoises appears, the command comes:

The prosaic American clipper, *Pass of Balmaha*, bound for Russia with a cargo of cotton, by the alchemy of war became the mysterious *Seeadler* preying on Allied shipping until a coral reef of the South Pacific ended its seven months' cruise of destruction.

The *Seeadler*, that carried the modern buccaneer whose dare-devil adventures were to outrival the high-handed days of the Spanish Main. From a sketch made from the photograph taken by the captain of the *Antonin*. See page 167.

Engineer Krauss and the mechanical crew picked for the pirate cruise.

"Get the harpoons ready!"

It takes a skilful harpooner to overhual a porpoise on its darting, leaping course. When one is taken, there is great rejoicing. Fresh meat will be served on board.

Near the Cape of Good Hope, Cape Horn, and the Falkland Isles you encounter many birds, albatross, cape pigeons, mulehogs, and all varieties of gulls. They feed on the waste thrown overboard and escort the ship halfway to Australia. You greet them as old friends whom you met a year ago and are glad to see back again. The gull and albatross are regarded as sacred, for it is the belief of the seaman that some day he will return to earth as a gull or albatross. Each one of these birds is the soul of a seaman. The white gulls are good souls. The brown or black gulls are bad souls, the "sea devils." When you are running before the trade wind south of the equator, the appearance of the albatross is a great event in the monotony of the voyage. Majestically the great white bird sweeps up and down, now before the bow now behind the stern, and circles the ship. He is the ruler of the Southern seas. It is a common belief among seamen that nobody ever succeeded in bringing an albatross alive to the Northern Hemisphere.

Sometimes off the coast of Africa hundreds of swallows that have lost their way in a fog alight on a ship's rigging, exhausted. Sometimes dozens of storks do. They never rise again. There is no suitable food on board for them. It is pitiful to see them waste away and drop dead on deck or into the sea. There is no help for it. They die a seaman's death, like sailors adrift without food or water.

Our ship lay idle in Tampico. A comrade and I got shore leave. We were allured by the romantic life of the lasso-throwing vaqueros, with their herds of long-

horned cattle, their fiery broncos, their silver-mounted saddles. A German settler put two horses at our disposal, and, to shame the idea that sailors cannot ride, we went galloping around the country on a tour that lasted several days. When we returned to Tampico, our ship had sailed.

In a country so rich as Mexico, it was not hard to make a living. All you had to do was to stand around the market-place and lend a hand. You earned enough to live and had a few coins left to squander in the gambling houses. For a couple of weeks, we made our living by carrying market baskets.

We joined the Mexican Army. Anybody could become a soldier. Life was pleasant and lazy, although the quarters were poor. We were sent to Mexico City, and there for several days stood on guard at the palace of the great Porfirio Diaz, under whose dictatorship Mexico was then enjoying her golden days.

We quit the army and worked on a railroad construction in the interior. In a gang of Italians, Poles, Germans, and Jamaica Negroes we transported sand, soil, and materials for railroad trestles. Then we worked for a German who had a ranch on which he raised poultry and fruit.

At Vera Cruz we signed on a petroleum tanker for Havana, and there shipped on a Norwegian craft which made the old New York–Australia run. The return voyage was via Honolulu to Vancouver, where we took a cargo of lumber aboard for Liverpool. On this voyage I acquired a fair knowledge of Norwegian, which was destined to play an important part in running the British blockade with the *Seeadler*.

Back in Hamburg I tried my hand as a tavern keeper and bartender. I frequented Mother Schroth's familiar old place. The *Frau*, a typical old friend of

Jack Tar ashore, suffered from asthma and had put on too much weight altogether. She wanted to go to a watering place. One of my pals, Ulhorn, and I, told her that we would take over her place and run it while she was away. She was greatly pleased.

It was easy enough to run the business, as only bottled beer was handled. The food was brought from a near-by restaurant, each portion in a pail, at sixty pfennigs a portion. All Ulhorn and I had to do was to circulate among the guests and see that they drank plenty of beer by drinking with them. In the evening a blind man came and played the accordion.

Business boomed. The sailors came, and felt at home. We had to get in an extra supply of beer. When we reckoned our accounts, however, we were astonished to find that we had a deficit. We chalked on a blackboard each bottle of beer that was drunk. That was all right so long as we stayed sober. Then, when we began to feel good, we allowed some of our guests to assist in the bookkeeping. They chalked up their own accounts, but instead of increasing their scores with every bottle of beer they drank, they reduced them. After a short while at this, we quit with less money than when we started. I decided that the saloon business was not the career for me.

After sundry other voyages, I shipped on the *Lisbon*, bound for the Mediterranean. By now, a little sense had been knocked into my head. I had saved 3,600 marks, which interest brought up to 3,800—enough to see me through a period of special training that would enable me to become a mate. This preparation called for a period of steamship service and a course at a navigation school. The *Lisbon* was a steamer, the first on which I had served. My voyage on her marked a turning point in my life

THE RUNAWAY COMES HOME

In the Café Niederegger in Lübeck I sat and drank my glass of beer, a trifle self-conscious. I had registered in Professor Schultze's School for Navigation, and felt that as a navigation student it was required of me to affect better ways than I had followed when I was a common sailor. I bought a decent wardrobe. I wore linen collars now, and neckties that you tie, and a scarf pin that you thrust into the necktie, instead of the eternally enduring celluloid collar which you share on board with a friend who wants to go ashore, and the indestructible tin necktie, made in America, with the scarfpin, a tiny revolver, riveted to it. I was conscious likewise that I must frequent better cafés than the saloons I had frolicked in as a sailor. That was what had brought me to the Café Niederegger, famous for its almond paste. The tables were covered with spotless white cloths, the waiters wore frock coats, and on a table, as a final mark of elegance, lay a handsomely bound book, the Almanach de Gotha.

Overcome with curiosity, I took up the volume and turned to the L's. Yes, there were the Von Luckners, and there was Count Felix von Luckner with the note attached—"missing." That was as I had thought. At home they had given me up for lost, dead.

"Phelax," I thought, "perhaps it is you who will be

missing before long. Perhaps before many months are gone Count Felix von Luckner will go home—as a naval officer in the Imperial Service."

For the present, I ordered another glass of Pilsener and drank to my demise.

At Professor Schultze's school, I was faced with that old and almost forgotten enemy of mine—study. I was past twenty now and more ignorant than the average ten-year-old child. The professor was tolerant and wise enough to expect almost anything, but I astounded him. When he examined me in fractional arithmetic I did not know what a fifth was. A half and a quarter I understood from the clock, but a fifth was a quantity unknown to me. And I was to acquire grammatical German, something of a general education, and the large amount of higher mathematics and astronomy necessary in the science of navigation. I should not have blamed the professor if he had despaired and turned me away. I told him my history, begging him to keep my identity secret, and he vowed, by Joe, that he would make a learned navigator of me.

I lived quietly. My face lost its tan and roughness. Month after month I had to buy smaller collars. I tried especially to keep my hands clean. By and by they lost their tarry wrinkles and calluses. I studied from morning till night. To reduce something to a common denominator is no joke. The whole Schultze family helped me and shared in my worries.

Examination day came, with all the professors in full dress. My handwriting was still clumsy. With my hard, big hands I used the bulkiest penholder I could find. It was as thick as a cane, an instrument designed for victims of apoplectic stroke who would have to grasp it with both hands.

Early one morning, a good citizen of Lübeck went

out to water his garden and saw a navigation student lying among his tomatoes.

"What are you doing there?"

The wretch, not knowing what to answer, merely asked in turn:

"What are you watering?"

For two days I had been celebrating the fact that I had passed the examination.

Again I was tempted to rush straightway to my parents. Professor Schultze had investigated quietly on his own account and found that my father and mother were alive and well and that my brother, like myself, had turned his mind to the sea. He was an ensign in the navy. Once more I denied myself, and remembered my vow not to go home save as a naval officer.

I got a post as petty officer aboard the Hamburg-South American liner *Petropolis*. I bought white kid gloves and white shoes, and can still see myself buying my first pair of cuff links. As I promenaded the deck of the *Petropolis* in my new uniform, I felt myself a god, only my cuffs kept bothering me and saluting seemed queer. I read all the learned books I could find, but there was much I could not understand.

After three quarters of a year aboard the *Petropolis*, I was eligible to enter the navy as a one-year service volunteer, for naval training and study. That was a method of training mercantile marine officers for naval service in case of war, of creating a class of reserve officers. After I had served my year as a volunteer and had mastered my studies, I would be entitled to wear a lieutenant's uniform. I would walk out a naval officer in the Imperial Service.

A comrade and I took the railroad from Hamburg to Kiel to be mustered in for volunteer service. It

was the first time I had ever been in an expensive railroad compartment. Opposite us sat a gentleman with a pointed beard whom we took to be a naval officer. That made us behave in very dignified fashion.

"Luckner," said my comrade, "is it not a fine view?"

"It is, indeed," I replied.

The gentleman with the pointed beard looked at me several times.

The daily drill at slow step on the parade ground at Kiel gave me a great deal of pain in the places where my legs had been broken before. An orderly came looking for a volunteer private named Luckner. I was required to go to the station. My officer asked me whether I had a relative at the station. I said, "No," and wondered whether it was a police station. Which one of my sins had been discovered?

I went to a red building and waited in an anteroom. A corporal bade me enter an inner office. Admiral Count Baudissin wanted to see me. How was I to behave in the presence of such a high dignitary? I supposed the principal thing was to stand at attention. The admiral was seated. He had gold braid on his sleeves. He was the same gentleman with the pointed beard who had looked at me on the train. I stood there at attention, elbows and hands held tight against me.

"Tell me, which Luckner are you?"

"The son of Heinrich Luckner."

"What is your first name?"

"Felix."

"He is missing."

"I am that Felix, sir."

"How did you get here?"

"I have passed my examination as mate, which

entitles me to volunteer service. I hope to become a reserve officer through good behaviour."

"How do you expect to pay your way?"

"I have 3,400 marks."

"You have earned that much?"

"Yes, sir."

"Why did you not write to your parents?"

"I want to go home an officer in the Emperor's service. I did not write because I did not want my parents to know I was a common sailor. I don't want them to know until I return home an officer."

Then the admiral said:

"I am your uncle Fritz."

"Eh," I thought, "what a noble uncle!"

I had never heard of this relationship. I rolled my eyes right and left, not knowing whether to address the admiral as Uncle then and there.

"Your Excellency," I said, "I wish it could be arranged that my parents do not learn of my being here until I have qualified as a reserve officer."

"Very well," he answered, "but you must not expect any help from me."

Not being able to say "Uncle," I replied:

"No, sir."

"Do not in any sense think that you are under my protection."

"No, sir."

"By the way, Felix, you may come to my house twice a week. My daughter will teach you a little, my lad. You speak a dreadful German."

I had considered myself, after all my studies, a tolerably educated man, but lapses in grammar have been my bane, more than storms at sea or shell fire during the war.

In the admiral's family, as a side line to my gram-

matical studies, I was required to write out a history of my adventures, which I did with judicious omissions, such as service in the Salvation Army and stealing a horse from a lighthouse-keeper. Such details would have spoiled my career at the outset.

I soon felt at home in the navy. There was a tremendous amount of studying to be done in mechanics, engineering, and the mathematics of gunnery. I was beginning to get used to study, as a slave gets used to the treadmill.

One day I tried to prevent a boat collision, and was too confident of my strength, alas. I was forced against an iron support, which pierced my abdomen and tore my intestines twice. That sent me to the hospital for a long spell. I was convalescing. A visitor brought some plums to a ward mate. I was starving. I begged some of the plums from him, and ate them. The next day, when the surgeon changed my bandage, he was dumbfounded to find the plums in the bandage. My imprudent act had caused a breaking of the intestines where they had been sewn. It was necessary to sew them again. I was threatened with arrest when I got well again, and a guard was placed over my bed to see that I ate no more plums.

Instead of arrest, however, and possible trouble about getting my commission, the naval authorities were kind enough to credit me with the time I passed in the hospital. In due time, I was mustered in as a reserve naval lieutenant. I called on my Uncle Fritz once more, and started out for home. I wore my uniform, a cocked hat, epaulettes, and a sword sash.

In Halle, the quiet home on the "Old Promenade" had changed not at all in those eight years. I climbed the steps to the door, quite a figure in my brilliant uniform. To the maid, whom I did not know, I

handed my visiting card, which she took inside. I heard the well remembered voice of the old gentleman questioning:

"Naval Lieutenant Felix Luckner? There is no such man of our name. But show him in."

I entered and said:

"Good-morning, Father. I hope I have kept my word to wear the Emperor's uniform with honour."

He could not find anything to say to me. He called for Mother in a choking voice.

She came down the stairs, looked at me for a moment, and sat down on a step in weak surprise. Then she began to cry, and came running to me. The old gentleman by now was wiping his eyes too.

Where had I been? What had I done? There were so many questions that I could not answer half. We sat there, and I told as much as I could. Soon the old gentleman had gathered his wits. He began to boast.

"You see, my dear wife. Did I not always tell you 'He is a Luckner—he will amount to something—do not worry about him'? Behold I was right. He is a Luckner."

Telegrams were sent to sisters, brothers, cousins, uncles, and aunts. There was a great family reunion, and I was petted like a child.

X

FROM PIG-STY CLEANER TO KAISER'S PROTÉGÉ

MORE studying and then more studying. It seemed as though I never would get through. I served as a mate with the Hamburg-American Line for two years, and prepared myself for the captain's examination. More mathematics, more astronomy, more mechanics. I plugged and plugged. Study is no good, but you've got to do it. Finally, I was ready for the test. I went to a school for a little more preparation, and succeeded in passing the examination with flying colours. I was proud, but I was also glad that there would be no more studying for me now. I was eligible to become a captain. What further rank was there to make me study again? I served the Hamburg-American Line until 1911.

Then more school and studies!

I often spent an afternoon with several comrades sailing on the lower Elbe near Neumuehlen. One day we saw a small catboat and in it a man who obviously did not know how to sail. He was, in fact, a merchant of Cologne possessed of more courage than sense. Pretty soon a jibbing boom knocked him overboard. He couldn't swim, either. He sank out of sight. I swam and dove for him. I got hold of him and pushed him up above me, so that he would reach the surface before I did. When I came up he seized me, wound his arms and legs around me, and dragged

me down. I struggled free, and everything turned black. I came to the surface, caught my breath, and dove again for him. I reached him, but an eddying current dragged us both down and down. Luckily, he was unconscious now, and I was able to grasp him and fight my way with him to the surface. I swam with my burden to shore. I was in reaching distance of the pier when I collapsed. Men waiting there pulled the drowning man out. An old gentleman claims he fished me out with his umbrella.

A week later, I was called before the authorities who awarded life-saving medals. They asked me to produce witness of my life-saving feat. That formality was necessary before they could give me a medal. I didn't want to bother producing any witnesses. The matter was dropped there.

I had the good fortune to be able to rescue three other people from drowning, and then a fifth. That occurred on Christmas Eve, 1911. I attended a celebration in Hamburg, and returned late to get aboard my ship, the *Meteor*. I waited on the slip for the ferry. Next to me stood a customs official. It was bitterly cold. In the flickering light I saw a man in the water some distance out. He was struggling faintly. I started to throw off my great-coat. The customs official held me.

"Are you crazy? Into that icy water? Is it not enough for one man to drown?"

"But surely I cannot let that man go down."

I slipped out of my overcoat, which he held, and jumped. By Joe, when I was in there I had the sensation of somebody holding a red-hot wire around my neck. After a hard swim, I reached my man. It was lucky for him that it was so cold and that he was so drunk. He was perfectly rigid now. If you lie still, you don't drown easily. It was no trouble to swim in

with him, except that it was so cold. The customs man pulled us on to the pier. I could never have got up alone.

"What a crazy fool," the customs man said. "If I had not been here you would have jumped in just the same, and you would have drowned."

They took us to a saloon, where they put us between blankets and gave us grog. I soon got my strength back, likewise my man, an English sailor named Pearson. He soon had his second load of liquor.

After that exploit, the Hamburg newspapers made much of me, particularly since I still refused to bother about producing the witnesses necessary before I could get a life-saving medal. The editors denounced this instance of red tape. The controversy came to the notice of Prince Henry of Prussia. A little while later, when I took part in the yearly manœuvres for reserve officers, I received an order to appear before him, and he asked me whether I should like to enter active service. That, I replied, was my greatest desire, but I was afraid I was too old. He kindly bade me not to worry about that, and on February 3, 1912, I received the official dispatch:

"Count Luckner is ordered to the navy for active service."

By Joe, now I would have to study. I would have to learn in a few months what cadets ordinarily learned in three and a half years. The Emperor had heard of me from Prince Henry and had interested himself in my case. My tuition was paid for out of his private purse. If I did not make good marks in my classes, what kind of a Luckner . . . well, by Joe. This was the climax of my whole unhappy career of study.

After an infantry course came a torpedo course. A torpedo has a thousand complexities for the student

to master. There were four kinds of torpedoes. One had a hundred and fifty screws. You had to memorize the names of all the parts and familiarize yourself with the apparatus so well that you could put it together without help.

"Luckner," I thought, "you will never learn all that. You are as stupid as when you were in the third grade."

I was afraid and felt pretty bad. I did not do so well with my studies.

One of my teachers was Lieutenant Commander Pochhammer, whose father was a professor of Italian literature. His especial subject was Dante. He gave lectures to the naval students on the *Divine Comedy*. Strange, I hated study, but I liked these lectures on Dante and I liked to study Dante. I did not understand much of it, but I found great pleasure in it. It was because of Beatrice, the Divine Maiden. I thought she must be the same as my fairy princess. Whenever Professor Pochhammer spoke of her in his lectures, or whenever I read about her in the pages of Dante, I was reminded of that fairy princess I knew must live on the green island the *Niobe* had sailed by, the fairy princess I had dreamed of aboard the *Cæsarea*, when old Smutje had whistled "My Heart Is Like a Beehive" and I had taken up the refrain. The fairy princess, of whom I had had visions many another time, had been a blessing to me before, and surely, in a singular way, she was a blessing to me now.

My interest in Dante and Beatrice, as propounded by Professor Pochhammer, made an excellent impression, not only on the professor himself, but also on his son Lieutenant Commander Pochhammer and my other teachers. For Dante's and Beatrice's sake they

winked at some of my most glaring deficiencies. They
built up my confidence. I passed the necessary examination. The Emperor ordered that my commission be antedated, so that I might have seniority
rights of a longer service than I had actually ren-
dered.

I was assigned to duty aboard the *Preussen*, and
there, during my leisure time, built models of sailing
ships.

One night, in a Hamburg café, I sat talking with a
friend, a shipowner.

"When I crossed the harbour to-day," I said,
"and saw the sailing ships, I remembered how I used
to sit on a spar while the sun was setting and listen
to a fellow playing a squealer. You know what a
squealer is? An accordion. I wish I could be a sailor
back on a ship again."

"Don't be foolish," my friend replied. "I have
never yet heard of a certified engineer wanting to go
back to the anvil."

"But," I insisted, "I want to be a sailor again if
only for a few days, and you must help me."

I made him give me a muster certificate for one of
his ships, the *Hannah*, which was lying in port and
taking on a crew. I went to a seaman's supply store
and bought a pair of overalls, a shirt, a blue and white
blouse such as sailors wear, a cap, a blanket, and a
mattress. The blanket and mattress I had sent to the
Hannah. The clothing I took with me. I took a cab,
and bade the driver go to the docks. Inside, I took
off my naval uniform and packed it in the bag I had
with me, and donned my sailor's togs. At my destina-
tion, I got out. The driver, a decent old fellow, opened
his eyes wide.

"Are you the naval officer who got in?"

"Yes."

"Say, what are you going to do? You have changed your clothes so they won't recognize you when they find you. You are going to drown yourself."

Rather baffled, I tried to assure him that I had no intention of drowning myself.

"No, don't tell me that. I know what you are going to do. Please tell me your troubles. You should not throw away your young life like that."

I had to give him a long and convincing story about some confidential mission for the government that I was engaged in, the truth of which statement I had to swear to solemnly. Then he agreed to leave me and take my satchel back to the hotel. As he started his horse, he turned around once more imploringly.

"You are surely not going to do it?"

I rubbed my hands in the dirt, rehearsed my old-time rolling sailor's gait, and tried to forget my fine manners. I practised an especial bit to see if I could still light my pipe and spit like a jack-tar. Hands in pockets, I sauntered on to the ship.

"Ahoy there," I called to the mate, and handed him my muster certificate.

After a few questions, he bade me the usual welcome.

"All right, Phelax Luedige, come on and get to work."

"No. In the morning I start."

You can tell an old-time competent seaman by his argumentative independence. The mate gave me a bad look, but was convinced that I would not go to work until morning.

I strolled back to the galley. The cook, a broad fellow with a red beard, was standing there. I watched a little fellow washing dishes, and thought:

"He is just as clumsy as you were once, Phelax."

The Sea Devil overtakes the *Charles Gounod*.

The end of the *Charles Gounod*.

The fake armament of the raider frightens a Canadian barque into submission.

Along came the *Antonin* on her way from Chile to France with a load of saltpeter. Her skipper was a savage old salt.

In the fo'c'sle two fellows were sitting on a box, smoking their pipes. They were shirking work, just as I had shirked it. I wondered whether they would find anything strange in me, and walked up to them. One of them named Hein said:

"What's your name?"

"Phelax."

"I guess you have been ashore a long time."

"Why?"

"Your hair is cut so neat. Are you married?"

"No."

"Well, I am. My old woman was married three times before, but never got the right mate. Now she says she has got the right one. How happy she is. She is a laundress, and when we are in port here she brings me my warm supper every night."

Now comes the mate.

"Get out of here and get to work. Phelax can unpack his things and get to work."

"No, I told you not until to-morrow morning."

The captain came on board and asked the mate what kind of help he had got.

"One who is mighty independent."

"Send him to me."

The cabin boy comes.

"Phelax, go over to the captain."

To the captain I say:

"Good-day, sir!"

"Good-day. How long have you been at sea?"

"Fifteen years."

"Do you know how to mend sails?"

"I know how very well."

"We have no time to mend sails at anchor. But you will have to do a lot of sewing at sea."

"I have done it often."

The captain sizes me up as a fellow who knows his

business and good at the sail-mending which he is anxious to have done. He agrees that I do not have to go to work until to-morrow morning.

Once again I eat bean soup, leaning over the table with a large enamel pot, my "mug." After dinner I lie in my bunk, and ask:

"Is there no squealer?"

"Hein has one."

"Play, Hein, and I'll treat to a case of beer."

A motor boat selling beer is alongside. I buy a case, and we drink. The squealer begins to wheeze, while the evening sun shines on the water.

At half-past six Hein's laundress arrived. She was passably good-looking except that she was all pitted with smallpox and her hair stuck out like a flying jib. She certainly loved her Hein. She brought him a pot of supper, some of which he divided among the rest of us.

I noticed that Hein had some paint and a brush such as artists use. Was he an artist? On the girl's arm he painted a big heart with an arrow. In the middle of the heart he signed his initials. He had to stop at times, because she could not bear the burn of the turpentine in the paint.

"She is a fine girl," said Hein. "She stands for everything. She is as true as gold."

She did not exactly look it.

Night came on, the stars appeared, and Hein's squealer gave forth music. That was the life. a sailor's life.

On the following day I worked. I could not get along with the mate. He thought me too independent, and tattled on me to the captain, who restrained himself and had patience with me, since he did not want to lose so experienced a sailor. At night Hein's

laundress came again, and the squealer sounded long and merrily.

On the third day my friend the shipowner came to the boat to get me. I managed to say to him without being observed.

"Don't give me away. Have the captain meet us for dinner at the hotel to-night."

The shipowner invited the captain, who accepted with alacrity.

That night at the Atlantic Hotel I dressed myself in full uniform, and joined the shipowner and the captain in the dining room. In such a glittering place, the captain was bashful.

"Captain Erdmann of the *Hannah*—Lieutenant Commander Count von Luckner."

Erdmann eyed me curiously and then looked down for a long time, turning his wineglass around in his hand. Evidently he thought he saw a certain resemblance. In a little while, I stepped out.

"Is he a count?" the captain asked the shipowner.

"Yes."

"And just think, I almost made the break of telling him he looked like a sailor aboard our ship. They might be twins, though. You never saw such a resemblance."

"It would be dreadful indeed to say anything like that," responded the other.

When I returned, we drank a little more and then I said to the captain:

"Don't you recognize me?"

He squirmed.

"Well—yes—but——"

"You mean you don't recognize me?"

"But, Count, have I really met you before?"

"Of course, don't you remember me?"

He wrestled with a temptation to speak out, but fought it down.

"Yes, Count, you do look familiar to me. But where have we met?"

He sat there, as the saying goes, with both feet in the trough.

"Don't you know me from the ship?"

"Man, man, are you Phelax?"

"Captain, Captain," warned the shipowner.

"Oh, excuse me, excuse me," stammered the captain.

"Well, I am Phelax," I laughed. "I went aboard your ship to see how it felt to be a sailor again."

"Well, well," stuttered the captain, "and now it is my turn to treat."

I told him my story, how I had been born a count, had become a sailor and then an officer of sailing ships, and now was an officer of the Imperial Service. He had tears in his eye.

"And my mate—think of it—my mate said you were too independent."

The old fellow became so enthusiastic that he insisted that we take a trip through Sankt Pauli with him. We went, and had a high old time. The captain got quite drunk, and he revealed a secret regret that lingered in his mind. What a sail-mender he had missed!

"Who will believe it on board," he muttered, "when I tell them that that my fine sail-mender turned out to be a count?"

XI

IN THE CAMEROONS, AND THE FAIRY OF FUERTEVENTURA

I HAVE told of how the Emperor transferred me to the *Panther*, which was then assigned to our West African station, the Cameroons. If my being aboard the *Panther* inspired, in itself, vivid recollections of my past life, my service as an officer of the ship presently brought me to another and far more delightful memory of my sailing-ship days. This was an incident that not merely returned to me in imagination, but one that brought to me that rarest gift of fortune, a dream come true.

The events that preceded the climax of which I speak were such as to provide the ever-striking qualities of contrast. The African jungle, the pursuit of savage beasts, black warriors, an extraordinary black king, fantastic war dances and all the unearthly sights and sounds that are Africa, and then . . .

The commander of the *Panther* was reluctant to have his officers go big-game hunting in the interior and, as he said, risk their lives uselessly. We were forbidden to take rifles on shore with us. But a comrade and I smuggled our rifles out, and took a big canoe upstream. With a dozen Negroes at the paddles, we raced against the sluggish current of the Mungo River, between giant, overhanging walls of trees. After eighteen hours, we reached Mundame. Our only

worth-while trophy so far was a crocodile—and crocodiles are hard to shoot, too, as they dive with surprising speed. We had also shot a few vultures, sea eagles, and monkeys. We could not quite bring ourselves to eat the flesh of the monkeys, which the natives consider a great delicacy. When wounded, a monkey cries and screams just like a child, but when skinned it loses its half-human appearance and looks like a big squirrel, or a woodchuck.

At Mundame the black people greeted us with eager cries:

"Massa, massa, plenty elephant."

We proceeded on an elephant hunt in which my friend Bryer and I must have cut rather poor figures as sportsmen! Our chase of the great beasts did not turn out to be quite what we had expected.

The elephants had broken into a Negro's plantation, and were not far away. With each a Negro as a guide, we went into the thicket of banana plants.

"Massa," my guide whispered eagerly, "massa, look, elephant."

I looked but could see no elephant. My guide kept repeating in tones of excitement that gradually turned into despair.

"Elephant, massa, look, elephant!"

I could have looked for a year and would not have seen the fraction of gray wall revealed between the leaves. Finally, the elephant began to move, and I saw at least the great disturbance among the foliage. I walked toward it, hoping to find some definite point of the beast's anatomy to shoot at. The elephant moved away at about the same speed, and I could get no closer to it. I came upon one of those huge ant hills you find in Africa, and clambered upon it. I now had a much better view.

"Ostriches!" I exclaimed.

There were many elephants plucking up at the bananas. Their trunks reaching high and curving and wavering gave me the impression of giant ostriches. One of the great beasts came out of the thicket right in front of the ant hill on which I was standing. Several others followed him. I remembered hastily that I must aim at the head a little lower than the eyes. I point the gun, pull the trigger, and then crash! The giant turned around in a circle giving a tremendous bellow. With a roar and a great sound of rushing, the beast plunged forward, right past the hill on which I was standing. The rest of the herd followed and passed very near me. I nearly fell off the ant hill, and made the deplorable blunder of losing sight of the elephant I had shot at. Fortunately, the natives, who were to get their share of the meat, did not allow themselves to become so readily confused. They followed the wounded animal, and found it with its tusks rammed deeply in the soil. It took several more shots in the head to kill the brute.

Nobody travelling in the Cameroons in those days ever passed up a chance to visit Banum Joja, the most intelligent chieftain in all Southwest Africa. He was an advocate of what modern improvements he could introduce into his kingdom, and had invented an especial alphabet with which to reduce the native language to writing. He was a great admirer of the Germans, and willed his beautifully carved antique throne to a German museum.

We went the long distance by train from the coast to the interior territories of Banum Joja. The palaver drums having advised him of our arrival, the chief met us with his staff. A long procession of cattle, goats, and other animals were paraded past us as a sign of his wealth. The old boy himself majestically arrived in his royal conveyance, a hammock carrie

by two slaves, slung on a long pole. We were considerably surprised at the figure he made. He wore a glittering cuirassier's helmet, a tremendous battle sword, and a tight-fitting red hussar's tunic on the breast of which was pinned the German Order of the Crown. His black, shiny legs, however, were bare. His pride as a sovereign increased visibly as he observed our surprise at his appearance.

In his palace, a large thatched hall surrounded by a high wall of loam, Joja showed us vaingloriously the many smoke-blackened heads of his ancestors' enemies and a large elephant's tusk decorated with the lower jaws of slain foes. Pottery is highly developed in those parts, for everywhere we saw vessels of clay. The only ornament in the palace, besides the grisly trophies of war and massacre, was the top of a European butter dish. It represented a setting hen. We drank palm wine, which was excellent.

In the courtyard of the palace, Joja ascended a stairway in a great hollow tree. Placed in the branches was the war drum which only the King may beat. Majestically he clambered out to it, and under the monarch's hand a muffled beat resounded. The four portals in the wall of the corral opened and files of black warriors rushed in, three thousand of them, a magnificent picture. They danced the war dance, a methodical evolution in which they rushed against each other with a tremendous clashing of shields. Then followed a spear-throwing contest with extraordinary displays of skill. The women entered, and there was another ballet, the women dancing around the men and then the men dancing around the women. Amid general rejoicings, the King treated his subjects to palm wine.

Joja arranged a buffalo hunt for us. A place is

chosen where the grass is brown and dry and fallen, else it would be so high that a horse and rider might disappear in it. On this open hunting field a dozen warriors take their place with big shields of buffalo hide. By means of fire and beaters, the buffalo herd is driven toward them. When they come to the open place, the male stares from the thicket with his dull brown eyes. He seems to study the black warriors waiting there. Now he sends his cows to safety through the thicket surrounding the open place. Then he attacks. The warriors' spears pierce him in the front. He comes thundering upon them, but with a fabulous speed they have thrown themselves on the ground, covering themselves completely with their staunch shields. The enraged beast passes over them without harming them. He is powerless now. The spears protruding from his front prop themselves against the ground, making running difficult. He cannot attack without driving the barbs farther into his flesh. He turns around. In a flash the Negroes are up, and the beast receives spears from the back. He can neither advance nor retreat now. He raves, wants to attack, the sweat streams down him. He throws himself on the ground. Some of the spears break off. But now the Negroes are on top of him, thrusting their spears into him. He receives the final blow and is still.

Religion was a much discussed question in Joja's kingdom. The German Evangelical missionary comes with Protestant theology. He asks Joja's people to picture an invisible God. This they are unable to do. The Catholic missionaries come, visiting the territories previously covered by their Evangelical colleagues. They talk little theology, but have a gorgeous display. A miraculous image is mounted and decorated with mirrors. The Virgin Mary with the

Child Jesus sits in the centre. To the right are the Three Wise Men from the East. These wise men are particularly interesting to Joja's subjects, because one of them is a black king. The priest, in gorgeous vestments, kneels before the beautiful display. The natives think:

"This is a real God. He is much richer than the Evangelical missionaries' God."

Joja was a skeptic toward the Christian religion. He asked me whether our God was black or white, but thought He could hardly be white, since He had made man in his own image and had made the black people too. He asked me when Jesus had come to Earth. I told him. Then he asked when America was discovered. I told him that. He asked me why Jesus did not go there too and preach his gospel.

While I was in the Cameroons, a German squadron circling the globe put in at Duala and anchored near shore. It consisted of the *Kaiser*, the *King Albert*, and the *Strassburg*. The black chieftains from the interior were entertained on the magnificent ships. They particularly admired the cannon in the turrets as they slowly swung around and fired. They asked whether the guns would shoot over the Cameroon mountains. When this fact was affirmed, their respect was great. The champagne with which they were served increased their respect.

The English instigated the Haussa, a mercantile tribe that roams the entire country plying trade, to spread the story that the ships were English ships which the English had merely loaned to the Germans.

Having to take the *Panther* back to Germany for overhauling, we steamed north. Our first stop was to be for provisions at Fuerteventura, one of the islands of the Canaries, a vacationing and health resort. I was on watch. Straight ahead, a speck of land ap-

peared on the horizon, Fuerteventura, the island for which we were bound.

It was a green island. Presently, through my glass, I could distinguish waving palms and white houses, white houses with green shutters and red roofs. A vague feeling made my heart jump.

"Luckner," I thought, "it is the same island, the island you saw when you were a cabin boy aboard the *Niobe*, the island of the fairy princess."

It was. There could be no doubt of it. So clear was memory impressed by a great feeling that I could recognize individual houses I had gazed upon seventeen years before while I had leaned on the rail dreaming a happy dream.

"Luckner," I said, "you are Phelax once again. They call you 'pig,' and you clean the pigs and the pharmacy. There is the island. Open your eyes wide. Is it not lovely and beautiful?"

It was as beautiful as when I had seen it from aboard the *Niobe*. The houses still looked pretty and clean. There were terraces with gardens and white paths lined with palms.

"Phelax," I thought, "it is fit to be the home of the fairy princess. It *is* the home of the fairy princess. She must be there, with her delicate blue eyes and golden hair, she whom you have thought about all these years."

We put into port. I attended to my duties. The other officers asked me why I was so preoccupied. I answered their questions silently to myself.

"Phelax, now you must go and inspect your island. Perhaps you may find your fairy princess."

I went ashore by myself, and sauntered over the island all day. It was small, with gentle hills and an abundance of vegetation. Flowers were everywhere. It was truly an island of flowers. I went on through

perfumed valleys and over breezy hills, lost in reverie, lost in my former life. A kind of hypnotism was upon me.

"Phelax," I thought, "of course you do not see the fairy princess. She is hidden beyond the flowers there. She will stay hidden. Is she to come to Phelax, a common sailor? Or even if you were a naval officer, would she come? She is too lovely for any mortal being."

So deep was I in fantasy that these thoughts inspired me to a sad regret and resignation. When evening came, I returned to the ship happy and yet downhearted.

That night we entertained on board members of the Royal Spanish Club and their guests. Some came for dinner, some afterward. It was a jolly meal. Then we gave an after-dinner entertainment, and I was called upon to entertain and amuse our guests. During my days as a sailor I was often in demand to amuse the company. The tricks I had learned among the Indian fakirs in Australia I had retained and cultivated. To this day I am somewhat skilful at various kinds of sleight of hand. I put on Oriental robes and turban. My face, freshly tanned by the sun of the Cameroons, needed no darkening. I had learned from the fakirs the solemn mystical demeanour and slow impressive movements that they cultivated. I must say that as I appeared before the guests in the salon of the *Panther* I cut quite an Oriental, wonder-working figure.

I had performed several tricks and had come to the one in which I snapped a ring on to a cane held at both ends by an assistant, when two newcomers arrived and entered through a door not far from me.

"Luckner," I thought, "are you going crazy? Phelax, there is she, your fairy princess."

She was on the arm of a stately old gentleman. She had the rosy lips, the short, pretty nose, the childlike eyes, and the rich blonde hair that had haunted my imagination. She came close to me and watched me with an expression of interest and something of awe. As I learned later, she thought I was truly an Indian fakir.

"Phelax," I said to myself, "she has come to you, your fairy princess. She knows you are on her island, and she has come."

I tried to go on with my trick, but my hands shook and were clumsy. I could not control them. Nor could I keep my eyes away from the blonde girl who stood there.

"I'm sorry," I said to my assistant, one of our officers. "The other ones went all right, but I can't seem to do this one. We've had enough anyway."

"Ladies and gentlemen," he announced jocularly, "the great fakir has reconsidered and thinks it would be wrong to disclose this last marvellous trick. He feels that it is his duty to retain it and exhibit it for the first time before his sovereign, the King of England."

Everybody laughed. I went out and changed into my naval uniform as quickly as I could. When I returned, I asked one of the other officers to present me to the blonde young lady. I have never felt so bashful as when I made my bow before her.

She was much amused at having taken me for a genuine Indian fakir, and talked merrily. Her laughter was very sweet. She told me her name was Irma. Her father owned great plantations on the island of Sumatra. She was with him at Fuerteventura on a sojourn for his health.

The remainder of my stay on the island was perfect happiness. Irma's father entertained us officers at

his bungalow. Irma and I were together all of the time. We took long walks among the white houses and through the green glades the sight of which had so gladdened poor Phelax long years before. When the *Panther* steamed north again, I was happy with the assurance that Irma had given me that she and her father were sailing for home in a short time and that I would see her there.

I did see her there, and we became engaged to be married. The *Panther* was to sail for the Cameroons again on July 17th. We were ready to start when we received an unexpected telegram from the Admiralty —"Do not start." On August 1st, Germany declared war on Russia, and the world was ablaze. I told Irma that our marriage must be put off. It would be wrong to have her become the wife of a man who might so soon leave her a widow. She wanted an immediate marriage, but I was determined.

XII

FAKE NORWEGIANS FOR A PIRATE CRUISE

It was in a gay café in Hamburg. In 1916, war times were growing hard in Germany, but still the cafés were astir with life and gaiety. A naval officer on shore leave could soon find surroundings that would enable him to forget the harsh life on dreadnaught and cruiser. My friend Dalstroem and I, over glasses of Swedish punch, chatted for an hour and then another hour. But our confab had nothing to do either with battle cruisers going down or with destroyers lifted out of the sea by exploding torpedoes, or the other sights I had beheld off Skagerrak. We talked of sailing ships, by Joe, and of the years I had served before the mast.

An orderly wedged his way through the crowd and handed me a message. It was from the Admiralty, ordering me to report at Imperial headquarters on the morrow. Such a summons to a mere lieutenant commander was decidedly unusual, and of course I was itching with curiosity. I never was any good at waiting.

The following morning found me in Berlin, entering the naval holy of holies, standing expectantly at attention before an old German sea lord with a face as stern as the cliffs at Heligoland. The orders I had come to hear were barked at me quick and short.

"You are to take command of a vessel," said the admiral. "We want you to run the blockade and raid

enemy commerce. Since we have no coaling stations, a sailing ship will be the best. Do you think you can do it?"

"Allow me," I felt like saying, "allow me to throw my arms around your neck, my dear fellow."

"Yes, sir! I'd like nothing better."

Good health and high spirits had given me boundless confidence. I was the sort of fellow who believes he can do almost anything—at any rate, anything with a sailing ship. The admiral replied that the mission was mine. And it turned out that I had been picked for this venture because I happened to be the only officer in the German Navy who had served "in sail."

But what if we should slip through? What then? What could one lone windjammer do against the naval might of John Bull and his allies? What chance had a romantic clipper ship in this era of giant ocean liners, of hush-hush armoured cruisers, of speedy destroyers, and against the combined strength of Jellicoe and Beatty's super-dreadnaughts? For that matter, what chance had a poetic sailing ship against an ordinary tramp steamer?

Well, it may sound mad, but the sea lanes of commerce can even be disrupted by a lone sailing ship in wartime. But whether the idea was mad or not, I was itching for action and ready for anything.

"What," the admiral asked, "should you consider of the greatest importance for the venture?"

"Luck," I replied.

"All right; then take the *Pass of Balmaha*. She has already carried British prisoners for us. She has been lucky for us once, she may be lucky for us again."

The Admiralty officials had picked the *Pass of Balmaha* because she was a staunch ship, an American

clipper, built in Glasgow.[1] They had also picked her because she had suddenly arrived in a German port with an unexpected present of some British prisoners for us. We sailors believe in good and bad omens, and we are right. Some ships are lucky and some unlucky. If something has happened to indicate a certain ship is lucky for you, take that ship. You want Lady Luck on your side when you put to sea.

Now, about the past record of this Yankee clipper that was to be converted into a German raider. The *Pass of Balmaha* had sailed from New York with a cargo of cotton for Archangel. Her commander was a Captain Scott, a well-known American shipmaster, a big-hearted, bushy-bearded, New England skipper with a very red face. Off the Norwegian coast, a British cruiser hailed her. Uncle Sam was then a neutral, and the blockade was getting tighter every month. The British were becoming suspicious of everybody, including neutrals and themselves. The overcautious commander of this cruiser, although he had no grounds for suspicion, ordered the *Pass of Balmaha* to turn back to the search port of Kirkwall in the Orkneys.

"Bah!" said Captain Scott, "here I am with a cargo for your allies, the Rooshians, and you patrol fellows order me back to Kirkwall. What do yuh mean by such nonsense? The wind is agin me, it'll take me three weeks to reach Scapa Flow and the Orkneys, and I'll be several months late in delivering my cargo to the Rooshians. Are you chaps trying to win a war or lose one?"

"Never mind," replied John Bull; "you do as you are told."

Leaving an officer and prize crew of six marines on board, with her funnels belching columns of black smoke, the British patrol cruiser continued on her

---

[1] See Note A, Appendix.

North Sea beat. As soon as the *Pass of Balmaha* had turned her nose toward Kirkwall and Scapa Flow, the British prize officer ordered the American flag pulled down and the British flag run up.

"Go to blazes," bristled the irate Captain Scott, and he refused to obey.

"Right ho," said the Britisher, and he told his men to haul down the Stars and Stripes and hoist the Union Jack.

"I wish the Germans would come," raged the Yankee skipper. And the very next morning his wish was granted! A U-boat popped up to the surface about a half mile away. Captain Scott waggled his beard in the Englishman's face.

"Serves you right! With the Stars and Stripes up there, they wouldn't bother us. Now they'll take us all to Germany. So far as you chaps are concerned, the war is over right now. You will get cocky, will you?"

The Britisher was alarmed. He saw visions of himself locked in a Prussian prison for "the duration." So he climbed down from his high horse in a hurry and meekly placed himself in Captain Scott's hands, begging the Yankee still to try and save the day.

"I ought to let you go as prisoners, by Joe, but I don't want to lose my ship," said Scott. "So go below with your men and hide in the hold while I put my flag back where it belongs. Maybe they haven't seen yours. Soon the submarine was alongside and one of her officers climbed aboard. The Germans had seen the Union Jack, all right, but they hadn't seen it hauled down. Now they found themselves on a ship flying the American flag, and they were puzzled.

"What's this?" the submarine officer demanded of Scott. "First we see a British flag, and now it's an American."

"You must be mistaken," replied the skipper, "this here ain't no Britisher."

The officer was bewildered and suspicious, so ordered the *Pass of Balmaha* to head for Hamburg. Leaving only a German ensign aboard, he announced that his submarine would follow close behind. Of course, this was only a threat, for the U-boat soon vanished beneath the waves.

Now the ensign grew worried. Something told him that everything was not right on the *Pass of Balmaha*. Had he known there were seven Britishers on board, he would have been still more worried!

"Captain," said he, "I am going to stay at your side all day and sleep with you at night. I've a hand grenade here in my pocket. At night I am going to fix it so that if anybody opens the door of our cabin it will explode."

Naturally Captain Scott lost no time in whispering to his mate: "Fasten down the hatches and don't let those Britishers come up. If they do, our goose is cooked. Don't say anything to them, or there will be trouble. This German smells a rat."

So the prize crew in the hold was kept there. Two days later, outside the entrance to the harbour at Cuxhaven, another party of Germans came aboard, so Captain Scott said to the U-boat ensign:

"You wanted to know what was wrong here? All right, now I'll show you." Then he opened the hatches and yelled for the Britishers to come up. The tall officer of the Royal Navy, one eye blinking and the other be-monocled, put his head up first.

"I say, where are we now?"

"You're in Germany. If you had left my flag alone, everything would have been all right. But you are prisoners now."

So you see how the *Pass of Balmaha* turned out to

be unlucky for Englishmen and lucky for Germans. That was just the ship we wanted, by Joe.

The American flag that the Englishman pulled down was still there when I took her over. So I kept it as a souvenir. We lost the ship in the South Seas, but not the flag. It served as mascot on two other ships that I lost. But on my present world cruise I hope to visit San Francisco and return it to the original owner and tell him what a fine raider his clipper made.

Our hope was to run the blockade disguised as a neutral—a thing entirely fair according to the laws of war. Although on land a soldier must wear service uniform, at sea you can fly a neutral flag and wear ordinary seaman's clothes. But you must hoist your true colours before going into action with the enemy.

We altered that British-built Yankee clipper from stem to stern, with concealed places for our guns, rifles, grenades, bombs, and other armament, with special quarters for prisoners, two ultra-modern 500-horse-power motors to fall back on in case of calm or when in a big hurry, a tank holding 480 tons of fuel oil, another tank containing 480 tons of sweet water, and provisions for a cruise of two years.

In addition to 400 bunks for prospective "guests," I had special de luxe quarters made for "visiting" captains and mates. These were spacious cabins to accommodate two or three. We also designed a separate dining saloon for them, with an assortment of books and magazines in French and English, and a gramophone with late English and French records. War or no war, I still considered all sailors my pals, and had my own ideas as to how our prisoners should be treated. A sailor is a sailor, no matter what his nationality, and if I took any prisoners I wanted them to feel as though they were my guests.

Then, of course, we had to arrange quarters for my crew of fighting marines as well as for the regular seamen required on a clipper of this size. Moreover, we had to do all this so it would not be noticeable to uninvited visitors.

When the work was done, below deck, the *Pass of Balmaha* was an auxiliary cruiser, armed to the teeth. Above deck she was merely a poetic old sailing ship loaded with a prosaic cargo of lumber.

Timber made the ideal cargo for our purposes, because a ship carrying lumber loads her deck as well as her hold. The piles of lumber even cover your hatches, so no one can go below until you unload. Hence no search crew would be likely to inspect us carefully at sea. They would either order us to Kirkwall, or let us go.

Norway exports lumber and Australia imports it. So we decided to pose as a Norwegian clipper bound for Melbourne. Having served on various Norwegian ships, I spoke Norse, and I knew I would have no difficulty finding men for my crew who could speak it also. But first I had secret doors and hatches cut in the floor of the closets in the officers' cabins, and another under the stove in the galley. From keel to top deck we converted this American three-master into a mystery ship of trick panels and trick doors.

But what would happen if we were ordered into Kirkwall to have our deckload of lumber shifted and our hold searched, you ask? Ah! we were ready for that.

Of course, if an enemy patrol vessel picked us up, a special prize crew of half a dozen men would be put aboard us to make sure we headed for the right port. I would have sixty-four men of my own to handle the small prize crew.

Dinner time would come. I would say to the Britishers: "Gentlemen, may you dine well."

"Cookie," I would call, "serve up the best we've got."

On their way to my private captain's quarters, they would leave their coats and weapons in the vestibule, within sight and just out of reach.

Right in the middle of the meal, I would signal to my fighting men hidden on the lower deck. Seizing their rifles they would jump to their appointed places. At another signal, the crew above deck would clamber up the iron masts, open small secret doors, reach down into the hollow chambers where their arms and uniforms were hidden, and a moment later German jack-tars would appear where humble Norwegian sailors had been a moment before. We would not attempt to recapture our own ship dressed in civilian togs.

Although the floor of my saloon where the prize crew would be dining looked like any other floor, it was in reality an elevator! All I had to do was press a secret button hidden behind the barometer in the chart room. Presto! down would drop floor, prize crew and all.

Before a man jack could jump for a weapon they would find themselves dining on the next deck below. With the difference that they now would be gazing down the barrels of twenty German rifles.

Then I would step forward, throw open my great-coat, and present myself as the skipper of a wind jammer suddenly metamorphosed into the commander of an auxiliary cruiser.

I had carefully arranged all this because I knew full well that British naval men will put up a stiff fight even with all odds against them. Most naval men will. Of course, it would be easy to overpower a prize crew of only six or seven men, but I wanted to avoid spilling any blood. It is better sport to capture men

than to take their lives. The Allies were calling us Huns, and I for one wanted to show the world how wrong they were.

And now, by Joe, suppose a British cruiser seized us and then we seized the British prize crew. Then supposing another cruiser should pick us up! We might have to do a bit of fighting, maybe take to the boats with our prisoners, and then sink our own ship. So we prepared for this by placing bombs where they could be touched off at a moment's notice. We had no intention of letting our raider fall into enemy hands.

I felt that it was so important to keep all of our plans secret that I even fooled the workmen who were altering the ship. Had they known what we were up to, the rumour might have gotten out. There were spies everywhere. You must admire the British. They had a great espionage system, and they paid their spies well. We Germans were stingy. Bah! That was one reason we bungled.

So I told everyone, including the foremen, that the *Pass of Balmaha* was being transformed into an up-to-date training ship, to be used in training mechanics' apprentices who later on were to run motors on submarines and zeppelins. That alibi was to explain our two motors. The war had shown that German cabin boys were deficient in knowledge of nautical rigging. So I also announced that one purpose of this sailing ship was to give them a chance to learn a little about handling sails. As to the accommodations in the hold for prisoners, and the bunks for our big crew, I explained that these were to be for apprentices and cabin boys. I even put up signs marking off one part of the ship "for 150 cabin boys," another "for 80 apprentices," and so on.

It would have looked suspicious for a naval officer

to be directing work of this kind with such infinite pains, so at the ship yards I posed as Herr von Eckmann, Inspector for the Naval Ministry.

An old retired captain of the Ship Inspection Service happened to be stopping in the same hotel. His love for his old profession caused him to take a most embarrassing interest in my work. One day, he met a bona-fide ship inspector and asked him whether he knew me.

"Von Eckmann? Let's see, I know everybody in the service. There is no Von Eckmann on the roster."

"Then," blurted out the old captain, "he must be a spy. I always said he had a typically English face. I'll watch him."

Through mistake, two letters came for me without the usual cover address. Both of them gave my full name and rank. I argued with the head waiter, trying to get him to give me the letters for delivery to "my friend, Count Luckner." The old captain happened to be snooping near by, although I didn't know it. By now, anything I did was suspicious. He already had me hung and quartered as his country's arch enemy.

"What did that fellow want?" he inquired of the head waiter.

"He asked me to give him the letters for Lieutenant Commander Count von Luckner."

"Ha!"

I suspected nothing. That evening I took the train for Bremen. A detective entered my compartment and demanded my papers. I gave them to him.

"Count von Luckner," he exclaimed, astonished and embarrassed, "I must have made a mistake. I am looking for a spy from Geestemunde."

I grew worried. Could it be that enemy secret/

agents were watching the work on my auxiliary cruiser?

"Where was the spy reported?"

"He lives at Beermann's Hotel."

That was my hotel. The spy was watching me. I told him that I would take upon myself the responsibility of saying that there were the most urgent reasons why this spy must be caught, and that he must wire his principals that the utmost vigilance must be used.

"We already have the railroad covered at both ends. But we will increase our precautions," he replied. "The spy will surely be caught."

In Bremen at Hillman's Hotel I was again stopped by a detective who demanded my papers. Again my papers confounded and bewildered him.

"The description of the spy fits you exactly," he said.

Once more I urged that the headquarters of the secret police be commanded to catch the secret agent at any cost.

At the Trocadero, I sat with a bottle of wine in front of me. A provost officer with two men in uniform came up to me.

"Come with us. You are under arrest."

I flew into a rage at these repetitions of stupidity, as I thought them to be.

"I am a naval officer."

"You are a spy. Come with us!"

The usual spy mania spread throughout the restaurant. Blows were threatened, chairs were brandished, and there were shouts of "Kill the spy, kill him!" on all sides. If the officers hadn't fought the crowd off, I would have been badly beaten.

At headquarters I was shown a description and

even a picture of myself. So there was no doubt but what I was their man.

"Under what name does this spy travel?" I demanded.

"Under the name of Marine Inspector von Eckmann."

"Why, I am he."

"But you just said you were Count von Luckner."

I was compelled, with great injunctions of secrecy, to take them into my confidence, and had them telephone the Admiralty for confirmation.

The prying old captain at Geestemunde soon took himself to other parts—by request!

As I explained, my plan was to slip through the British blockade as a neutral and if possible disguised as some other ship that actually existed. There happened to be a Norwegian vessel that was almost a dead ringer for the *Pass of Balmaha*. She was scheduled to sail from Copenhagen. I decided that we would take her name, and sail the day before she sailed, so that if the British caught us and wirelessed to Copenhagen to confirm our story they would receive word that such a craft had left port at the time we claimed. This other ship was named the *Maleta*. For some time she had been discharging grain from the Argentine. From Denmark she was to proceed to Christiania and there pick up a cargo. Why not a cargo of lumber for Melbourne?

I went to Copenhagen, donned old clothes, and got a job as a dock walloper on the pier where the real *Maleta* was moored. That enabled me to study her. There was one thing that promised to be difficult to counterfeit. That was the log book. This precious volume contained the life history of the *Maleta*, when she left the Argentine, what kind of cargo she carried, what course she steered, the wind, the

weather, observations of sun and stars, etc., etc. That log book must be in the captain's cabin and I must have it. But a watchman was stationed aft, so how could it be done?

I discovered that the captain and both mates were still in Norway with their families. So it would be some days before the loss of the book would be noticed—if I got it.

So one night, in the uniform of a customs inspector, I stole aboard the *Maleta*. The watchman, as usual, was sitting near the captain's cabin. The ship was moored to the pier with ropes fore and aft. Stealthily I tiptoed to the bow and cut the ropes, not quite through but almost. A stiff wind was blowing. The ropes cracked and broke. The ship swung around. The watchman ran forward shouting, and at the same moment I ran aft. Fumbling around the captain's cabin I at first failed to locate the log. Finally, I discovered it under the skipper's mattress. Shoving it beneath my belt, I slipped out.

On board now, and also on the pier, half a dozen men were shouting and throwing ropes to haul her back so she wouldn't side-swipe a near-by ship. I joined in the shouting, pretended to help them for a minute, then clambered on to the dock and hurried off in the dark.

We now put on the final touches that were to turn the *Pass of Balmaha* into the *Maleta*. We painted her the same colour as the *Maleta*, arranged her deck the same, and decorated the cabins with the same ornaments. In my captain's cabin, I hung pictures of the King and Queen of Norway and also of their jovial relative, King Edward VII of England. The barometer, thermometer, and chronometer, and all the other instruments were of Norwegian make. I had a Norwegian library and a Norwegian phonograph

and records. We had enough provisions from Norwegian firms to last us through the blockade. It would hardly do to have any Bismarck herring, sauerkraut, and pretzels in sight if the British boarded us, would it?

The names of the tailors sewn inside my suits and my officers' suits were replaced with labels from Norwegian tailors. On my underclothing we embroidered the name of the captain of the *Maleta*—Knudsen.

I had learned in Copenhagen that a donkey engine was being installed on the *Maleta*. Very well, we got a donkey engine of the same make from Copenhagen and installed it on our ship. The log book of the *Maleta* was solemnly put in place, and the first entry was made, "To-day put in a new donkey engine."

We got up our cargo papers in regular form, signed and sealed by both the Norwegian port authorities and British consul. We also had a letter signed by His Majesty's consul at Copenhagen stating that the *Maleta* was carrying lumber for the use of the Government of the Commonwealth of Australia. The letter requested all British ships to help us if any emergency arose. To prove that this document was genuine, it was even stamped with the British Imperial Seal (made in Germany!).

I also had a letter which a British officer had supposedly written to my shipowner and which my shipowner had forwarded to me, warning us against German search officers, but advising us to place our trust in the British!

A sailor with the loneliness of the sea upon him nearly always takes with him on his voyages photographs of his people. Now the crews on British warships know sailor ways, so I inquired all about the procedure from captains of neutral ships who had had their ships searched. They told me that the British

always inspected the fo'c'sle to see that everything looked right there. I immediately got together a lot of photographs to pass as those of Norwegian sailors' parents, brothers and sisters, uncles and aunts, sweethearts, wives and mothers-in-law. What did it matter whether the sweethearts were good-looking or not? Sailors' sweethearts are not always prize beauties. We sent a man to Norway for the pictures in order to have the names of Norwegian photographers stamped on them.

The British are smart people, by Joe, and they know how to search a ship. They attach special importance to sailors' letters. The sailor eagerly looks forward to the letter he will receive at the next port. He never throws the letters away either, but always keeps a stack of them in his sea chest. Sometimes you will see him reading a letter that his mother sent him eight years before. So we had to get up a whole set of letters for our "Norwegian" sailors, each set totally different from the other.

Of course, the stolen log of the *Maleta* gave us a lot of useful information about her crew, and our fake letters were made to tally with this information. Women in the Admiralty and Foreign offices who knew Norwegian wrote them for us. We got old Norwegian stamps and Norwegian postmarks and postmarks of various ports the letters were supposed to have been sent to. Then we aged the letters in chemicals, and tore and smudged some of them.

I picked as my officers men who like myself had spent long years before the mast, who knew Norwegian, and were of the right spirit. First Officer Kling had been a member of the Filchner Expedition, in which he had distinguished himself. The officer whom I selected to go aboard captured ships was a former comrade of mine, a fellow of six feet four,

whom I met by chance on a dock. In response to my question whether he wanted to accompany me, he asked:

"Is it one of those trips that is likely to send you to heaven?"

"Yes."

"Then I'm with you. My name is Preiss, and you are after prizes. So I'll bring you luck."

My artillery and navigation officer, Lieutenant Kircheiss, was a wizard navigator. Engineer Krauss was our motor expert. The boatswain, the carpenter, and the cook, the three mainstays of a voyage in a sailing vessel, I picked with like care. Of the men who were to go with me I only needed twenty-seven with a knowledge of Norwegian. There were just twenty-seven aboard the real *Maleta*. In selecting, my men, I interviewed each candidate personally but gave him no hint of why I wanted him. I tried to read these men's souls in order to discover in them the qualities of courage and endurance that would be needed.

Without giving them any clue concerning the adventure on which they were soon to engage, I sent them home on furlough to prevent them from meeting one another and talking over the questions I had put to them. Not until the hour of departure did I send for them.

Now we needed a name for our raider. We needed one that she could take for her official name as an auxiliary cruiser after running the blockade. I wanted to call her the *Albatross* out of gratitude to the albatross that saved me from drowning when I was a lad. But I discovered that there was already a vessel with that name, a mine-layer. Then I wanted to call the ship the *Sea Devil*, the name by which I personally was afterward to be called. My officers favoured

some name that would suggest the white wings of our sailship. So we compromised on *Seeadler*, or Sea Eagle.

On a pitch-dark November night, the *Seeadler*, with a small emergency crew, raises anchor and sails out of the mouth of the Weser into the North Sea. There, some distance offshore, we drop anchor.

At a remote place along the docks at Wilhelmshaven, men appear one by one. By the light of a dimly burning lantern I gather my crew. None of them has any inkling of what is afoot. I hear them ask:

"Where are we off to? What is it?"

We piled them into a little steamer, and off. Soon they saw an imposing ship riding through the night.

"Hello, what sort of craft is this, a sailship?"

Aboard everything is ready, and everything is Norwegian. Their bunks are all prepared. Photographs are on the walls. Norwegian landscapes, photographs of Norwegian girls, Norwegian flags hang draped. A fully equipped Norwegian ship awaiting the arrival of its crew.

"Do you speak Norwegian, Karl?"

"Yes. Do you?"

"Yes."

"Strange business this!"

Some of the men do not speak Norwegian. The ones that do, have their bunks above deck. The ones that don't, have their bunks below. Germany below decks. Norway above. Strange!

We were away from all communication with land now. There was no longer need for secrecy.

"Boys, the British say not even a mouse can get through their blockade. But we will show them, by Joe, and under full pressure of sail. Then, once we reach the high seas, we will sink their ships, by Joe. Can we do it?"

"Sure, Count, we can do it! By Joe, you bet we can do it!" Not a man quailed, and I was happy to be in command of such a crew.

Next morning a scow of lumber lay alongside, and we stacked timber to a height of six feet over all the deck, and fastened it down with wire and chains.

Every man had his rôle. Every man must now prove his mettle as an actor. Officers and sailors were given the names of officers and sailors aboard the *Maleta*. They had to get used to their new names. Fritz Meyer was now Ole Johnsen, Miller became Björnsen, Hans Lehman became Lars Carlsen, and they knew me only as Captain Knudsen. We had long practice drills until the new names slid off our tongues without getting stuck.

Each man also had to learn a lot about his native town that he never knew before! I had already assembled as much information as I could about the towns listed in the stolen log book, and the rest we invented. Each man had to learn the names of the main streets of his town, the principal hotels, taverns, and drug stores, as well as the names of the mayor and other officials. Much of this sort of material had already been woven into the letters we had prepared for the sailors. Each man had to familiarize himself with the set of photographs that had been allotted to him, and the names of them all, the contents of his letters, and fix in his mind a whole new past life, according to the life of the sailor of the real *Maleta* whose rôle he was to play.

One of the mechanics' helpers, Schmidt by name, I had taken for a principal rôle in our strategy. He was slender, beardless, and of delicate appearance, and could pass well enough in woman's clothes. Norwegian skippers often take their wives with them on their voyages. The captain's wife aboard the false

Maleta would seem natural and tend to disarm suspicion, and, besides, British naval officers are always
courteous and considerate toward women. In the
presence of the captain's wife, a prize officer who
might board us would be more obliging toward us all.
We had a blonde wig for Schmidt and an outfit of
women's clothes. We took great pains in schooling
him to play the part of the captain's wife correctly.
One difficulty was his big feet. Not even a Norwegian skipper's wife had such feet. There was,
unfortunately, no way to make them smaller, so we
arranged that the captain's wife should be slightly
ill and remain seated during any possible search and
have a rug thrown over her feet to keep them warm.
The other difficulty was Schmidt's voice. It was too
deep, and he knew no Norwegian. Well, the captain's
wife can't talk because she has an awful toothache.
A wad of cotton stuffed into Schmidt's cheek, and
there was the swelling. He did know enough English
to say "all right." We trained him to say a high-
pitched "all right" something like a woman with a
toothache. Except for that phrase, he was to keep
his mouth shut. We had a large photograph made of
Schmidt in his costume, signed it "thy loving
Josephine," and hung it in my cabin. Now the Britishers could compare the photograph of the captain's
wife with the lady in person. So from now on poor
Schmidt's name was "Josefeena" as the Norwegians
pronounce it.

We were ready to sail when, by Joe, what comes
but a telegram from the Kaiser's aide. I am to report
immediately direct to His Majesty. I guessed what
was up. I had gone into the navy from the mercantile
marine instead of through the usual cadet route. I
had been a common ordinary sailor, and this had
aroused a lot of antagonism in naval circles. There

had been jealousy about my getting an independent command—highest of all naval honours. So attempts were being made to have my assignment annulled.

And now they had gone to the Emperor! Maybe I would lose this fine sailship of mine. Already it had given me a new lease on life, just by getting back into the old life, the life that had been so difficult to survive and so delightful to recall. Maybe I would have to go back to the navy, to the modern war of hissing steel, and deafening guns of superdreadnaughts. I had an affection for them too, but it was the enthusiasm of the mind. Here on the sailship was my heart. Well, I would fight them.

"Luckner," I thought, "you always have to fight, or you sink. That's life."

The Emperor had been very kind to the man who had risen from a common sailor to a naval officer. He had paid for my naval training out of his own private purse, and had taken a personal interest in my promotions. Many a time on board ship he had commanded me to tell stories of my adventures. I could talk to him. I could talk to him more boldly than other officers dared. I knew that he understood me.

Even to appear in the Imperial presence was a trying ordeal for most officers. Many took refuge in rigid "attention." Well, I had never quite got used to high class manners at sea, and the ramrod "attention" left me more embarrassed than otherwise. Even in the Emperor's presence, I kept the same free, brusque manner of an old-time seaman that was natural to me.

The Kaiser spoke bluntly.

"Well, Luckner, at the Admiralty they now tell me it is madness to attempt the blockade with a sailing ship. What do you think?"

"Well, Your Majesty, if our Admiralty says it's impossible and ridiculous, then I'm *sure* it *can* be done," I replied. "For the British Admiralty will think it impossible also. They won't be on the look-out for anything so absurd as a raider disguised as a harmless old sailing ship."

The Emperor looked at me with a frown, and then his face relaxed into a smile.

"You are right, Luckner. Go ahead! And may the hand of the Almighty be at your helm."

I knew now that there would be no more official interference. The true *Maleta* was now due to sail in a day, so we made ready to pull up anchor. Then a wireless came from the Admiralty:

Wait till the *Deutschland* makes port.

Our giant merchant submarine, the *Deutschland*, was on her way home from her famous transatlantic cruise to America. In an attempt to cut her off, the British had set a double watch. So the *Seeadler* would have to slip past twice as many cruisers and destroyers as otherwise. I still hoped that, if only detained a day or so, we might yet be able to slip across the North Sea ahead of the *Maleta*. But we lay there for three and a half weeks, and the sad news came that the real *Maleta* had sailed and passed through the blockade. If we now attempted to use her name and a search party boarded us, the jig would be up.

So we hurriedly examined Lloyd's Register in the hope of finding another Norwegian ship that might correspond to us. We picked out one called the *Carmoe*. We had no idea where she was, but hoped she might be in some distant port unbeknown to the wary British. It was a long chance, but we could think

of nothing better. Now we had to change our ship from the *Maleta* to the *Carmoe*. Painting out one name and substituting another was easy enough, but changing all our ship's papers was far more difficult. But with much use of chemical eraser we finally accomplished it, and we had papers that would pass if the visibility was not too bright during the search. Then, when we were all set again, we picked up a copy of a Norwegian commercial paper and found that the real *Carmoe* had just been seized by the British and taken to Kirkwall for examination.

"By Joe, and they said this *Pass of Balmaha* was a lucky ship! We must have a Jonah on board!"

Now, if you haven't any luck, you must go and get some! All you have to do is know how to do that, and you will be a great success at sea, or anywhere!

So away with Lloyd's Register! Let's take life's register and name our sea eagle after the girl of my heart. Surely she will bring us luck. So, out with the paint and on with another new name—the name of my sweetheart, *Irma*.

In that name was concentrated most of the beauty that I had found in life. It symbolized strange moments of beauty that had crossed my path during the most trying days I had so far known. It seemed to be a lovely silken thread that had run through the years since that first voyage, when as a miserable cabin boy I sailed to Australia on that Russian tramp.

Of course, there was no such name as *Irma* listed with Lloyd's, and all any British officer would have to do would be to consult his Register and the jig would be up. But somehow I had a premonition that the name *Irma* would bring us through.

When we applied eraser and ink to our shipping papers and wrote in the name of *Irma*—disaster. Two erasures were too much. The ink blotted. If we should

be stupid enough to take the British for fools, then we ourselves would be the real fools. Where was our luck now? Fate seemed to be against us, but I had no intention of giving up. Calling the carpenter I said:

"Come on, Chips, I am going to make you admiral of the day. Get the ax and smash all the bull's-eyes, windows, portholes, and everything."

Poor Chips! He thought I had gone off my head, but he obeyed. The smashing began.

"Bo's'n," I called, "half a dozen men with buckets of sea water! Throw it around, drench everything."

And now the water flew in the cabins, in the drawers of chests, in the officers' bunks, all over my Norwegian library, water everywhere. I took my shipping papers and put each page between sheets of wet blotting paper so that not only the name of *Irma* and the other entries we had changed were blotted, but every line. I even soused the log book in a bucket of water.

Then I called the carpenter again.

"Now repair everything you have smashed, Chips. Nail everything."

He hammered planks over the smashed portholes and bull's-eyes, and put the smashed chairs together as well as he could.

Now, if the Britisher came aboard, he would say:

"By Joe, Captain, you must have had a hard blow to get knocked about like this."

And I would growl, "Yes, by Joe, everything is drenched, even my papers."

Two days later a southwest wind sprang up. The moment was at hand. To go raiding in a sailing ship and that sailing ship with the name of *Irma* painted on her bows—ah, it seemed more like a dream than like setting out on a real adventure. It seemed as

though all the events of my life had been designed to converge to this one glorious point. Our one hundred-and-seventy-foot masts creaked. Our nine thousand square feet of sail bellowed before the wind. We sailed north under a full spread.

XIII

SAILS bellied and motor humming, we parted the waves and left a path of foam in our wake. On deck we devoted all our spare time to more dress rehearsals. My boys took a particular relish in putting me through the "third degree," as you call it. One of them played the part of a British search officer.

"Now, Captain, what is the name of your ship?" he bellowed.

"She is the *Irma,* and as good a full-rigged ship as ever crossed the North Sea."

"Have you any brothers and sisters, Captain?"

"Oh, yes, a lot of them. There are Olga, Ingaborg, and Oscar who live in Hatfjelddalen. Dagmar and Christian are seamen like myself. Lars runs a salmon cannery in British Columbia, Gustaf and Tor are lumbermen somewhere in America. And then we have another brother, Eric, whom we've lost track of."

While trying to make the narrow channel of Norderaue we hit a sand bank. The ship creaked and the masts trembled, but somehow we pushed across—further proof that the Scots of Glasgow still know how to turn out a sturdy clipper ship.

At ten o'clock we passed the Horns reef and continued along the Danish coast. At eight bells we hoped to reach the Skagerrak, and then turn her west to give the enemy the impression that we had

come from a Scandinavian port. Shortly before daybreak, the wind shifted abruptly from southwest to
due north. Against such a stiff breeze, we could make
little headway. On our right were the low rocky fjords
and reefs along the coast of Ringkjöbing and Thisted.
To the left were British mine fields. We didn't dare
run into a Danish harbour for fear of being interned.
So we must either turn back or take a chance on
slipping through the mine fields. It is always possible
to sail through a mine field—provided you sail under
a lucky star with a guardian angel at the helm.

"Hard aport! We'll risk it, boys." With a full
spread of sail, we turned straight west.

Now, a tacking ship heels over. The more sail you
carry the more she lays over, and the less water she
draws. That was our chance. The mines were nearly
always planted several feet under water, just out of
sight. Perhaps we could slide right over them. Lifeboats were lowered, and every man adjusted his life-
belt. Before the mast, the sailors; aft, the captain. But
we all kept to the foreship. We were lower aft than
fore, and if a mine went off it probably would be aft.
But our luck held and we got through in safety.

Our course lay around the northern end of Scotland, along the usual shipping route from Norway to
the Atlantic. To be sure, we could have hugged the
Norwegian coast, but the blockade was even tighter
there. That was the natural course for one of our
raiding armoured cruisers to take, so, if she were
headed off by Beatty, she could turn quickly into
a neutral Norwegian port and accept internment
rather than capture. We didn't even keep to the
middle of the North Sea, but with the idea that our
one path of safety lay right under John Bull's nose,
we followed the coast of England and Scotland.

There were three lines of the blockade. The first

lay across the North Sea from the Scottish to the Danish coast. We must run this one first.

The wind grew stronger. The barometer fell. Anyone on the North Sea on the twenty-third of December, 1916, will remember the hurricane that came. It was one of the worst storms of years. The wind was cyclonic in force, and lashed the shallow North Sea into a cauldron. Running before it we carried every foot of sail we dared, every stitch except the royals and gallantsails and smaller staysails. We could take chances. We had no shipowner to answer to. Every mile through the storm now meant a mile through the blockade. The ship lay over so far that all our leeboard was under water. Every plank quivered from the strain on the rigging. The rigging sang like a violin. Heavy waves swept over us. It looked at times as if Niagara Falls were descending upon us. Two men were needed to hold the helm, and had to be lashed there. Some of our stays broke and some of our canvas ripped. But we made fifteen knots, and that hurricane was a godsend to us, for we knew no British cruiser could search us or even keep track of us in such a heavy gale.

We sped right through the first line of the blockade without sighting a ship and as though the whole North Sea were ours. Instead of going up, the barometer continued to fall. Louder roared the storm, and more and more mountainous became the waves. We passed the second line of the blockade. Still not a ship in sight.

"At twelve o'clock, boys, we will know whether we are going to get through or not. At this speed, we will pass through the third and most important line. Half the Grand Fleet is said to guard this third stretch from the Shetlands to Bergen."

Midnight grew near, and still that wild heaven-

sent hurricane kept up. We ran before it like a frightened bird, fearing every minute that our sails and masts would go overboard. We lay on the yards and scanned the horizon with our glasses. Half-past eleven! We were in the midst of the blockade line. Where were the cruisers and destroyers? All we could hear was the whistling of the wind and the rushing of the water beneath our bows. All we could see, the blackness of the night. Twelve o'clock and still no sign of the enemy. Even our binnacle and compass lights were out, for any ray of light might betray us. By one o'clock we knew we had passed the last line.

The British, warned by the falling barometer, had taken their guard ships to shelter in the lee of the islands. There was nothing else for them to do in such a storm. Even if they saw a ship, it would be hopeless to try to board her. And if Beatty's fleet had kept to sea, there would have been grave danger of their running one another down. We couldn't help recalling the old saying that it is indeed an ill wind that blows no one any good.

I thought now that, under cover of darkness and with the aid of the storm, we might shorten our voyage to the Atlantic by cutting through the channel between the Orkney Islands and the Shetlands. I was about to order the helm changed, when the hurricane shifted abruptly from southwest to southeast. The change came so suddenly that the twisting winds nearly ripped our masts out by the roots. Somehow, that seemed to be a warning to us, a warning not to go through that channel.

A sailor believes in signs. And something told me to take a more northerly course, nearer the Arctic Circle and the Faroes. Later, we learned that the German submarine *Bremen* had tried to pass through

that channel and was never seen again. The channel
had recently been mined. But for that sudden shift
of the storm, we too would have shared the fate of
the *Bremen*. With sails still full spread, we continued north, nearer and nearer the Polar zone. It
grew bitterly cold. The waves dashed over us, and
the water froze where it fell. Our timber cargo was so
coated with ice that not a stick of lumber could be
seen. The deck was like a skating rink, and the ship's
bow one huge cake of ice. Everything froze, including the sails. The ropes became coated and would
no longer run through the blocks. We tried to thaw
them with oxygen flame, but they froze again the
moment the flame was removed. Unable to change
the sails, we were helpless. To turn on the motor
would only make matters worse, because that would
carry us toward the Pole all the faster. We knew that
unless the Hand of God intervened within a few days
we would be hopelessly caught in the Polar pack and
probably never heard of again. So long as the wind
blew from the south, we were sure to continue on
north. We were in the region of eternal night now,
except for a few minutes each day. The sun rose at
eleven and set at half-past eleven. If we continued
this crazy, frozen voyage to the North Pole we would
be smashed in the ice, by Joe.

Christmas Eve came, and we prayed God to send
us the one Christmas present, the only one that
could save us—a north wind to blow us south. My
men in the hold, my fighting crew, huddled together
to keep from freezing. They were prisoners, for the
waves and spray had swept over everything until
our secret hatches were frozen as solid as concrete.
My false Norsemen on deck slid about on the icy
planks, and every man suffered from frostbite. No
one tried to turn in to sleep. The tension on our

nerves was too great. Only one thing was warm and steaming—the kettle of grog. You landsmen have no idea of what grog means to a sailor under such conditions. No wonder seamen call a glass of schnapps "an ice-breaker!"

At heart every sailor is a child, and he has a child's love of Christmas. And how he enjoys a Christmas present! He turns it around in his hands, and says:

"By Joe, it's good to have Christmas."

And surely the present that came to us was the finest that any sailor ever had.

As suddenly as it had come, the south wind died down and a breeze sprang up in the north. Our frozen ship creaked, laid over, and came around with the new wind, and our hearts sang for joy. Each day we seemed to thaw out a bit more. Soon we passed to the east of Iceland and reëntered the Atlantic. Axes and picks were busy chipping away the ice. It was hard work, but who cared now that we were getting warm again? We were through the blockade and out of the Arctic—and now to test the "Freedom of the Seas" and give the Allies a touch of high life.

"By Joe," I said to my boys, "and they call it a blockade!"

You would have thought the fellow in the lookout was answering me.

"Steamer ahoy," he sang out.

What? A steamer in these parts?

I climbed aloft with my glasses. Sure enough, there was a British armoured cruiser steaming toward us at full speed. She had the signal flying:

"Stand by or we fire!"

Such bad luck after such good luck! This second Christmas present was not so amusing. But now for our test.

"Hustle you non-Norwegian chaps. Get below

deck! Throw water everywhere to explain why our papers are blurred and wet. The storm we just passed through will make it seem the more natural. Schmidt, get into your finery. Remember, from now on you are the shy 'Josefeena' (Josephine), the Captain's wife. If they put a prize crew aboard, we will capture the prize crew. If they suspect we are an auxiliary cruiser, bombs fore, midship, and aft, and we blow up the ship!"

Now for a big quid of tobacco in my mouth. I have never had the habit of chewing tobacco, but a Norwegian skipper would not be true to type without his quid. Besides, a chew of tobacco gives you time to think. If somebody asks you an embarrassing question, you can roll your quid around in your mouth, pucker up your lips slowly, and spit deliberately and elegantly. I had practised rolling the quid and spitting until I thought myself a past master at the art.

But that smell, by Joe! The unexpected always happens to mar the best-laid plans—and help the worst. We had been running our motor full open. Because of the cargo of wood that sealed the deck, there had not been enough ventilation to get rid of the fumes. The characteristic reek of crude oil burning in a Diesel engine seeped up through the secret entrances placed in my cabin, and everything smelled of it. What will the search officer think when he smells a Diesel engine aboard a sailing ship? No use to burn punk or sprinkle eau de cologne.

"Stuff a rug in the chimney of the kerosene stove," I yelled, "and turn up the wicks of the oil lamps as high as you can."

Stench against stench, kerosene smoke against the fumes of the motor. In five minutes my cabin smelled to high heaven of kerosene smoke.

The Britisher had hove to now, and we saw that she was the *Avenger*, an armed merchant cruiser of some 15,000 tons.

"How's that?" I thought. "Why are the guns pointing? We are a peaceable Norwegian sailing ship. Why the guns?"

She had her big guns trained on us, and her officers were on the bridge looking us over with their glasses.

"Can we have been betrayed?" I asked myself. "Of what use is the best mask, of what use are the best men, if a traitor has done his dirty work?"

The thought of treachery always makes the fighting man tremble. I went into my cabin, and like the drowning man who grasps at a straw, I remembered how before leaving port a friend gave me a parcel, saying:

"My boy, take this package with you. But never open it unless you are in a tight fix. Then it may save you."

Well, we were in a tight fix all right, so I opened the package. I took off one wrapper after another. Ah! It was a bottle of rare old Napoleon brandy, almost priceless, made more than a hundred years ago.

"What was good for Napoleon ought to be good for me. He fought against the British, too. Maybe this is just what we need."

I took sixteen or eighteen swallows, and with each gulp felt my cares getting lighter and lighter. Never did I thank God so much that I am not a teetotaller.

The cruiser had put out a small boat. Two officers and sixteen sailors were rowing toward us. We must receive them cordially, I thought. Going to the gramophone I put on, "It's a Long Way to Tipperary." That will make the officers feel good. I also told the cook to stand in the door of the galley with a bottle

of whisky in his hand. I know the British! I know what they like, and I guessed that while the officer proceeded with his job, his jack-tars would go poking about to see if they might find anything suspicious. I also suspected that they would go to the galley and sing out:

" 'I there, Cookie, got any grog?"

Always give a British sailor a drink, or a German sailor, or an American sailor, or any kind of a sailor, for that matter.

The boat was alongside. I began to swear at my men. It was hard for them to forget their naval habits, and, with an officer coming aboard, they were standing as stiffly as if at attention.

"Take the line, by Joe. Give a hand, by Joe. Don't stand there like wooden men, by Joe."

Then, too, it would sound natural to hear a Norwegian skipper swearing at his men.

The search officer clambered aboard.

"Merry Christmas, Captain."

"Merry Christmas, Mister Officer," I replied, using the kind of broken English I thought a Norwegian skipper would use. I talk English with an accent, luckily about the same brand you would hear in a Scandinavian port. "But," I continued, "if you want to see what kind of Christmas we have had come along down to my cabin."

"A bit of a nasty blow this past week, eh, what!" agreed the officer, "and from the look of your deck you've had more than your share of it. We went in behind the islands and waited for her to blow over."

"Yes, luckily for us," I thought to myself.

"I must see your papers, Captain." He got right down to business. Just then the gramophone struck up "Tipperary," and he began to whistle the tune

while his men made for the galley. I ushered the two officers to the cabin. The one who stuck his head in first retreated holding his nose.

"What a hell of a smell!"

"Excuse me, Mister Officer, but my stove is out of order. I could not know you gentlemen were giving me a visit to-day."

"Oh, never mind, Captain, that's all right, that's all right."

I had purposely hung my underwear up to dry so it would be in their way and so that, in stooping to get under it, they would see the name "Knudsen" embroidered on it. As the chief search officer crossed the cabin he suddenly saw my charming wife Josephine, with her blonde wig, her swollen jaw, and the rug hiding her big feet.

"Oh, excuse me."

"That is my wife, Mister Officer. She has been having a bad go with the toothache."

He was chivalrous, just as most Englishmen are. He might have been talking to a court lady, instead of that rascal Schmidt.

"Sorry, madam, to intrude like this, but we must do our duty."

"All right!" said my lovely but somewhat distorted better half in a high falsetto voice out of one corner of her mouth.

"By Joe, Captain, you haven't much cabin left, have you? You *have* been through some rough weather!"

"I wouldn't mind the rest, Mister Officer, but look at my papers. They are soaked, too."

"I can understand that, after the weather you've had."

"Yes, Mister Officer, it's all right for you to see them in this condition, because you saw the storm

yourself, but later, if I meet some of your comrades who didn't hit the blow that we had, they may not take my word for it. That's what's worrying me."

"Oh, don't worry, Captain, I'll give you a memorandum explaining the condition of your papers. You are lucky to have saved your ship."

That memorandum was just what I wanted. There was no telling when we might be searched again.

I had the papers scattered all over the cabin to dry, and each time I handed one to him I spat a stream of tobacco juice on the cabin floor. He examined the papers with a practised eye and made entries in his notebook. Each page in his book was for a ship, and I could see that thirty or forty pages had been used already. Yes, he was an experienced officer.

When he came to the last document, the one signed with the false signature of the British Consul at Copenhagen and sealed with a false British Imperial seal, and read the formal statement that the *Irma's* cargo of lumber was destined for the use of the British government in Australia, he turned to me suddenly.

"These papers are all right, Captain."

In the excitement of the moment I suddenly swallowed my chew of tobacco. I was afraid this might give our whole sham away. So I coughed and coughed as though with a bad cold, trying to cover up what had happened. What would a British search officer think if a Norwegian skipper got seasick? My mate Leudemann was standing next to me holding the log book. I had told him to have it ready in case the Britisher should want to examine it. Leudemann saw there was something wrong with me, and was quick-witted enough to divert the search officer's attention, by handing him the book.

"Oh, yes, the log," exclaimed the officer, and opened the wet pages.

The quid of tobacco seemed to be moving up and down my gullet. I struggled with myself, and to show an outward calm I said to Leudemann in Norwegian:

"I wish I'd had that officer's camel's hair cape and hood. It would have been fine to keep a fellow warm while up there north of the Circle."

"For rain and spray, too." The Englishman spoke up in Norwegian to show that he knew the language.

You must admire how careful those English are. The officer examined every page of the log.

"How is this, Captain?" he exclaimed. "You were laid up three weeks and a half?"

There was a discrepancy in dates which represented our wait after the Admiralty had ordered us not to sail because of the return of the submarine, *Deutschland*, and the consequent increased vigilance of the blockade. I had not thought of it. Here was the one detail that we had neglected to provide for in our elaborately detailed preparations. Even if I had been in the best of health, I should not have known what to reply. With that tobacco quid running around inside of my body I could only pray to God for help.

Again Leudemann saved the situation. He was a little fellow and simple-hearted, but a great character. When bad times came, Leudemann was at his best.

"We didn't lie there for pleasure," he said in his dry way as he looked up at the big Englishman. "We had orders from our owner not to sail until we got word."

"How so?"

"Haven't you been warned then about German cruisers?"

"What's that?"

"Haven't you heard about the *Moewe* and the auxiliary cruiser, *Seeadler?*"

The search officer turned to me.

"What about this that your mate is saying, Captain?"

My stomach felt much better, now that Leudemann had spoken. So I thought I might as well give the Englishman a good dose.

"There were rumours at home in Norway that two cruisers and sixteen German submarines had put out of port."

The search officer's comrade, who had been looking around the cabin, came over to us when he heard all this.

"I think we had better be going," he spoke up suddenly.

"Yes," replied the other, and they went on deck.

They made no attempt at questioning the sailors or investigating the sailors' belongings.

"Your papers are all right, Captain," said the search officer, "but you will have to wait here for an hour until you get a signal to proceed."

"All right, Mister Officer."

One of my boys, who was of a pessimistic turn of mind, heard this. As he walked away from my cabin he said out loud to himself:

"Everything is lost."

Down below were the members of my other crew, waiting in the dark. They were right beneath the floor of the deck, straining their ears to catch any word that might give them an idea how things were going on deck. They heard the exclamation, "Everything is lost," and took it for the official word

that we were discovered and for the command to do what was to be done in that case. They lit the fuses of the three bombs that were to blow up the ship, and waited for the hatches to be opened to let them on deck to the boats. The fuses would burn for fifteen minutes.

The British were in their boat now, trying to push off. But you can't hold a sailing ship in one place like a steamer. She keeps drifting. And the suction of the *Seeadler* as she drifted held their boat so it couldn't get away. What was still worse, it kept slipping aft, and if it got under our stern, they would have been sure to see our propeller. A sailship with a propeller? Yes, sometimes, but we would have been done for, as there was nothing to that effect in our papers. Seizing a rope, I tossed it overboard toward them.

"Take the rope, Mister Officer, take the rope," I shouted as though clumsily trying to help them.

That made them look up, so that the rope might not fall on their heads. I heaved the rope just as they were sliding around our stern and away. The officers thanked me, and one of them, angry with his men for not being able to push the boat off, exclaimed:

"I have only fools on my boat."

"Yes, maybe you have," I thought, "and maybe you are the worst-fooled one of all!"

My stomach was quite normal now. I was so happy that I even felt as though I could digest that quid of tobacco. The men on deck felt like cheering and singing, but they had orders to go on about their jobs as though nothing unusual had been going on, until the cruiser was far and away. They just grinned, but so broad were the grins that I thought they would split their faces.

My first thought was to bring the happy news to

the boys in the darkness down below. I went to one of the secret hatches, which they had fastened from within.

"Open," I shouted.

There were vague sounds below.

"Open up," I called again.

Then I heard a muffled voice say:

"Open the flood valves."

"What's that?" I yelled. "What's the matter? Open the hatch!"

The hatch opened. I saw troubled faces. I could hear water rushing into the ship.

"By Joe," I shouted, "are you trying to sink my boat?"

I could hear men running below to all parts of the ship. I climbed down roaring. One of the men spoke up.

"They are cutting the fuses and closing the flood valves."

"Fuses, flood valves, by Joe. How's that happen, by Joe?"

Then one of the men said: "But someone called down that all was lost! Afterward you called 'open' and we thought you meant open the flood valves."

The fuses had been burning for eight minutes out of their fifteen, and hundreds of gallons of water were pouring into the ship.

By Joe, I looked for the fellow who said "All is lost." He came forward at once and confessed.

"I wasn't calling to the men below. I merely said it to myself."

"Why do you say 'all is lost,' by Joe, just when everything is fine?"

"Well, Captain, when the Englishman said that we would have to wait for an hour, I thought to myself that the game was up. It means that he is keep-

ing us waiting while he sends a wireless to Copenhagen asking about the *Irma*, when there is no *Irma*."

"By Joe," I said, "that's right."

In our excitement, neither I nor my officers had thought about the wireless. It had not occurred to us to ask ourselves why we had been ordered to stand by for a whole hour. We didn't even think of Lloyd's Register. The search officer might have gone back to his ship to look up the *Irma* in the Register, where there was no *Irma*.

For days I had been on deck in the storm and in the ice regions. For the past half hour I had gone through worse turmoil even than that. And now, when everything seemed clear, the sky looked black again and that quid of tobacco started getting in its dirty work. I went to the rail and hung there on my elbows, staring through my binoculars at the *Avenger* and watching for the flag signal. My hand shook, and instead of only one I could see three cruisers in my glass. I handed it to Leudemann and while he took a look I leaned there with the code book in my hand, ready to decode the signal when it came.

I don't know how long it was, fifteen minutes or an hour, but finally three little flags went up the signal rope. Old imperturbable Leudemann steadied his glass. At last he made out the signal:

"T-M-B."

I thumbed the book clumsily. It seemed as though I would never find T-M-B. But there it was. It meant "Planet." Nonsense. Read the signal again.

I was getting weaker and weaker, whether from the anxiety or from that quid, I don't know. This time he read:

"T-X-B."

Pages, columns, and then the right place. . . .
Continue voyage.

I felt as though my heart had two valves instead
of one and was pumping madly through both. I sat
down and breathed heavily. Instead of going about
their ordinary tasks, my men wanted to yell like
Indians.

Hello, what's this? The *Avenger*, with her 15,000
tons driven by 100,000-horsepower engines, was racing straight at us. Huge streams of smoke and great
flames like torches poured out of her three funnels
as her safety valves blew out from the over-pressure
of her boilers. Just as she got on top of us she swerved
off. At her stern flew a signal. I did not need a code
book. I knew that signal by heart—Happy Voyage.
We raised the signal—thanks—and dipped our Norwegian flag three times.

The British had behaved like gentlemen toward
us. I think the way they pointed their guns at us when
they came up to us was a bit of a joke. The hour they
made us wait was, I think, to enable them to make
wireless inquiries about the story we told of German
cruisers and submarines. The search officer did his
work courteously and well. No seaman should try to
make another seaman ridiculous. We were disguised
so well that he could have suspected nothing. In his
place, I should have been fooled exactly as he was,
and so would any other officer.

"And now, boys, let's celebrate Christmas!"

We dumped our deck load of lumber into the sea,
and cleared the deck for a big time. I had a Christmas
tree that I had brought from home. We set it up.
Before the *Seeadler* left port, Fraulein Bertha Krupp
had sent us a huge box full of Christmas presents,
something for every man. We opened it and found

clothing, cigars, pipes, cigarettes, cigar holders, knives, liquor, soft drinks, and musical instruments.

It was the merriest Christmas of our lives. Singing "Yo-ho" and cheered up with many good bottles of rum, we headed south to play our rôle as buccaneers.

WE CAPTURE THE *GLADYS ROYAL* AND THE *LUNDY ISLAND*

ALL hands on deck!"

Aloft my boys flew, into the rigging and up the ratlines like monkeys.

"Loose the fore-taups'l!" boomed up from the quarter deck.

"All gone, the fore-taups'l," they sang out.

"Loose the ga'nts'ls and stays'ls!"

The sails were sheeted home and were filling out. We didn't lose much time in getting her away. Lying over on her beam ends and running before the wind, we set our course for Madeira.

We knew that just off Gibraltar would be one of our best hunting grounds, so we cleared away the remains of our Norwegian camouflage, and after a few days we were as spick and clean and orderly as a German auxiliary cruiser should be. We were the *Irma* no longer, but the *Seeadler* now, although I felt a pang of regret at letting go the name that had served us so well and brought us luck.

There was constant labour on the motor. The lubricating oil we had was of poor quality. Oil, like many other things, had become scarce in Germany. Our enterprise had the enthusiastic support of only a few of the officials at the Admiralty. The others thought it certainly foredoomed to failure, and did not want to risk too much on it. Among these were the heads of the department that supplied us with oil. A sailing

vessel under the pressure of sail nearly always lists to one side. The work of the motor was hampered by a leaning position. We sailed most of the time throughout our cruise with the motor dismantled and under repairs.

We had only two guns, and only one at a time could be brought into action against an enemy. Our orders were to attack sailing ships only. Windjammer against steamship was considered a ridiculous idea. We would not need great broadsides of cannon in capturing sailing vessels. We tried to make up for our lack of gun power by skill and precision in handling the guns we had. Our gun crew worked incessantly at drill and target practice, and schooled themselves to such quickness and accuracy of fire that the power of our armament, in effect, was doubled.

Our lookout posts were excellent. We had a crow s nest with a comfortable seat high up on the mast. Only a man at ease watches well. A second lookout was on the foremast, where a petty officer was perched. I offered ten pounds sterling and a bottle of champagne to whoever should report a ship first. A jealous rivalry grew up between the lookouts. In each raged a tremendous thirst for that bottle of champagne. All day long eager eyes swept the horizon.

On January 9th, off Gibraltar, the shout rang out: "Ship ahoy."

On our larboard side was a large steamer heading toward us. Flying our Norwegian colours, we turned to meet her. She flew no flag and carried no name. The British were the only people who sent their boats out without names. She looked of British build, too. Our orders were not to tackle steamers. Well, you can promise a lot. We raised the signal:

"Chronometer time, please."

A sailing ship long away from port rarely has the correct time. Our request was reasonable enough. The steamer signalled that she understood us, and came to the windward so that we could heave to. I wore my great-coat to conceal my uniform. Those of the crew that had rifles hid themselves behind the railings.

The steamer came near, ready to give the sleepy old Norwegian the time.

"Shall we tackle him?" I asked one of my sailors who was crouched next to me peering through a loophole.

"Sure, let's take him. He's an Englishman."

I shouted the command, and the drum beat "clear for action." A section of the rail could be lowered and raised as a gun shield. It dropped clattering and revealed the muzzle of the cannon. Up with the German flag and fire, one across her bows.

It was the *Seeadler's* first shot against the enemy.

What's that, by Joe? Nothing happened, no movement on deck, no slowing down of the ship. Then a flag went up the mast, the British flag. It was like the fantastic things that happen in a dream. I thought I must be asleep. Another shot across her bows. She suddenly changes her course. Hello, she wants to get away. A shot over the stern, another over the smokestack, and now she hove to.

A boat was in the water rowing toward us. We all put on our best manners, and I welcomed Captain Chewn aboard the *Seeadler*. What did we want of him, he asked, so bewildered that he stuttered. "Well, first a friendly chat," I replied. He was an old salt with a scraggly gray beard. I liked him right off. His ship was the *Gladys Royal*, bound from Cardiff with five thousand tons of coal for Buenos Aires.

I told him that, much as I disliked sending any ship to the bottom of the sea, nevertheless, we must sink the *Gladys Royal*.

"Oh, no," he argued, "we are bound for a neutral port and won't harm anything. It will be bad for me to lose my ship, and I have a wife and children at home."

"Do you believe, Captain Chewn, that, under the same circumstances, a British naval officer would show any mercy to a German ship?"

He made no reply.

We now got an explanation of the queer behaviour of his ship that had so puzzled us after our first shot. Captain Chewn, an old-timer at sea, simply thought we were trying to compare time in the old traditional way, by firing a blank mortar. He had raised his flag to serve as the mortar shot on his side. He would afterward lower it to give the exact moment. That is the way in vogue to-day. But when our second shot was fired, the cook on the *Gladys Royal* saw the shell strike the water and thought we had sighted a submarine and were firing at it. He gave the alarm, and the captain started to zigzag. It was only after the third shot that they saw our cannon pointed at them and the German battle flag at our masthead.

"By Joe," and the captain pounded the rail with open admiration, "you fooled me bloody well. It was the damnedest trap I ever saw."

I sent a prize crew aboard the *Gladys Royal* with orders to have her follow the *Seeadler*. I wanted to wait and blow her up after nightfall. Cruisers might be roaming somewhere in these parts, and it would be unwise to run the risk of attracting their attention with the sound of an explosion.

We photographed our capture carefully. At dusk we transferred the steamer's twenty-six men, white

and black, to our ship. The captain brought his belongings aboard. I also sent Lieutenant Preiss to pack
up everything aboard the captured vessel that he
thought we might need and ferry it over. He displayed excellent judgment, too, and turned up with
a welcome store of excellent provisions. We sailors
could be content with a sailor's fare whenever need
be, but we wanted our guests to dine well at all times
to help make up for the sorrow of losing their ships.

Preiss and his men planted a bomb in her hold,
lit the time fuse, and took to the boats. Fifteen
minutes passed. Then the *Gladys Royal* trembled
fore and aft.

She went down stern first, and in ten minutes her
forward quarter stuck straight out of the sea. Her
bow remained above water for a long time. A steamer
hove into sight. She carried side lights, and from that
we judged her to be a neutral. Suddenly a second explosion, from the accumulation of air pressure, burst
the bow of the *Gladys Royal*. With a final quiver, she
took her last plunge into the depths and slid out of
sight, while we scurried away into the night with
all sails set.

We wanted nothing of neutral ships. We would not
bother them even if we thought their neutrality a
pretense. If we stopped one and searched her and
found her really to be a neutral, we could only release her, and she would spread the news about us.
We had a trump card in our hand—nobody imagined
that an old sailing ship could be out buccaneering
in this age of fast battle cruisers. It was our plan also
to molest only those ships that we were fairly certain
did not carry wireless sets and therefore could not
broadcast our attack before we had boarded them.

Captain Chewn was agreeably surprised to find himself assigned to a cozy cabin. His only complaint was

that he had no one to enjoy it with him. This sociable mariner liked company. So we promised to supply him with companions as soon as possible.

Much as we wanted to please Captain Chewn and show him that we were accommodating hosts, we allowed the next ship to sail by in peace. She was a British passenger steamer bound through Gibraltar. We had room enough for all her passengers, but we did not want to be bothered with women and children. Having lived at sea among men nearly all my life, I regarded all women as flowerlike creatures sent to beautify and soften the harshness of this world. In my opinion, women should see nothing of war. Their lovely eyes should only gaze on the beautiful, the pleasant things of life. Women are too graceful and delicate for the sights of war, with men shot down, wounds and blood, and men dead and dying. I had resolved to carry out my raiding cruise without any killing, if I could help it, but in my nautical career I had found many a thing I couldn't help. Anyway, to me women were synonymous with romance and love—not with war.

At noon, with a heavy sea running, we sighted a steamer cutting diagonally across our course. No flag, no name. We signalled her for information, but there was no response. Surely she must be an Englishman with a hard-boiled efficient skipper. You know how a British captain often is, with his nose right down on his job, with no thought except his cargo and his lookout for submarines and cruisers? Well, evidently this chap couldn't be bothered with a funny old Norwegian windjammer. Sails set and motor running, we held across his course and got in front of him. Now, at sea, a sailing vessel always has the right of way over a steamship because the latter

can manœuvre more rapidly. But that meant nothing to this steamship. She swerved not an inch, and seemed quite content to run us down.

"This businesslike skipper must have an important cargo, since he doesn't care a rap, by Joe, about ploughing into a clumsy old Norwegian bumboat," said I to myself. And I could imagine how he was swearing there on his bridge.

"Stupid blighter, by Joe," no doubt he was saying, "get out of my way or I'll ram you!"

We had to jib and let him go in the wind, or there would have been a collision. The Englishman passed us at three hundred yards.

The German flag was climbing swiftly to our masthead.

"Fire," I commanded, "let's see if that will make him change his mind."

The gun boomed and a shell went screaming over the steamer.

"By Joe," I said, "he sticks to his opinions."

The steamer's stacks belched fresh clouds of smoke. Her course changed not at all. Another shot, this one, by way of emphasis, just over the smokestack. The steamer turned into the wind.

"A wise baby, that skipper," commented Leudemann sarcastically. "He knows a windjammer can't sail against the wind."

We, of course, couldn't catch him in a chase, but our range was still point-blank. A shot through the smokestack and a couple into the hull. We could see the crew running around wildly. A siren was screaming. A shell exploded on deck. The propeller stopped, and the steamer slowed down and lay rolling in the trough of the sea.

"This new invention of war without killing, what

do you think of it now?" Leudemann looked up at me satirically. "I guess you'll find there are a couple of casualties over there."

The Englishman must have known that he hadn't a ghost of a chance to escape under fire at such close range. First of all, he had been discourteous in ignoring our friendly signals. Then he had violated the rules of ocean traffic in not giving our clipper the right of way. And now in cold blood he had endangered the life of his crew. According to the unwritten rules of etiquette among pirates and raiders, it was up to us to put out a boat and board a prize. But instead I signalled the steamer:

"Captain, come aboard!" Let him come over to us. If he's such a tough guy, we'll show him who rules the waves in this part of the Atlantic.

It was funny. Finally, I had to laugh. The ship was the *Lundy Island* bound for France with a cargo of Madagascar sugar. An important cargo, sure enough. Sugar was scarce in all the countries at war, and we Germans, whose supply of sugar consisted mostly of a great longing for it, could sympathize with the captain's eagerness to get his precious merchandise to port. When the first shot struck the *Lundy Island*, the crew, black, brown, and yellow, fell into a panic. With shells falling, running the ship or staying with it meant nothing to them. The captain roared and stormed, but that was all the good it did. So he seized the helm, himself. Just then a shot hit the rudder chain, and when he turned the wheel nothing happened. The crew started taking to the boats, and the tough old salt was left alone on deck. Our signal for him to come on board left him helpless. His boats were out there with the crew floundering at the oars. The sea was pitching and rolling, and they were so frightened they could hardly row

A strange encounter. The old *Pinmore*, on which "Phelax Leudige" had served, appears on the horizon.

The modern buccaneer sends his old ship to her last port.

The latter day corsair in a poetic setting.

He paced the bridge with his handbag in his hand, a solitary, woebegone figure. We finally had to send a boat for him.

On our deck he got a stern, formal reception.

"Any casualties among your men, Captain?"

"No, worse luck. Not a man scratched, by Joe, and the blighters scurried around like rabbits at a dog show. Look at them in the boats out there. They haven't got here yet, the beggars. Let me at that gun, by Joe, and I'll sink them."

It was hard not to sympathize with him, but still his conduct had apparently been inexcusable.

"Why did you endanger your men's lives like that, Captain? It not only was the height of folly, but it was inhuman!"

Just then our ship's surgeon, Dr. Pietsch, came along.

"Hello, Captain."

"Hello, Doctor."

They greeted each other like long-lost friends, save that there was a shadow of uneasiness in the captain's fraternal demonstrations.

Dr. Pietsch had gone out with our armoured cruiser *Moewe* on one of her freebooting expeditions. Among the captured captains of that cruise was our present guest, who, while aboard the *Moewe*, had struck up a pleasant comradeship with the doctor. Now he, along with the other captains, had been released on parole. They had signed written promises that they would engage in no further war activity. Believing he had broken his parole, he thought the Germans would hang him from a yardarm if they ever caught him. When he saw we were an auxiliary cruiser, he already felt a rope tightening around his neck. That was why he had tried so desperately to get away.

We amused ourselves with a formal discussion,

after which I addressed our guest with suitable gravity.

"We are of the opinion, Captain, that your parole did not cover your calling as a merchant captain. Only direct combatant service was included under the heading of war activity. Therefore, we feel ourselves under no unhappy necessity of hanging you."

Well, the smile on that hard, weather-beaten face was like a sunrise. We now understood the all-too-human motives behind his actions, and we respected his plucky attempt to get away in the face of point-blank gunfire. Sailors ourselves, we could only salute this skipper who, with a worthless, spineless crew, had to take the wheel himself, and then only to find his rudder chain smashed.

"All right, Captain," I said, "it's the way things go at sea when there's war on. God help us sailor chaps."

After he had roundly cursed his crew when finally they came aboard, we took him below and introduced him to his new quarters with Captain Chewn. The two skippers found themselves mutually agreeable and became great old sidekicks. Some of the crew found old friends among the sailors we had already captured, and none of them appeared particularly grieved over the loss of their ship. We now had fifty-odd guests, apparently representing half the races on earth. The *Seeadler* was becoming populous and quite convivial.

The sea was so rough now that we did not send a bombing party to board the *Lundy Island*, but sank her by direct gunfire.

That night Leudemann and I sat over bottles of beer and talked about our prospects.

"Well, old chap," said I, "everything has begun well. It's a fine cruise. But when will they sink us?"

"Not, at any rate," he replied, "until our hotel is full."

You see our buccaneering raid was pretty certain to remain a secret until the time came when lack of space would compel us to release our prisoners and send them to port. Then the news of our freebooting jaunt would be out, and cruisers would be hot after us in every part of the world.

"And if we don't capture any more ships," I reflected, "we can go on cruising indefinitely."

"Then let's catch some more quickly," laughed Leudemann. "It will be great sport to play hide and seek with cruisers."

That mate of mine was always itching for trouble. But then that was what we had all come through the blockade in hope of finding, so if we wanted plenty of excitement, then the sooner we sent the crews of eight or ten ships into some port the sooner would the alarm go out—"German raider in the Atlantic!" Then, too, Lloyd's insurance rates would start to soar when the news got out, and ships with supplies that the Allies needed badly would be held in port. Also, a number of cruisers would no doubt be detached from blockade patrol duty across the North Sea. That was the interesting part of it—those cruisers and how to elude them.

"Leudemann," I said, "the better the lookout, the more ships we will catch. We already have a good lookout, but I've thought of a way to have a better one. A hundred pair of eyes are better than two pair."

"What do you mean?"

"Well, from now on, I'm going to change that offer of ten pounds and a bottle of champagne that we promised to the first of our two lookouts to spy a ship. I'm going to open it to everyone on board!"

"To all of our crew?"

"Yes, to our crew, and to all of our prisoners, too! Ten pounds sterling and a bottle of champagne! I'll bet that'll send everybody into the rigging, including the captains."

"By Joe, you're right," said my mate, slapping his knee, "particularly since they know that, as soon as we are full up with prisoners, they will all be sent into some port."

"Exactly," I responded. "It won't be long before we have several hundred aboard. That will make a fine flock of birds perched in the rigging, forces of the Allies on the lookout for Allied ships to sink!"

Leudemann and I roared with laughter the longer we thought of it. I at once had notices posted up:

"Ten pounds and a bottle of champagne to the first man who sights a ship. Offer open to all."

You should have seen the rigging crowded with crew and prisoners from then on. Every man who had any kind of glass brought it out. There were up-to-date binoculars, old-fashioned spyglasses, and cheap opera glasses. Even those without any glasses took their places on the yardarms, trusting to luck and the power of the naked eye. The two captains, with the dignity and poise that became their exalted rank, climbed aloft and sat next to each other on a yard, sweeping the horizon with their excellent binoculars.

Never had a ship such a lookout. I often stood and watched the curious flock perched in the rigging, all colours, sizes, and styles of beauty. And, believe me, they were wonders at spotting ships. Sometimes two or three would spot the same ship at the same moment. Then there would be an argument, a riddle for Solomon himself to answer. Once or twice the argument got so hot that I had to pay two rewards for

a ship, and then the champagne flowed freely. That night, if the weather was balmy and a gentle breeze was blowing from the Gulf Stream, the deck of the *Seeadler* became a veritable beer garden, and our guests frolicked like tourists on a Mediterranean cruise.

RAIDING ALONG THE EQUATOR, AND AN INTERRUPTED HONEYMOON

THERE are some memories that are painful to recall. To this day I can see the *Charles Gounod* going down, her bowsprit plunging first and her tall masts sinking slowly, first one spar disappearing and then another. It fills me with sadness, for she had behaved like a gallant craft, and she was a large barque with all the air of an argosy, and as we bore toward her, she proudly saluted our Norwegian flag by raising the tricolour of France.

"What news of the war?" she signalled.

We steered close to her, unmasked our gun, and raised the German battle flag.

"Heave to," was our reply.

Incredulity, consternation! The officers and sailors on deck stood paralyzed for a long moment. Then the barque hove to.

Our prize crew went aboard and commandeered a batch of fine red wine from among the ship's provisions, and three fine fat hogs. The Frenchmen packed their belongings, and came aboard the *Seeadler*. They were a glum-looking, disgusted lot.

The French sailor bitterly hates to leave his ship. He is almost as attached to it as the average Frenchman is attached to his native land. No French sailor willingly serves on a foreign ship. The crews of other nations are made up of men from every corner of

the world, from Chittagong and Malacca to Senegal and Jamaica, from Hull to Helsingfors, but no foreigner is taken on a French ship. The French sea laws are more severe than those of other nations. Desertion from a French ship is a very serious offense, while on most German ships it is punished by a mere fine of twenty marks.

The captain was painfully correct in his manner toward us. He was a tall, impressive fellow with deep voice and black beard. A man of fine education and studious mind, he was scrupulously polite, but knew how to make the hostility he felt toward us clearly and rather amusingly evident. He was our prisoner. Very well, he conceded that. But we were the enemies of his country and the destroyers of his ship. Therefore he preserved a demeanour appropriate to that attitude of mind throughout his entire voyage with us. For our part, we could not but admire him for his superb, unbending spirit.

His barque was loaded with a cargo of corn and bound for Bordeaux. Now, I don't know much music, and I don't care for this modern jazz school at all. Faust I enjoy. Give me the duet in the Garden scene, and, since I am called the "Sea Devil," I don't mind admitting a secret fondness for old Mephisto and his serenade beneath the window. Now I had to sink my favourite composer. The thought of it made me hum a phrase of Valentine's dying lament.

But the sinking of the *Charles Gounod* meant much more than any such superficial melancholy. One shouldn't ever have to sink a sailing ship. They are the last survivors of the golden days at sea, crueler days and finer days. Take any old salt who has sailed before the mast, and ask him. The shipyards are not building many of them any more, and the day of the schooner, the barque, the clipper, and the barquentine

is fast passing. Every one that goes down to Davy Jones is a loss that will not be replaced. I have an old-time seaman's love for sailships. A steamer? Train the guns and light the fuses. I could sink a steamer and laugh as she takes her last dive. But I never did get used to sinking sailing ships, although we had to send many of them on their last voyage before our own final adventure in the South Seas.

Our bombs exploded in the hold of the *Charles Gounod*. She lurched like a living thing. Her tall masts trembled. The majestic ship seemed to bow her head as she nosed down into the sea. The last we saw of her was a glimpse of her tallest mast and waving from it the tricolour of France. With her departure, I somehow thought I saw the passing of the whole age of sailing ships.

Three days later, a tremendous commotion in the rigging. Six men were reporting "Sail ho!"

"Hold there," I roared, "let's have done with the argument until we've settled with the ship."

She was a fine three-masted schooner. We thought she might be an American. The Americans favour that type of ship. And the United States was not yet in the war. However, the Canadians also have a weakness for the three-masted schooner. We raised our flag, hoping to induce the skipper to raise his flag, which would be the polite response for him to make. But her skipper didn't seem to be in any mood for returning compliments that day. Perhaps he had had a bad night and was saying to himself:

"What do I care for that old Norwegian tub?"

We backed our main-topsail and dipped our flag three times as a salute, hoping that this exceptional courtesy would induce the schooner to follow the amenities of the sea.

It happened now that our freebooting led us to intrude unwittingly into the rose-covered field of romance, where our rough pirate's boots were not adapted to walk among the delicate plants. However, buccaneers that we were, we were not without a high regard for the tender sentiment. Aboard the schooner, the captain had his newly married bride. The voyage was their honeymoon. He saw no reason why he should bother to raise his flag in response to ours. She, however, inspired by the enchantment of a honeymoon voyage, was full of romance and the spirit of the sea. She remonstrated with her bridegroom for his impoliteness toward the Norwegian ship.

"Oh, to blazes with the —— old Norwegian," grumbled the bridegroom, and she thought him a very cruel and hard-bitten husband, and told him so.

When we dipped our flag three times and he still proposed not to answer the salutation, she felt it was an outrage. I don't know whether she broke into tears, as brides always do in books, but, at any rate, she talked a lot. He got angry, and they had a real row—their first quarrel, we afterward learned.

Leudemann and I stood on the bridge.

"Better leave the lubber alone," I said.

Just then the ensign in the lookout on the mainmast sang out:

"That's no American. They're raising the British flag."

Sure enough, there were the British colours. Up went our battle flag! Across her bows went a shot from our gun. But it required a second shot before she hove to.

"Hey!" cried Leudemann, "there's a woman."

The captain's bride was running around the deck in a tailspin, as aviators say. I don't know whether

she was afraid of shot and shell or the righteous ire of her husband. Maybe he was chasing her.

Prize Officer Preiss had an added dignity as he climbed into the boat with his boarding crew. He was always a great hand at quieting excited people —especially the ladies. With his six feet four, his deep voice, and his imperturbable manner, he was the kind of man to raise his hand and calm the tumult of the howling mob. He had a certain streak of gallantry, too, which made him a second Siegfried when it came to the task of quieting an excited young woman.

The schooner was the H. M. S. *Percy* bound from Nova Scotia with a cargo of gaberdine. The captain told me he saw our first shot splash into the water in front of his ship, and thought it merely a whale spouting. With our second shot he heard the report of the gun, and saw that we were an auxiliary cruiser. The *Percy's* cargo was so light that we did not use bombs, but shot her full of holes.

We were worried about having fair company aboard. There might be rough work that would not be good for the eyes of woman. And then a woman needs attention. She must be treated with care and consideration. Suppose this new and undesired captive should start to complain. Women like to complain. Suppose she should grow angry at being kept a prisoner. What could we do? You couldn't put her in the brig.

"Well, Leudemann," said I, "the only thing we can do is to treat her so well that she will be happy all the time."

"I treated a dame well once," growled Leudemann, "and then she ran off with another man the first time I left her alone."

The skipper's bride turned out to be the best fellow you could want. She had one of those sunny temperaments that simply spread mirth and good cheer everywhere. She had a smile for everyone and in every circumstance. She took her stay aboard the *Seeadler* as an unexpected, exciting, and appropriate phase of her honeymoon, and resolved to get the greatest possible fun out of it. We all made much of her, did everything to make her comfortable, gave her presents, and got up amusements for her. Her husband was a little annoyed with her at first for having caused the loss of his ship, but he could not stay angry with her for long, and when he saw what a reigning queen aboard she was, he became very proud of her—and seldom left her side.

When she got back to Canada, she gave the newspapers long stories about her stay on our terrible pirate raider, the *Seeadler*, and told what a delightful time the freebooters had shown her. When I returned to Germany after the war, I found an envelope full of clippings from her awaiting me.

We lay in the waters off Africa five degrees above the equator and thirty degrees west longitude. That region is right on the path of all sailing ships that run before the southeast trade winds and head north. The weather is seldom bad there, the air is clear, and from our masthead we had a range of vision of thirty miles.

A Frenchman, no doubt of it. The ship was scrupulously clean, her rigging trim and neat. Her hull was decorated artistically with gunports, after the manner of an old-time war frigate. Only the French keep their ships so thoroughly shined up, and there was one firm of French shipping owners whose custom it was to decorate their vessels man-o'-war fashion.

She was the four-masted brig *Antonin*. We came up behind her diagonally, and then after her. Our motor was having one of its off days, but we did not care. What's the matter with canvas? The *Seeadler* was one of the fastest clippers ever turned out by an American shipyard, and there was nothing I liked better than a race under sail. We'd see if this Frenchman could outsail us. Fine chance he had. But if he did not exactly outsail us, he sailed with us. We could not gain on him. That bark was fast, and so we went on, mile after mile, quite evenly.

A sudden wind squall arose. It blew like a fury. The captain of the *Antonin* was a sensible skipper. He immediately lowered sail, took in his royals and upper gallant sails. That was where we had it on him, for we had no miserly shipowner to be afraid of. Our masts wouldn't break, anyway.

"Keep every stitch on, boys! After her, my hearties!"

Of course, we gained rapidly on her now.

The wind continued to howl. The gale raged, and the captain of the *Antonin* thought we were quite mad. Gallants and royals up during a wind squall —he had never seen such a thing in all his days at sea. The sight was so funny that he wanted a picture of it. We watched him standing in the stern of his ship and gazing down into the finder of his camera.

"Leudemann," I said to my helmsman, "we must capture that snapshot for our collection of photographs, if we have to take a trip to Davy Jones doing it."

We were attempting to keep a thorough photographic record of our cruise, for the Imperial archives, and a picture of the *Seeadler* running with all sails set through a squall, particularly if that picture were

snapped all unwittingly by the captain of a prize, would indeed be a gem for our collection.

We were close behind the *Antonin* now. The captain's picture seemed to have been satisfactorily snapped. A machine gun began to rattle. We were often bored during those long days at sea. Anything for a bit of amusement. It would be funny to watch that captain's face when he heard the typewriter of Mars rattling in his ear and when he saw us sending a stream of lead through his rigging. First he started, and then he glared. What did these lunatics mean? This kind of insanity was too much. His rigging might be injured, ropes cut or spars smashed. He began to roar at us in the most profane French. When a Frenchman swears, you can hear it far off. Then he saw the German flag at our masthead. He staggered back with a dramatic gesture that only a Frenchman can achieve.

We sank the *Antonin* just as we sank the others, but first we seized that kodak and roll of film, by Joe.

We added another Allied nation to our list of prizes when the *Buenos Aires* came bowling along. She was an Italian ship built in England, a fine vessel but filthy dirty. Everything was untidy from stem to stern. Her captain, a fat, unkempt man of about fifty-five with a bristly moustache and a month's growth of scraggly stubble on his face, came aboard the *Seeadler* carrying an umbrella! Can you imagine a skipper of a windjammer carrying an umbrella at sea? We couldn't, and my men all burst out in rude guffaws. I suppose he had it to protect himself during a hurricane, eh? I had once seen a photograph of the Italian commander in chief, Count

Cadorna, carrying an umbrella. So we immediately dubbed our new skipper Cadorna. He was a genial fellow, full of good nature and fun. You should have seen his astonishment when he saw the fine quarters we provided for our captive skippers. He never did quite get over it. Apparently, he was better off as our prisoner than he had been before.

We sailed night and day. During the day we tacked south into the steady trades, and during the night we ran with the northeast trade winds. At nights, when we ordinarily could not see them (because in wartime they all sailed without lights even in the Pacific), we went in the same direction as the ships bound for America, so that none passed us, and it was up to us to catch them. During the day, with our zigzag tacking, we were pretty sure to come in sight of any vessel sailing along that shipping lane in either direction.

*   *   *

One night, our lookout saw a tiny flash of light astern. A ship was coming along behind us, and somebody on her had looked at his watch with a pocket flash. We kept along on our way. No doubt in the morning she would still be close to us. Dawn came, and there she was, a magnificent French barque, the *La Rochefoucauld*. We signalled her:

"Important news."

She hove to. The captain, who was on deck in his carpet slippers, saw our gun but thought we were the mother supply for a squadron of British submarines. Seeing that he was under some illusion, I decided to have a little fun with him. I called our captured sailors to deck in batches. First up came the Chinamen. They lined up along the rail so that the Frenchman could get a good look at them. Then I called the West Indian Negroes on deck. After them the

white men. Now Chinese, now black men, now Caucasians—the captain of the *La Rochefoucauld* thought he must be having a nightmare. And a most disagreeable nightmare it was when he saw the German flag run swiftly to the tip of our mainmast. You should have heard him swear.

He climbed on to the *Seeadler's* deck a picture of wrath and despair. He still had on his carpet slippers, and had brought nothing with him. His name was Lecoq.

"Don't you want to send for your belongings, Captain Lecoq?" I asked.

"If I have to lose my ship, *mon Dieu*, I want to lose everything," he replied.

"You don't want to take anything with you?"

"No, let everything go down with the ship."

I sent a couple of his sailors back aboard the *La Rochefoucauld* to pack his luggage and bring it aboard the *Seeadler*.

One of my sailors came to me, saying:

"They met a cruiser a couple of days ago."

My men had orders to circulate among captured sailors and talk with them to see what they could pick up. This sailor had heard mention of a cruiser in the talk of the French sailors.

That was funny. I had asked Captain Lecoq whether he had sighted any ships within the past week, and he had replied no. In his log I had found no mention of being searched by a cruiser. One of my officers examined the log again and found that a page had been torn out. A thorough questioning of the French sailors brought out the fact that they had been thoroughly searched by a British cruiser. This warship had taken her position three hundred miles south of us and was cruising back and forth across the Pacific ship lane, examining every vessel

that passed. So you see, we, apparently, were picking them up after she had O.K.'d them. Captain Lecoq had bidden his men to say nothing about the cruiser. Apparently he hoped that we would wander far enough south to run afoul of the Britisher and be captured.

I was momentarily displeased with him for his deception, but, after all, he was a Frenchman, and we were the enemies of his country. His action was a bit heroic, too. If we ran into the cruiser, we might be sunk, and he would go down with us. I was destined to have trouble later with this same irreconcilable Captain Lecoq.

The stately *Cambronne*, commanded by an equally stately skipper.

Captors and captives aboard the raider enjoying the plunder of the
champagne ship. Von Luckner second from the left.

The South Sea island home of the shipwrecked buccaneers.

XVI

WINDJAMMER VS. STEAMER

Now the biggest ship we captured in the Atlantic was a 9,800-ton British steamer loaded with champagne—the *Horngarth*. That was our banner day.

She was well armed and had a wireless. She hove into sight one morning, and we could see that she would make a tough customer for our sailing ship to handle. But why not have a good look at her? We set the signal:

"Chronometer time, please."

The way she paid no attention to the request said very clearly:

"Let that old windjammer go and buy a watch!"

But we had other devices. We had a smoke apparatus to send clouds rolling out of the galley, and on the galley roof was a dish loaded with a quantity of magnesium which when lighted produced a wicked red flame. We set the smoke and fire going, and ran up distress signals. The *Seeadler* now was the most dramatic-looking ship afire you ever saw. Thirty of my crew armed with rifles hid behind the rail, and Schmidt quickly dressed up as the captain's wife, the beautiful but simpering "Josefeena" of the big feet. We had another piece of apparatus which we now used for the first time. It was a kind of cannon made out of a section of smokestack. It was loaded with a charge of powder, and you touched it off with a lighted cigarette. It was quite harmless

but made a terrifying noise. You would have thought it a super-dreadnaught's full broadside. I picked three sailors who had the most powerful voices aboard, gave them large megaphones, and stationed them on the topmast yards of the mainmast and mizzen.

If that steamer was short on courtesy, she was long on humanity. She came rushing heroically to the aid of the old sailship that was blazing so dramatically just astern. She had a powerful wireless set, and as I stood on my bridge watching her as she steamed toward us I could not take my eyes off the five-inch gun on her deck. What was our little pop-gun beside that piece of ordnance? One shot would blow us right out of the water.

The steamer had a big fat captain, who had his cap pulled down over one eye. His voice, even when he whispered, was a deep bellow. You should have heard it through the megaphone! The steamer drew near. The fat captain raised his megaphone.

"What the hell's the matter with you?" His voice boomed across like the rumble of our old cannon.

We cut off the smoke and flame. It looked as if we had fought our fire successfully. Schmidt, the captain's beautiful wife, tripped along the deck with coquettish movements of shoulders and hips. The officers on the steamer's bridge eyed the fair vision and exchanged smiles with that rogue of a Schmidt. Nor was the fat captain insensible to feminine charms. He rolled his eyes and grinned with the expression of a skipper who can easily "cut his officers out."

"Look at the wireless, Leudemann," I said, "and the five-inch gun."

"Knock the wireless over," he replied, "and let's have it out with the five-inch gun."

"Clear the deck for action," I roared.

Instantly, the beautiful Schmidt threw off his silken dress, and in the uniform of a German gob kicked his blonde wig around the deck. The Britishers stared aghast. The German flag ran up, our riflemen arose from behind the rail, ready to pick off anyone who tried to handle the five-inch gun. Bang, crash, and our gun knocked over the wireless shack. A tremendous detonation, and our false smokestack cannon added its voice to the general effect.

The steamer's crew swarmed on deck and ran around like crazy animals. The captain telephoned his order to start the engines. His engine crew was on deck as panicky as the others. He ordered the boats swung out. His men were already doing that as well as their fright allowed.

"Clear the deck for action," he howled.

That only gave the crew a greater scare than ever. I shouted to him:

"Lay to, or I will sink you."

I had to admire that captain. The fat fellow dominated the frightened mob by sheer force of lung power. His voice seemed to sweep the deck and master everything.

"Gun crew to their posts. By Joe, you scalawags. Gun crew to their posts, I say, by Joe."

We stood watching. I didn't think he could do it, but the panic stilled. The frightened men stood at a kind of attention. The gun crew separated itself from the crowd. It looked as though there would be a fight, his cannon against our rifles. Well, we could pick them off, and that fat "soul of the situation" would be an excellent mark to shoot at.

We had one more device left. I gave the signal. From the mastheads boomed three voices through the megaphones in unison. The shout was in English and seemed to dominate the ocean to the horizon.

"Torpedoes clear!"

On the deck of the steamer a crazy yell arose:

"No torpedoes, for God's sake, no torpedoes."

Handkerchiefs, napkins, towels, and anything white was waved. The cook frantically waved his apron.

"Lay to," I shouted, "or we discharge our torpedoes."

There was no further sound. The fat captain was licked, licked by the terror the torpedo inspired in everyone who sailed on ships. He made no further protest. He could not have done anything with his men now, but I don't think he liked torpedoes either. He sat down on a deck chair, cursing and wiping the sweat off his face.

We still had to be careful. There were plenty of firearms aboard that ship, rifles, grenades, and what not. I kept our riflemen at the rail, ready to cover our boarding party and to shoot down anyone who went near the five-inch gun. Still with the idea of keeping the men on the steamer overawed, I sent my eight strongest men as the boarding crew under the command of my giant prize officer. They had been among the strongest men in Germany. One was the wrestling champion of Saxony, another the wrestling champion of Westphalia. One, a Bavarian who had been a sculptor's model. He had been in much demand for posing because of his prodigious muscular development. Any one of these fellows could bring up the 220-pound weight with one hand. They went with bare arms and shoulders. They had long bamboo poles with hooks at the end. They reached up with the poles, caught the hooks over the edge of the deck of the captured ship, and climbed up hand over hand. The men on deck looked down as they ascended.

"What fellows, by Joe. No, by Joe, we're not going to fight with those fellows!"

Our prisoners came aboard. Among them were eight British marines who had been assigned to the steamer as a gun crew. The fat captain looked around our deck with a sort of belligerent curiosity. He walked up to our smokestack gun, and you couldn't have told his face from a beet.

"Captain, is that the thing that made that hell of a racket?"

"Yes."

"Where are your torpedoes?"

"Torpedoes? We have no torpedoes."

"No torpedoes? That was a fake, too?"

"Yes."

"By Joe, Captain, don't report that, by Joe."

I promised him I would not report it, and told him heartily that he had behaved like a true British skipper, and no man could have done better

Aye, things have changed on the sea. When I went aboard that steamer, I had to sit there and look around and think. She was a freighter, and what were freighters like when I was in the fo'c'sle? That wasn't so long ago, twenty-odd years, but ships and customs change rapidly. I was in a magnificent saloon, with heavy carpets, glittering candelabra, and big, luxurious club chairs. Paintings in heavy frames hung on the wall. In one corner was a Steinway grand piano and beside it a music rack. There were other musical instruments, a melodeon, a violin, a guitar, a ukulele. Freighters nowadays often have better officers' accommodations than passenger ships. They have more space for them and their voyages are longer, sometimes a year or more. The shipowners provide comforts and luxuries to make the long periods at sea less

burdensome. The sailors, too, are put up in far better style than formerly. In my time, even on the biggest freight steamers, the officers had simple quarters and the seamen had little more comfort than they had on the sailing ships. I remembered the various ships on which I had hauled at ropes and swabbed the deck.

"By Joe," I thought, "if they had told you of anything like this, you would have thought them ready for a lunatic asylum."

The hold of the steamer was no less interesting than the officers' saloon. The cargo was valued at a million pounds sterling. It included five hundred cases of rare cognac and twenty-three hundred cases of champagne, Veuve Cliquot. That was something.

"Ho! boys," I called, "lend a hand. There's a bit of work here."

We took the musical instruments, the piano, violin, 'cello, melodeon, and all. We had aboard the *Seeadler* a pianist and a violinist, both excellent musicians out of the German conservatories. We had no room in our cabins to hang the paintings, so I gave them to our captive captains to take with them when they left our ship. Some of the expensive furniture fitted nicely in the *Seeadler's* cabins. Of the cognac and champagne we ferried aboard as much as we could stow away. We opened the sea cocks of the steamer, and she settled down peacefully beneath the waves.

XVII

THE LAST CRUISE OF THE POOR OLD *PINMORE*

ONE night, the breeze having become light, we proceeded under a cloud of sail. It was a night such as you rarely find anywhere but in the tropics. The four scintillating stars of the Southern Cross twinkled merrily down upon us. Our sails were full, and the waves murmured past our bow. The sky was a gorgeous spread of blinking stars, and Old Man Moon was so bright that he seemed to be laughing and chuckling. The buccaneer's deck was crowded. We sat around in genial fraternity, officers, prisoners, and crew, each with a goblet of champagne. Midship was the orchestra, violin, 'cello, melodeon, and Steinway grand. Perhaps it was the spell of the tropic night, but as I paced the quarter-deck it seemed to me that they played as well as the musicians at the Stadt Opera in Berlin.

"Oh, lovely south wind, blow." The melody drifted along on the wind of the Southern ocean.

How remote the war seemed then! The day was not far when we would be shipwrecked, but to-night all thought of what might be our fate was wafted away by the spell of the music, the champagne, and the poetry of night beneath the tropic stars.

"What ho, a light!"

My night telescope at my eye, I saw a ship. On the horizon, brightly outlined by the light of the moon, stood a stately three-master.

"Hard aport!" We were on the dark side of the horizon, and she could not see us. After a bit of scrutiny as we approached her, we guessed her to be an enemy ship.

Our flash signal flared out across the water.

"Heave to—a German cruiser." Unable to make us out, she little guessed that we were nothing more than a sailing ship, from which she could easily escape by slipping through the night. We were confident she would take us for an armoured cruiser easily able to catch her and blow her out of the sea with a broadside.

We waited at the rail to see what would happen. Presently, we heard a splashing of oars. Out of the darkness came a hail, the jolliest hail I have ever listened to. It was in nasal seaport French.

"What a relief! Instead of a Boche cruiser, I find you are an old windjammer like ourselves. But why the joke? Your signal fooled us completely. I suppose you want to tell us something about the war."

I did not wonder at his surmise. Ships long at sea, particularly Allied ships, were always keen about news from the various battle fronts, and it was common enough for vessels to stop and exchange news.

"Come on aboard," I replied. "We have lots of news."

We were in our shirt sleeves, and looked like ordinary seamen. On deck he said proudly:

"I am a Frenchman." As though we couldn't have guessed it.

"A Frenchman? Fine. How is France doing?"

"Ah! France, she is victorious, or will be very soon. *Ravi de vous voir.*"

He fairly bubbled over with delight when we offered him a bottle of champagne. Being homeward bound, he was in a frolicsome mood. A generous taste of

the champagne, and he was ready to embrace us. He thought our supposed joke, which certainly would have been somewhat cruel, was the result of our being tipsy. He slapped me on the back, as one cheery skipper to another.

"Captain, what a terrible fellow you are to have fooled me like that. But now I feel as though a stone had dropped from my heart."

"Beware," I thought, "that your stone does not come back twice as heavy."

He was such a cheery, convivial soul that I hated to break the bad news to him. I left the progress of events to do that. He wanted to have a look over our ship. So I ushered him aft to my cabin, and threw open the door. He took a step forward and recoiled. On the walls were pictures of the Kaiser, Hindenburg, Ludendorff, and Von Tirpitz, and a large German flag.

"*Des allemands!*" he groaned.

"Yes," I said, "we are Germans."

"Then we are lost, *per Dieu!*"

"Yes, *per Dieu*, you are lost."

He stood with his forehead in one hand. His despair was both tragic and comic to behold. I tried as best I could to say a few words of cheer.

"Well, Captain, you are not the only one to lose your ship during the war. To-morrow I, too, may be sunk, or the next day."

He replied in the most doleful tone imaginable.

"It is not so much the loss of my ship. But it's that I feel I have only myself to blame for it. In Valparaiso, where I lay in port with my *Dupleix*, two of my fellow captains warned me not to start until they had cabled our owners for final instructions and news about U-boats and cruisers. Possibly our owners would instruct us to keep off the usual

course, they said. But the wind was fair, and I
thought it best to take advantage of it. So, without
waiting for a reply from our owners, I sailed from
Valparaiso ahead of the other two captains. And now,
because I did not take their advice, I have lost the
Dupleix, my ship. *Mon Dieu*, what an ass I was!
Now they will report it to my owners, and I will
never get a ship again."

"What were the names of your friends' ships?"

"The *Antonin*——"

"The *Antonin* under Captain Lecoq?"

"Yes. And the *La Rochefoucauld*."

"Orderly," I called in German, which the captain
did not understand, "bring up captains numbers five
and nine."

While we waited, I invited my mournful guest to
have some more champagne, but he refused and
continued holding his head and moaning.

A knock at the door.

"Come in."

And in walked the captains of the *Antonin* and
the *La Rochefoucauld*. They had been on board ten
and three days respectively.

The captain of the *Dupleix* gaped.

"*Eh, tout la France!*" he cried.

Full of ironical enthusiasm, he raised his glass of
champagne and saluted them. Then with joy that he
made no effort to conceal, he clasped the hands of
the two captains whose advice he had scorned and
who had encountered the same fate as he. They returned his welcome with a grim humour.

The presence of these three captains aboard the
Seeadler represented a loss of ten thousand tons of
saltpetre destined for French powder mills, and a saving of hundreds, perhaps thousands of German lives.

*   *   *

One Sunday morning, we sighted a large British barque and started after her. She thought we were playfully challenging her to a race, and tried to run away. I don't know whether we could have caught her in a straight sailing ship against sailing ship contest; at any rate, our motor gave us the edge.

A strange feeling came over me as we gained on her and as her lines became more distinct. It was a sense of sadness and of vague, dimly dawning recollection. Had I seen that ship before? Was it possible . . .

"Signal and ask her for her name," I called.

Our signal flag went aloft. The reply came back: "*Pinmore.*"

Ah, my old *Pinmore*, on which I had made the longest and most harrowing voyage of my life. Memories swept over me of those endless storms and of the disease on board, beri-beri, scurvy. My whole being seemed to leap back to the days of my youth. Homesickness seized me. I could not say a word to Leudemann, who stood beside me.

"No use, the ship must be sunk," a harsh inner voice told me.

It was hard for me to sink any sailing vessel, but doubly cruel to have to sink my old ship. I felt as though she were a kind of mother. No sailor with any kind of sailor's soul in him will raise a hand against his own ship.

We took her as we had taken the others. When her crew came aboard, I looked for familiar faces. There were none. The skipper, Captain Mullen, came up to me with a humorous, seamanly air.

"Well, Captain, our hard luck is your good luck."

"Lucky?" I felt like saying. "Do you call this lucky?"

He was a typical old seaman, afraid neither of

enemy in war nor storms at sea. The seven seas had been his home. Like the sailing ship, the old-time windjammer captain is vanishing. Captain Muller was indeed like the king of a vanishing race. He swaggered down below, and saluted our other skippers with a jovial air. He soon became the leading figure of the "Captains' Club."

When everyone had left the *Pinmore*, I had a boat take me over to her. I clambered aboard and sent the boat and its crew back, telling them I would give them a hail when I wanted them again.

"Why does the Count want to remain alone aboard her?" I heard one of them say.

I went to the fo'c'sle. There was my bunk, the same old bunk where I had slept night after night for months and had tumbled out countless times at the command "all hands on deck" while those endless storms bore down upon us. I paced the planks on deck where I had stood watch so often. It seemed as though I had never seen that deck save in a storm. Those gales had left so deep an imprint on my memory that it gave me a sense of strangeness to see the sun shining on the *Pinmore's* planks and a slowly heaving sea around.

I remembered a cunning little cat I had once owned on board her. The captain's wife wanted it. The steward got it for her. I told the steward that if he did not bring it back to me I would go to the captain. The steward laughed at me. I determined to complain to the captain about the steward and his wife and demand my cat back. I could see myself as I had wrathfully strode along the deck to the cabin. The sight of the door made me stop. I mustered up my courage and advanced again. I ventured just far enough to peep in at the door, which was ajar. The skipper was sitting there reading a paper. One

glimpse of the master, and all of Phelax Luedige's bravery oozed away. He turned and tiptoed away. I never did get my cat back, and forever after held a grudge against the steward.

I could still feel the old enmity. If I could have found that steward, I would have let him know how the end of a rope felt. I went to the cabin and half opened the door. It was much as when I had seen it last. The bright rainbow glow of the coloured sky-light gave me an old familiar feeling. Something restrained me from entering. I did not dare go in then. I would not now.

At the stern I looked for my name which I had once carved on the rail. I found it, half effaced by time and weather. I read it slowly, spelling it out as a child spells its first lessons: P-H-E-L-A-X L-U-E-D-I-G-E. I looked at the compass, beside which I had watched for hours. The compass is a sacred place to a sailor.

"This ship," I thought, "carried me safely. The storms were wild all the way from 'Frisco around the Horn to Liverpool. They wanted to take us, every man aboard, but the good old *Pinmore* fought against wind and wave over leagues and leagues of dreary waste and brought us safely to port. Yes, she was our mother, our kindly protecting mother."

The deserted ship with an unguided helm rolled back and forth. The rigging creaked and groaned. It seemed to be a voice, a voice that hurt me. Every spar seemed to say:

"So here you are, Phelax, back again. Where have you been all these years? Where is all the crew? What do you want here, alone? What are you going to do with me?"

Little had I dreamed when I was a sailor on this fine barque that one day I would walk her decks

again, not as a seaman, but as the commander of a raider.

Returning to the *Seeadler*, I shut myself up in my cabin. In the distance I heard the roar of a bomb, and I knew that my old *Pinmore* had started on her last cruise.

XVIII

THE LIFE OF A MODERN BUCCANEER

Ever taken a trip at sea where the company aboard was dull and dead, the passengers uncongenial to one another, and everybody sitting around day after day and bored to death? You have? Well, then, you know what it's like, eh?

Give me a lively, companionable crowd of shipmates, and I don't care how long or how stormy the cruise. On land, if you don't like the company, you can seek better mates elsewhere. On shipboard, do your darnedest and you can't get away from 'em. You have to take your company just exactly as you find it. You are married to it. A genial lot of shipmates and a long cruise, say from New York to Melbourne, and what more can any man ask for at sea?

Although our old jolly-boat was a raiding auxiliary cruiser, she also degenerated into a breed of passenger ship, too. Our passengers were our prisoners. That made the situation somewhat unusual and added a bit of spice. I've served as an officer aboard a dozen or more liners, and have seen all kinds and strata of society aboard, including dull, delightful, ill-natured, jovial—both the quick and the dead. Yes, I have had some splendid passenger lists on voyages where every hour was gay and bubbling with fun. But no group of passengers on a liner ever enjoyed such happy comradeship as did we aboard our buccaneering craft. The fact that we were cap-

tors and captives only seemed to make it all the jollier. We took the greatest pleasure in making the time agreeable for our prisoners, with games, concerts, cards, and story-telling. We tried to feed them well, and I think we did, which helps a lot, as you'll agree. We didn't throw it at them either. In fact, we served special meals for all the nations whose ships we captured. One day our own German chef cooked, and that boy was *some* cook, as you say. The next day an English cookie, then the French chef, then the Italian to make us some *polenta*. The English food was the worst. It usually is. On the other hand, the Americans fed their sailors best of all. It's long been a tradition on Yankee clippers. In the old days, the American sailing ships were famous for frightful work and much brutality, but the food was good. To-day the work is not bad and there is no brutality, but the food is still good.

The prisoners seemed to appreciate our intentions thoroughly. They wanted to do everything they could for us in return. Feelings of patriotism should have made them hope for our early destruction. But more elemental sentiments of gratitude and friendship obliterated the more artificial passions of war hatred. I am sure that very few of our passengers wished us any ill or gloated in the hope of our being sunk by the cruisers of their nations. I think it really hurt many of them to realize that the day probably would come when we would be caught and go down under a rain of Allied shellfire. That magnificent Frenchman, the captain of the *Charles Gounod*, kept aloof from the general fraternizing, and scrupulously kept up his manner of cold politeness and stately hostility toward us, but even he thawed out a few degrees, although he tried hard to keep from showing it.

There was only one of our prisoners who behaved

himself in any way that could be considered improper. That was Captain Lecoq of the *La Rochefoucauld*, that same Captain Lecoq who had cherished hopes that we would run afoul of the British cruiser. You see, the skippers aboard were quite free to go where they liked on the ship, except that I asked each one, as he came aboard, not to go into the fore part of the ship, and I explained why.

"My magazines," I said, "are in the forward half of the boat. I do not want you to know exactly where they are placed. After you are released, you might reveal the secret. Then, one of these merry days, if some cruiser takes a shot at me, and if the location of my magazines is known, they'll aim right at that spot. A shell there and up in the air we go. I must ask you to give me your word of honour that you will not go into the foreship, else I will have to keep you confined."

Each skipper gave me his word, including Lecoq.

Captain Lecoq broke his promise. He not only went secretly into the foreship, but he made sketches of the layout there. Captain Mullen of the *Pinmore* saw the sketches, knocked Lecoq down, and reported him to me. I berated Lecoq soundly.

"And as a result of your dishonourable action," I said, "when I release my prisoners and send them off to some port, there will be one Frenchman who will remain behind, and that Frenchman will be you. You will continue your cruise with us. You know where my magazines are, and I cannot trust any promise that you now give me."

He turned a bit green around the gills at that, but there was nothing he could say in reply.

Our only woman aboard, the skipper's little bride, grew melancholy. We did everything we could to make the time pleasant for her, but she pined for the

society of other women. It was rather a trial for her
to be so long the only woman among several hundred
men.

"Count, I do so wish there were a woman aboard
that I could talk to," she said to me a bit coaxingly
one day. "Why don't you catch me one?"

I always like to oblige a lady, particularly one so
charming and agreeable as she, but catching another
woman was a game of chance with us. You don't
often find fair company aboard freighters, especially
in tropical waters. However, I said:

"Madam, we will do our best."

At times I used to amuse myself by joining the
crowd on the lookout in the rigging. It was a misty
day, and nobody had much of a chance of seeing
anything. Then it cleared a little in the west, and
Boarding Officer Preiss, who was beside me, thought
he saw a ship. I instructed the helmsman to steer
in that direction, and after fifteen minutes a large
British barque appeared through the mist. As we
drew near her, I saw a white figure on the deck. Sure
enough, a woman.

"Madam," I shouted, to the Canadian skipper's
bride, "get ready to welcome your companion.
She'll be paying you a call in a few minutes."

Everybody, prisoners and all, swarmed on deck to
witness the exceptional capture. The *Seeadler* bore
down on the unlucky barque.

The captain looked curiously at the crowded
figures standing at our rail, of every colour and race.
They waved gaily. Our gramophone blared out, "It's
a Long Way to Tipperary."

"Hello," he shouted through his megaphone,
"collecting volunteers?"

He thought we were picking up war volunteers
from the Atlantic islands.

"Volunteers?" I called in return. "Oh, yes."

Our prisoners laughed a bit.

"Any news of the war?" he asked.

Officers and sailors and the woman on his deck craned their necks for a reply.

"Much news of the war," I responded. "I will signal it."

They stared, awaiting the signal.

"C-I-D," our signal flags went up; "heave to or I will fire."

I could see the captain rapidly thumbing the pages of his book. His head jerked up suddenly. His binoculars focussed themselves on our masthead where the German flag now waved. Our gun mask dropped, and the cannon peered forth. By Joe, but it raised a commotion on the deck. When she saw it, the woman darted into her cabin. The sailors ran to the boats. Even the helmsman deserted the wheel. The captain was the only one who kept his head. He seized the helm with a firm hand, and the ship hove to.

Our guests were always interested in the prospect of having new additions to their company. They had an ever-ready, cordial welcome for fresh arrivals. This time, the coming of a second feminine passenger made the occasion a gala one. Everybody put on his best manners. The members of our "Captains' Club" marshalled their forces on deck, ready to greet the officers and the lady from the captured craft with suitable dignity and formality.

Our little woman put on her best clothes and asked me for a nosegay from a supply of artificial flowers we had captured. The newly arriving woman, who scarcely knew what to expect aboard our dreadful pirate craft, was surprised when she was greeted not only by our Captains' Club with all of its stately

courtesies, but also by a brightly smiling young woman who presented her with a bouquet of flowers that made up in brightness of colour what it lacked in sweetness of perfume, since they were imitation ones.

The two women immediately became the best of friends, and the convivial spirit aboard made our happiness complete.

The captured barque, the *British Yeoman*, carried a rare store of provisions, including some live pigs and chickens. She also had two pets, a curious pair—a rabbit and a pigeon. We promptly adopted them and called the pigeon "the dove of peace" in honour of the spirit aboard our raiding ark. That rabbit and pigeon were inseparable. If the rabbit strayed, the pigeon would coo and coo for it to come back, and the rabbit would obediently respond.

Then we also had two dachshunds aboard, Piperle and Schnaeuzchen. Piperle was a friendly little rascal and most intelligent. He seemed to understand what our work was, and grew most enthusiastic. He went out with the boarding parties, barked furiously if anything seemed to go wrong, and wagged his tail with a tremendous enthusiasm when things turned out all right. He seemed to take it as his especial task to give a friendly welcome to prisoners brought aboard. He would bark and leap upon them, as though saying:

"Hello, you'll have a good time here."

Schnaeuzchen was an ill-natured specimen of dachs bitch. She looked on satirically at Piperle's demonstrations, and people had to make many amicable overtures before she became friendly. She and Piperle were of discordant temperaments. They got along together in a resigned sort of way, with

many a quarrel in dog language, something like husband and wife. I think she nagged him a lot.

We gave the rabbit and pigeon quarters in Piperle's kennel, which delighted the good-natured dog. He welcomed his guests with cordial demonstrations. He licked the rabbit's fur continually, which at first made the pigeon jealous. The bird sulked and made angry sounds. The unfortunate rabbit seemed in a quandary, torn between his liking for the new friend and the old. He must have been a diplomat, though, for presently he found a way to reconcile the pigeon to his fondness for Piperle, and the three became excellent friends. When the three were asleep in the kennel, they made an edifying picture of harmony, Piperle on his side, the rabbit huddled against his belly, the pigeon perched on his side.

Schnaeuzchen, malign and crafty, watched this beautiful friendship with a jaundiced eye. She was the villain of the piece. She often made attempts to devour the rabbit or the pigeon or both, or at least to take a bite out of them. She was quick and cunning with her snapping jaws and sharp teeth. I spent a great deal of time trying to convince her that she had better leave the three pals alone, and Piperle had to be on the alert all the time to protect his two friends. One night Schnaeuzchen, with bold and bloody resolve, raided Piperle's kennel. I suppose she reasoned that she had better end the obnoxious situation with one fell blow. She got in before Piperle knew what had happened, and the rabbit barely escaped her jaws. Piperle turned on her and chastised her properly. After that she resigned herself to the inevitable. She kept the peace with the other pets, and while she never became really friendly with them, the pigeon and rabbit were at least safe.

Talking about animals brings to mind one remarkable piece of good fortune that blessed our entire adventure. Before it was over, we were destined to suffer pretty nearly all the hardships that the sea can bestow upon the sailor—arctic ice and tropical sun, storm and calm, frightful labour and deadening idleness, shipwreck, life as castaways on a desert island, the terrors of weeks in an open boat, hunger, thirst, and scurvy. But we never had any bedbugs. I had had enough experience with those vermin in my early days before the mast. I was determined to have none of them now. Bedbugs are a constant pest aboard sailing ships, and doubtless some of the vessels we captured had plenty of them. But aboard the *Seeadler* we had a magnificent fumigating plant, and every article that was brought aboard was given a thorough treatment. That fumigator was one of our most treasured possessions. Without it, we would surely have been in a fix. We could not have put comfortably into a port and called for the vermin exterminator, and if we had taken aboard any bedbug guests, our long voyage would have given them plenty of time to multiply and overrun our ark. We would have been eaten alive.

I remember a time during my jack-tar days when we had a magnificent collection of bedbugs in the forecastle. A comrade and I went to the captain, a mean old German skipper, and told him we were being eaten alive and begged him to go to the slight expense of getting a vermin exterminator.

"Bedbugs," he grunted, "*Gott im Himmel*, catch them."

We did catch them. We caught a match box full of them, and put them in his bunk.

The next day the vermin exterminator came aboard.

XIX

HOW WE MADE OUR PRISONERS WALK
THE PLANK

OUR floating hotel was about full. If we wanted to take any more guests aboard, we would have to get rid of our present company. The old pirates would have had a plank-walking ceremony. That was a sure way to prevent inconvenient information from getting around. Undoubtedly, it would have enabled us to keep our existence still secret. We were buccaneers in a sense, but not quite that bad. We would have to take other measures. When our prisoners got to port and our freebooting career became known, cruisers, of course, would set out after us. They would make the narrow Atlantic much too hot for us. We would have to seek other waters. The broad Pacific remained. We did not want to hold our prisoners for the always rough passage of Cape Horn, where, in addition, there were likely to be cruisers on watch, keeping a guard for suspicious ships that might be trying to take the shortest route from European waters to the Pacific. We might be shelled and sunk, but it would have been scarcely humane to take a chance of going down with all our prisoners on board. So we arranged it in a way that would enable us to get a good start on our trip around Cape Horn before the cruisers could get word of us.

The French barque, the *Cambronne*, came along. You should have seen her heave to and her yards

come banging down when our German flag went up and we signalled the inevitable: "Stop or I shall fire."

Her captain exhibited all of the usual Gallic despair at the prospect of losing his ship. We looked the craft over. She was large and roomy and had aboard a large stock of provisions.

"No," I said to her skipper, "we are not going to sink your ship. She will go right on to port."

"Eh?" He was immensely surprised.

"She will take our prisoners."

"I will be delighted, monsieur, to have them as my guests."

"They won't be your guests, Captain. You will be the guest of the new captain of the *Cambronne*."

"I will not command my ship?"

"Not at all. I have a Captains' Club aboard. You, as a prisoner, are now a charter member. Your ship is my prize. I will select a member of the Captains' Club as her skipper."

He was very angry. It hurt him nearly as much to be removed from the command of his ship as to have her sunk.

It was a touchy matter to select a skipper from among a dozen captains, each of whom was full of sensitive dignity and thought he was the best navigator of the lot. The French captains thought a Frenchman should be selected, since the most numerous nationality among the prisoners was the French. The traditional principle of seniority, however, pointed to the selection of the oldest skipper. My belief in that principle was confirmed by the fact that the oldest skipper was Captain Mullen of the *Pinmore*. He had shown himself to be the finest of gentlemen, and then there was the memory of my old ship, which I had been compelled to sink. I appointed Captain Mullen master of the *Cambronne*. Since he

was a Britisher, it was reasonable that his ship should sail under British colours. That necessitated the ceremony of hauling down the French flag and hoisting the Union Jack. The French captains did not like it at all.

I was rather glad that it was not I who would command the *Cambronne*. With all those captains aboard, especially the disgruntled French captains, the skipper of the *Cambronne* was certain to have an uncomfortable time. One skipper always knows more than any other skipper. Nor is any skipper ever reticent about the mistakes of another. The skipper of the *Cambronne* had better navigate with a perfect correctness, or there would be plenty of talk aboard.

We lopped off the *Cambronne's* upper masts, so that she could set only her lower sails. She could not make any speed now, and it would take her from ten to fourteen days to get to Rio de Janeiro, which was the nearest port. Then I exacted a pledge from Captain Mullen:

"Captain," said I, "we are releasing our prisoners, and they are under your command. I understand perfectly well that when you get to port our existence will be known. We will be a sailing ship in a world of armoured cruisers. We will be chased like a wild deer. We need a start. We have taken care that you do not get to port too soon. One thing remains, though. You may meet a ship within a week or within a day—it may be a steamer with a wireless plant. I ask for your word that you will not communicate with any ship until you reach port. We have, I hope, treated our prisoners fairly, and I ask this of you in return. I must have your solemn word on it."

"Count," he replied, "I give you my word that the *Cambronne* will not communicate with any ship until she is in port at Rio."

We shook hands on it, and my mind was at rest. It was no risk to take the word of the *Pinmore's* old skipper.

He played his part nobly. He passed several steamers on his way to Rio, but steered clear of them. One comical thing happened. A big steamer came toward the *Cambronne* one morning, and then her captain noticed the crowd of prisoners on the ship's deck. He was a cautious soul. It looked suspicious. The steamer turned and fled at full speed.

There remained the case of Captain Lecoq of the *La Rochefoucauld*, who had broken his word to me and whom I had promised not to release with the other prisoners. He tried to dissuade me. He was aghast at the thought of being kept aboard the *Seeadler* throughout her long cruise, the end of which no one could foretell. He vowed by all the saints that he would keep the position of the ship's magazines locked sternly within his bosom. I would not listen to him. I told him that the others would go but he would remain. I intended to hold him until we had caught and released our next batch of prisoners. He enlisted the other captains to intercede in his behalf. They came and asked me to relent.

"Gentlemen," I replied, "I have just now rested the safety of my ship on Captain Mullen's word. You are all ship masters. You know a captain's duty to the vessel he commands. Very well, I know that Captain Mullen's word is good. I have taken the others of you at your word, and you have not failed me. But Captain Lecoq broke his word. Can I trust him not to break it again?"

They argued so hard for their unfortunate fellow skipper that I finally gave in. After all, even if he did break his word again and tell of the position of my magazines, it did not necessarily mean disaster. I

made him sign a promise and made the other captains sign as witnesses to his promise. Then I gave orders that he should go with the rest.

We paid our prisoners off, just as if they had been working for us. Each received wages for the time he had spent aboard, and each was paid the wage he ordinarily received from his shipowner. By Joe, that made them happy. We had a final banquet. The sailors feasted in their quarters. I entertained the officers and ladies in my cabin. Toasts of champagne were drunk, and at the end there were cordial handshakes. We transferred the crowd to the *Cambronne* in boatloads, and each boat, as it pushed off, gave three cheers for the *Seeadler*.

Evening was coming on. The *Seeadler* lay watching while the *Cambronne* raised sail. Now the stately barque was sliding through the water. Hands waved and farewells were shouted. The two ships saluted each other. With her snow-white canvas bellied out by the brisk wind, the *Cambronne* sailed toward the horizon. Aboard the buccaneer, we watched till the last tip of her mast disappeared below the skyline.

We had been away from port for eight weeks and had sunk eleven vessels, representing a total of more than forty thousand tons of Allied shipping. The Atlantic had given us its share. Now to the Pacific. And God save us from the cruisers.

XX

THE BATTLE OF THE FALKLAND ISLANDS

THROUGH an oily sea we sailed south and west toward the Falkland Islands. Many a time had I passed this way in the old days when bound for Cape Horn. These islands of the South Atlantic have long been the base for whaling schooners. But to every German the Falklands will be forever memorable as the scene of a one-sided naval engagement in which one of our best beloved admirals was overwhelmed by a British fleet.

Had you seen our deck as we sailed south during these days, you might have wondered what we were about. Along with other plunder, we had looted captured ships of several great sheets of iron. We had ripped them from iron walls and roofs of forecastles and stowed them on our deck. Now the mechanics of the *Seeadler's* motor crew got busy with acetylene torches, and from those sheets of metal they welded a great iron cross, ten feet high.

We drew near a spot on that lonely ocean just a bit to the east of the Falkland Islands. My navigation officer and I figured out the point carefully on our chart, and when our instruments told us we were there, I called all hands on deck. Somewhere far below on the floor of the ocean were the bodies of hundreds of our comrades and the battered hulks of a once proud German fleet. It was in these very waters that our gallant Pacific Squadron under Count von

Spee sank in three thousand fathoms. For here it was that our light cruisers, the *Scharnhorst*, *Gneisenau*, *Nuremburg*, and *Leipsic*, with odds against them, fought it out with a more powerful British squadron.

With flag at half mast, we stood at solemn attention. The sky was gray and melancholy. The sea rolled with a gentle swell. In our mind's eye we could picture that disastrous day when, outranged by the guns of the great British warships, our cruisers, two large and three small, had fought a losing and hopeless fight. One, a scout cruiser, escaped. The others went down. Pounded from the distance, they trembled under the blows of the shells that rained down upon them. Exploding projectiles raked the decks and pierced the hulls of the ill-fated vessels. As if in a last struggle, trying to keep afloat for one more shot at the enemy, they staggered, lurched, and then, one after the other, plunged into the depths, entering port on their final voyage far below on the ocean floor, eighteen thousand feet beneath the surface. Every man aboard three of the ships was lost. A high sea happened to be running at the time, so the victors had little chance to rescue the men from the doomed ships. Two hundred and fifty members of the crew of the *Gneisenau* were picked up and got to the Falklands alive.

As if in a dream, I thought of the last time I saw my friend Count von Spee. It was in the days before the world went mad. The Navy Yard at Kiel was in gala mood. Every warship in the harbour had sent three hundred men. They stood at rigid attention while Von Spee and his staff strode by. Then he addressed them.

"By order of the Emperor, I am to take command of our cruisers in Chinese waters. My officers and men sail with me to-morrow."

The sailors all give three cheers. They think the Admiral and his men are merely going for a pleasant vacation to the Orient. It is in 1913. No war is in sight. Yet a darker note intrudes: Even then military and naval men were unable to escape the thought of war:

"We are leaving home and country for two years. We who part from you to-morrow will do our duty, knowing that every man at home will do his. If war should come, we will be across the world and you will be here. We will be too far away to lend a hand to you, and there is little that you will be able to do for us.

"Ours is a young navy, but we have had a great teacher. When England built her mighty fleet, she taught us how to build ours. The English have great naval traditions, and both their fleet and traditions have been our model. If war should come before we meet again, we along the far-off China coast may be but a few ships against many enemies, but from you of the High Sea Fleet we expect great deeds."

We of the German Navy knew and constantly gave expression to the thought that Britain was our guide on the sea. Her great seafaring tradition was our conscious and admitted pattern. We German naval men liked the English and were in sympathy with them. Our navies were alike in spirit. The French Navy was somewhat different. Its morale was perhaps not so good. French naval officers all come up from the ranks. The British and German come from cadet schools and are recruited mostly from the first families. That is best. It provides a finer corps of officers. I, myself, came up from the forecastle, but I believe that, unless you have officers and men from different worlds, your men will have little respect for their commanders. It must either be that, or

your officers must inspire respect with their fists as in the old sailing-ship days. The French Navy no longer has a rich tradition. It is true that the French had far greater sea fighters than we in past centuries, and they had their fine old naval traditions. But during the Revolution the old Royal Navy of France was swept away and remained abolished for twenty years. At the end of that time, a new navy was formed, but by then the fine old French traditions seem to have been forgotten and new traditions had to be formed. We Germans, with a new fleet, took over the old, solid tradition of the British and made it our own. We did everything we could to implant it in our men, and make it a real, living thing ingrained in our people. Our sea leaders understood the importance of a tradition. That was why we were determined to keep a fleet after the war. When our great ships went down at Scapa Flow, our Socialists favoured the total abandonment of the naval arm, but fortunately enough of our people came out of their post-war trance long enough to prevent such a fatal error. Perhaps it might be only a few small ships that we could retain, but it would serve to keep traditions alive until we could again build up a fleet as great or even greater than the one we lost.

Von Spee was a sailor's admiral. He was a seaman by temperament, open, honest, and jovial, uncomfortable on land and only himself when on the bridge of his flagship. Too many of our professional fighting men, I regret to say, were more ornamental than useful. They were good at wearing gold lace and that is about all. But not Von Spee. He was at his best on a quarter-deck in a storm. I still can see him pacing back and forth, with his bushy brows and piercing blue eyes.

The day after he said *auf wiedersehen* to us at Kiel,

he and his officers and men left by transport for the
Orient, there to relieve the officers and men aboard
the cruisers of our small Pacific Squadron at Tsing
Tao. What was to have been their two-year term
overseas began as commonplace, quiet routine. It
ended under the salvos of British guns off the Falkland Islands.

Von Spee's plan, when the war caught him 15,000
miles from German waters, was to harass the Allies
in the Pacific and then try to slip back through the
North Sea to Kiel. Lady Luck smiled on him for a
little while and then deserted him. After crossing
the Pacific, he caught Craddock, the British admiral,
off the coast of Chile. Von Spee's star was in its
ascendancy at this time and Craddock's on the wane.
A German secret agent in Chile flashed a wireless to
Von Spee giving him the information that Craddock
was waiting for the arrival of the big but old battleship *Canopus* that was rounding the Horn. Without
the *Canopus*, Craddock's forces were weaker than
Von Spee's, and Von Spee instantly dashed to the
attack so as to engage Craddock before the *Canopus*
came up. Craddock and his men met their fate like
true British sailors. Outgunned, the British cruisers
continued to fire until they sank. Only one, a small
boat, got away. But their conqueror's days were
numbered.

Von Spee now began his long race toward Kiel.
Only two routes were possible, one by Cape Horn
and the other by the Cape of Good Hope. Of course,
he knew the British would be laying for him at
both places. He knew also that they would be after
him with swifter and more powerful ships than his
own. His one chance was to beat them to Cape Horn,
lose himself in the broad Atlantic, make a run for it,
and probably fight his way through the blockade.

By now he was short of both munitions and coal. A wireless from Germany brought the good news that a supply ship had slipped through the blockade and was now on its way out to meet him. What a tremendous voyage he might now have made! What a hair-raising dash at the Allied blockade line he might have made! But he never got the chance.

As he rounded the Horn, Dame Fortune tempted him, and he made what proved to be a fatal error. He stopped a British collier and took all her coal. This delayed him for three days. Meanwhile, a fleet of Britain's mightiest battle cruisers had arrived at the Falklands. He still might have run by them unnoticed had he not determined to shell and destroy the wireless station on the Falklands. Thus he stumbled into that nest of battle cruisers. He tried to run, but they caught and sank him. That day the British had their sea giants, the *Indefatigable*, the *Invincible*, the *Indomitable*, and along with them a number of other battle cruisers, that later were to fight gallantly at Jutland, and then find their way to rest on the floor of the North Sea.

Only one of Von Spee's ships, the light but fleet cruiser *Dresden*, showed her heels to the British leviathans and slipped back around Cape Horn. But the Fates were merely playing with the poor *Dresden*, and a few days later she was sunk by the more powerful British cruiser *Kent* off San Juan Fernandez, Robinson Crusoe's island, in the Pacific. She was lying in neutral waters and should have been sheltered by the laws of war. Her captain signalled to the commander of the *Kent:*

"We are in Chilean territory."

"My orders are to sink you on sight," replied the *Kent*, "and no matter where you are."

The captain of the *Dresden* blew up his ship, and

with his officers and crew swam ashore. The island was not quite so deserted after this shipwreck as it was in Robinson Crusoes' day!

That in brief was the story of the plucky Von Spee and his gallant men. Hence this dreary waste of waters off the Falklands was sacred to us. We hove to, and from my quarter-deck I presided over a brief memorial service above the watery graves of our comrades and their ships. First I told my boys the story of my friend Count von Spee and his men, and every one of us knew that we, too, might soon be on our way to join them. But with the difference that we might not even have a chance to fight it out.

On German ships, the captain is also the chaplain. Every Sunday aboard the *Seeadler* we had our hour of prayer and song. When we had "guests" aboard from enemy ships, we invited them to join with us in the worship of the Great Ruler of the Waves. Our service followed the ritual of no particular creed. It was as simple as we simple seamen could make it. The table which bore the ship's Bible was draped not only with our German flag but also with the flags of all the Allied nations whose ships we had captured and under whose colours our prisoners had sailed. I wanted to make our prisoners feel that the service was as much theirs as it was ours, and that we did not feel ourselves any more a chosen people before the Altar of God than any other people.

My life has not been altogether a pious one. On the contrary, it had been decidedly blasphemous. My character was then, and still is, far from saintly. However, I may not have been wholly unfit for the office of ship's chaplain. I am religious at heart, easily swayed by sentimental appeal. Had I not been a member of the Salvation Army in Australia? Those testimonial meetings in Fremantle were still

vivid memories to me. So I was not exactly a green-horn at conducting a prayer meeting.

Before concluding our little memorial service, I addressed our comrades three thousand fathoms below us. No mounds were raised over their graves, no green grass or kindly flowers had been placed to cheer them on their journey to the land from which no traveller has yet returned. Only the waves of the sea. I spoke to them as though my voice could somehow find its way to their resting place among the mountain ranges at the bottom of the South Atlantic:

"Glorious fallen comrades, we bring you a message from home. Your comrades have kept their promise to your commander. On sea and on land they are fighting for the Fatherland. We of the *Seeadler* salute you and solemnly swear that we, too, will endeavour to live and die as gloriously as you. We, too, are hunted on the sea, even as you were. So perhaps it will not be long ere we join you down there in Davy Jones's Locker. If we do, our one hope is that we will be able to fight our last fight as gallantly as did you."

I then led the sailors in a prayer that we repeated aloud, and while the chorused invocation travelled southward on the winds that blew toward the Antarctic, four men came forward bearing the great iron cross.

"A decoration for the graves of heroes!"

At this signal from me the massive emblem slid into the water with scarcely a splash and flashed swiftly down, down, three thousand fathoms, to carry our message to Admiral Count von Spee and his men.

XXI

RACING THE ENEMY AROUND CAPE HORN

Aʜᴏʏ, shipmate," I said to Leudemann, "you are the fellow who likes yacht racing. By Joe, it's to be a race now—a race to see who gets to Cape Horn first."

We knew that, as soon as our former prisoners made port, the news of our presence in the South Atlantic would be flashed abroad. Then the British would send their cruisers on the double-quick down the coast of South America to keep us from doubling the Cape. To be sure, we had taken care to give ourselves a mighty good start. But in a race of wind-jammer against swift cruisers, what is a start of a thousand miles or so? With decent weather, we had hopes of making it. So far we had had fair winds and had made good time. But the most difficult stretch of sea in all the world now lay before us. The storms for which the Horn is famous often delay sailing ships for weeks.

"And then," responded Leudemann, "even if we do get to the Cape before any cruisers that may be sent down from the North, they may have a cruiser or two nosing around at the Pacific end of the Straits. Unless we round the Horn before those chaps reach Rio, the jig may be up."

Just south of the Falklands, we caught a wireless from a British cruiser, a warning message to Allied merchantmen.

Steer clear of Fernando Noronha. German cruiser *Moewe* reported there.

"*Moewe*" means "sea gull" in German. "Hail to you, far-distant Sea Gull, may you fare as well on your warlike flight as we hope to fare in our Sea Eagle!"

A feeling of homesickness for the old *Moewe* came over me, as it does over any sailor at the mention of a ship on which he has sailed. My service aboard the *Moewe* had been neither long nor eventful, but already she had made for herself a heroic reputation. I have always regretted that I was not with her on her raids. She made several, slipping out through the blockade, sinking quantities of Allied shipping, and stealing back into German waters.

She was built just before the war, and originally designed to carry the exotic banana from Southwest Africa and "German East" to Hamburg. Plans had just been made to flood Germany with them. Her sister ship in the banana trade was the *Wolf*, and she, too, became a famous raider.

All manner of ingenious devices were invented in fitting out the *Moewe* for her career as a raider. She was altered so that she could disguise herself and change disguises while steaming at full speed just like a quick-change actor. One day she would be a three or two funnelled steamer, the next she would look like a slow tramp with one funnel. The line of her deck could be changed in a few minutes also. She also had fake superstructures that could be raised or lowered at will. She could even be made longer or shorter in a few moments by means of a fake section that slipped out from her stern. One day she would be a tramp, the next, with fake bulls'- yes, a liner. These startling metamorphoses were a

great success and enabled her to dodge many an Allied cruiser.

Of course, the British soon got on to the *Moewe's* quick-change habits, and were not to be fooled by them. On one of her adventures, the *Moewe* was trapped off the eastern coast of South America. The British cruisers *Glasgow* and *Amethyst* were warned by wireless that the *Moewe* was steering south from Fernando Noronha to take coal. So they rushed out from Rio de Janeiro to trap her. Presently, the *Glasgow* spotted the *Moewe* on the horizon. The German ship had on one of her innumerable disguises, and the captain of the *Glasgow* could not recognize her. He was wary, however, and on to the *Moewe's* tricks, so he wirelessed her to stand by to be searched. The *Moewe* turned and ran south. The *Glasgow* could make twenty-five knots and easily outrace her. The *Moewe* was well armed with guns and torpedoes and would fight, but she would be no match for an armoured ship. The men aboard the *Moewe* seemed as good as at the bottom of the sea. The *Glasgow* knew that the fleeing ship must be the long-sought-for raider, and prepared to sink her.

The two ships steamed with straining boilers, and the *Glasgow* was fast creeping up on the *Moewe*. When almost within range, the hunted raider ran into one of those sudden rain squalls that sweep over the ocean. Like the Biblical cloud, it hid her from the pursuing cruiser. Of course, the *Glasgow* followed her into the squall. But as the *Moewe* ran through the swirling storm, she passed another steamer, this one steaming north. The cruiser saw emerging from the squall this new ship. She had three masts. The *Moewe* had had but two. The captain of the *Glasgow* thought only of the *Moewe's* ability to disguise herself. He presumed that the *Moewe* had taken advantage of

the squall to run up a third mast and then double
back on her trail in the hope that the Englishman
would not recognize her and that she might pass
safely and even have an opportunity to torpedo the
Glasgow. The cruiser instantly opened fire, and blew
the poor, inoffensive cargo steamer out of the water.
It was only when they examined the wreckage that
they discovered that they had made a mistake and
sunk a British freighter! Meanwhile, the *Moewe* had
escaped once more.

Nor was that the only ship the British sank by
mistake. They shelled two harmless sailing vessels to
pieces, mistaking them for our *Seeadler.* It all came
about because of one of those familiar war rumours, a
rumour to the effect that we were already somewhere
off the Australian coast. An Australian cruiser encountered a Scandinavian three-master, and they
seemed to think she was behaving queerly. Word
had been passed around that the *Seeadler* carried
torpedoes. So the cruiser thought she had better not
run any chance of being blown up. She opened fire
at long range. Only ten men aboard the Scandinavian
ship were saved. Later on, the armoured cruiser *Kent*[1]
sank another sailing vessel under similiar circumstances in the Pacific.

Sailors since Magellan, by Joe, have talked about
the storms around Cape Horn. Sea stories usually
have something about the tough times rounding the
Cape. I had seen those storms myself when I had
sailed in the forecastle, and as a naval officer I had
many a time told tales to my brother officers of
gales and tempests I had witnessed in an old windjammer rounding Horn. But our trip this voyage was
to be the most unusual of all. If the storms held us
back, the cruisers would be almost certain to catch
us. We had sailed south in fine time, and if we

---

[1] See Note B, Appendix.

made a quick passage round that boisterous tip of South America, we might slip into the wide Pacific and continue our raids.

Well, we ran into the dirtiest weather off the Horn, gales and hurricanes. Why, there were days when even with our motor running we could make no headway at all. It took us three weeks to beat our way through the gales and around the point. By that time, the cruisers lay there in wait for us, not just one or two, but a whole half dozen of them.

Ordinarily, a sailing ship tries to hug Cape Horn as closely as it can, keeping quite near land. If you veer too far to the south, you run into icebergs. Navigating among icebergs with the wind whistling through your rigging is enough to give any skipper the chills. So the storms had held us up, and now our best chance probably would be to steer as wide a course to the south as possible, whether safe or not. The mountains of ice were there, and a hurricane was blowing. But we considered the ice the lesser of two evils. The British watch to the far south was bound to be less vigilant than up nearer the Cape. We must try to sail around them. So, ho for the Antarctic!

On our way through the blockade, we had steered into the Arctic. Now here we were heading into the Antarctic.

To make it pleasant, by Joe, the weather, which had been quite decent to us on the way south, changed in order to give us a regular Cape Horn welcome. It turned into a veritable hurricane. Nevertheless, we were determined to carry as much sail as possible. Risky, but we had to take chances in the hope of getting through. As the tempest increased, not even the *Seeadler* dared carry more than a rag or two of lower sail. With this we tried to hold our

way. Through the mist we saw a great wall. It came moving toward us. A vast wall of white, an iceberg. The wind was driving this white spectre through the water, and we had to veer off in order to avoid collision.

To the north were the cruisers, and here, but a few hundred yards away, an equally relentless enemy bearing down upon us, as though determined to turn us into the arms of our pursuers. A shout to the helmsman. Determined as we were to go no farther north, we knew we could do no more than hug the Antarctic ice field.

The mountain of ice nearest us seemed coming closer and closer—nine times as much ice below the water as above. As every schoolboy knows, if a berg looms up two hundred feet above the waves, its base extends eighteen hundred feet below the surface! How far its sharp hard edges and spurs may extend on either side you never can tell unless one of them rips open your hull. The best way to avoid running into a spur is to turn and run the other way. An iceberg carries neither lights, lighthouses, buoys, nor sirens. She is a cold, calculating, merciless Circe, and the wise mariner gives her a wide berth. Some of us thought the berg was six thousand feet long while others thought it much more than that. We were so near it that we could hear the clattering and squawking of the thousands of sea gulls that swarmed around the ice mountain. In the wild, heaving sea, the berg rolled like some mammoth ship. There were cracking sounds as the heaving ice strained and split. Once, under the stress of the movement, one whole vast corner broke off with a tremendous rending and tearing. The block, as big as a skyscraper, crashed into the sea, and before it could start off on a cruise of its

own the waves dashed it into the berg with a noise like thunder, and this continued time and again as the parent berg drove its husky offspring before it.

Suddenly, there came an even more ominous scraping sound. The *Seeadler* quivered, and our blood fairly froze. We had grazed a submerged snout of ice. In such a sea, there would have been no chance to launch lifeboats. Although we had not staved in our hull, nevertheless, the ship had sprung a leak. No matter who was captain. Everybody to the pumps. I took my place with the sailors in the hold, and we all fought to keep the water in check. The brush with the ice was a warning. We veered a bit more to the north, and with pumps working madly, passed the berg. The wind wrenched us, the waves struck us hard, but we kept on, beating our way to the Pacific and pumping.

"Cruiser ahoy!"

I saw through the storm a 23,000-ton auxiliary cruiser. I believe it was the *Otranto*, a converted passenger liner, fast and well armed, capable of blowing us out of the water before our little gun could throw a shell halfway to her.

"Hard aport," I shouted.

The ship shook as the helm was forced over, and the wind nearly turned us bottom side up. Storm or no storm, we were all dead men if that cruiser ever caught us.

"Set all sails."

We must risk it and run with all our canvas before the hurricane, and perhaps, somehow, we knew not how, in the shelter of the storm, we might be lucky enough to evade the cruiser.

Only men who have been to sea in windjammers can imagine what it is to set sail in a hurricane. The canvas whipped as though a devil had taken hold of it.

The masts bent under the force of the wind as it blasted against the sails. The ship and its rigging creaked and groaned as though crying out against the sudden strain.

"The cruiser is coming," Leudemann shouted in my ear. "She is making straight for us."

"More sail on, by Joe," I sang out to the men aloft.

Never mind the hurricane. To the south we go. We'll bury ourselves in the Antarctic ice before we let them catch us, if the wind doesn't snap off our masts.

So, with the combined force of the gale and our 1,000-horsepower motor, we scudded southward. Suddenly, a flooding rain broke over us, a providential squall if there ever was one. It was like a gift of heaven. It blotted us out from the cruiser, just like the squall that rescued the raider *Moewe*.

"It is the hand of God," I shouted. "Our hour hasn't struck yet."

Under cover of the squall, we got away from there as fast as we could go, and after a few hours we felt certain we had given our pursuer the slip. In reality, we had not been pursued at all. The cruiser hadn't even seen us, and our lookout had been sharper than hers. We learned this from later reports. The ironical thing now would have been for us to have impaled the *Seeadler* on an iceberg in that mad sprint southward. But luck was with us again. The storm blew itself out.

Still, we were not out of the danger zone. Days went by before we were safely out of that boisterous region and spreading our wings on the broad expanse of the Pacific. Cruisers were still watching for us, and we had to keep a constant lookout. Our problem now was how to put them off the scent.

The *Seeadler* carried twenty lifeboats and a corre-

sponding equipment of life preservers. These were much more than enough for our crew. We had taken ten of them off captured ships to accommodate our prisoners in case of necessity. Now we threw all these extra lifeboats overboard, taking care that on each boat and each life preserver was painted *Seeadler*. Our hope was that some of them would be picked up, and that the report would then be sent out that we had gone down off the Horn. That was exactly what happened. Two days later we picked up a wireless. It carried the news that a coastguard cutter had found one of our little boats. Later, two more were picked up. Then three. All along the coast of South America we were now given up for lost. The cruisers abandoned the chase and steamed north.

This left the way clear for us, and now we sailed out to continue our adventure on the greatest of all the seven seas.

Fourteen days after rounding the Horn, we picked an interesting and rather puzzling wireless out of the air:

Seeadler gone down with flags flying. Commander and part of crew taken prisoners and on their way to Montevideo.

"What's that?" I thought. "By Joe, Johnny Bull is telling a whopper."

Now, when old John Bull tells a fib, you can bet, by Joe, that he has good reason for it. We tried to figure it out, and came to the conclusion that it had something to do with the scare we had created. The news that our prisoners had given out at Rio had sent Lloyd's rates skyward and caused many ships to lie in harbour until the danger from the German raider had blown over. The British, in order to bring

Lloyd's rates down and to liberate all the shipping that had been tied up, took pains to spread a highly coloured report of our disaster dressed up with suitable imaginative trimmings to make it more convincing.

"Well, Johnny Bull," I thought, "we'll fix you."

Our wireless operator, a very capable fellow, worked out a scheme with me. "Sparks" sent out the following message purporting to come from a British ship:

SOS—SOS—German sub . . . .

He cut the message short, as if interrupted, to make it seem as if at that moment the ship had been torpedoed.

After a suitable interval he sent out another call, this one merely reporting German submarines off the coast of Chile.

Did Lloyd's rates go up again? And did those ships that were getting ready to put to sea put back to their berths? Well, you can bet your boots they did. And we sent out other submarine warnings every so often just to keep our little joke alive.

These were all small injuries, but we had been sent out to harass the enemy, and this was one way of doing it. What more could you expect of a lone windjammer? And then, it's these injuries all added together that more often than not win the day. It was good sport for us, anyhow.

XXII

RAIDING THE PACIFIC

THE wireless continued to be interesting. We picked up many messages from the cruiser *Kent*,[1] which was right in our waters; in fact, much too close for comfort. Our course was northward, with the Chilean coast and the Andes almost in sight. We steered almost to the Galapagos Islands, and at Robinson Crusoe's island, San Juan Fernandez, we trimmed our sails and turned our bow west. We sailed for weeks on the broad expanse of the Pacific without sighting a ship. Except for the occasional crackle of the wireless, we were alone in the world.

Our wireless antennæ kept us in touch with the latest phase of the international situation. Nor was it particularly pleasant on those long idle days at sea to sit and meditate on the fact that the United States was going into the war against us. We sailors knew better than some of our people at home the tremendous power of the great republic of the West. There were closeted statesmen and generals who might talk as they pleased about the American lack of military preparedness and the impossibility of American troops being mustered and sufficiently trained in time to be of any service in the critical hour of the war. We sailors had travelled. Many of us had been in the United States and had served on American ships. All fine technical points aside, we had had opportunity to sense the might of the North American giant with its numerous and virile population and

---

[1]See Note C, Appendix.

its incalculable wealth. With such strength behind it, even an awkward, poorly aimed thrust was enough to push almost anyone over.

We caught one radio dispatch that caused us to sit and gaze hopelessly into the sky. It told of the famous Zimmermann note. What madness had dictated that extraordinary state paper, which proposed to Mexico that she join Germany in the war and receive in return a slice of American territory including Texas? I had served as a soldier in the Mexican Army, and knew something of its probable prowess in a war. A few American regiments on the Rio Grande could hold back the Mexican Army as easily as I can hold a child. And did our statesmen think the Mexicans were such fools? The folly was one that could only enrage the people of the United States and make the Mexicans laugh. We of the German fighting forces could only curse the luck that had given our country such diplomacy. All it succeeded in negotiating was new enemies and fewer friends.

The American declaration of war came as a blow expected, but hard nevertheless. Some of the more pessimistic of us could spell the doom of Germany in it. It altered the position of our buccaneering expedition somewhat, too. It reduced the number of neutral ports into which we might sail. It also increased the number of cruisers we had to look out for. However, neutral ports did not enter into our calculations much. All ports really were hostile, anyhow. Neutrals would limit us to a short, inhospitable stay, the wireless stations near by would broadcast our presence, and the cruisers would come flocking. The American naval ships didn't mean much either. They would doubtless be kept, nearly all of them, to guard the Atlantic shipping lanes for the passage of American troop transports and leave what patrol

of the Pacific was necessary to the British and Japanese. The principal change of circumstance for us was that now we could take American prizes.

We steered across the Pacific past the Marquesas, far to the south of Hawaii. We made the waters near Christmas Island our cruising ground. There, near the equator, the eastbound and westbound routes for sailing ships crossed. We sailed backward and forward, crossing the equator two and three times each day.

We captured three American ships in these waters, the *A. B. Johnson*, the *R. C. Slade*, and the *Manila*. Our prisoners numbered forty-five men, one woman, and a pet opossum. The captains were not half so astonished and bewildered as the former captains when we unmasked ourselves as a buccaneer. They knew that the sailing ship raider was abroad. So we were deprived of some of our former amusement of astounding and befuddling officers and crews by suddenly hoisting the German flag, unmasking our cannon, firing a machine gun into their rigging, and similar pleasantries. Everything went off according to routine.

On one occasion we ran into a most intricate complication. We had expected the complications of war and piratical strategy. That was part of the game. But at the time to which I refer we were faced with a new and tender complication, a romantic complication.

"He's got his wife along," Boarding Officer Preiss informed me.

He referred to an officer of one of the ships. Indeed, we had noticed a woman aboard the captured ship.

The officer in question presently introduced me to his helpmate, and a knockout she was, pretty, petite, and—well, just a bit roguish.

"By Joe," I thought, "the sailors of these days are marvellous fellows. Where do they get these swell-looking wives? When I was in the forecastle, it was different."

In those days, an officer's wife was something to run away from, usually fat, usually savage, and always sloppily dressed. I thought of all the windjammer captains under whom I had sailed, and I couldn't think of one who had a wife that looked like a chorus girl. Well, times do change! There was the captain we had captured in the Atlantic who had such a pleasant little bride, and now here was this officer and his sprightly beauty.

I guess I can also add myself to the list. Here I am, skipper of a peaceful windjammer now, taking my three-master the *Vaterland* around the world, and I have my wife along. I have already described Irma, the fairy princess of my green island in the Canaries. Yes, sailors' wives have improved in looks these days.

Aboard the *Seeadler* we greeted the pretty little lady with great cordiality. Our former fair company had been so pleasant that we anticipated another similar brightening of the dull monotony aboard. The monotony was indeed broken somewhat! But in a decidedly different way than we had expected. The officer had not been long aboard before he took me aside and made an awkward and somewhat embarrassed confession. He had been thinking things over.

"Count," he said, "in your reports you may say something about my having my wife along."

"Yes," I replied.

"Well, by Joe," he continued, "I wish you wouldn't say anything about it. Don't say anything about my having a wife along. My real wife might find it out, and then there would be hell to pay."

"Oho," I exclaimed, "so that's the way the wind blows, eh?"

"I said she was my wife," he continued lamely, "because I thought it might help to save her from your sailors. But I don't want my wife to find it out."

"All right, sir," I said, "I won't report it, and I won't let my officers or crew know anything about it. That will be best. Treat the girl as your wife. I will keep my mouth shut, and you keep your mouth shut."

It was a difficult point of morals aboard ship. If the sailors found out that the girl was not the officer's wife, but only a kind of stowaway, they would lose all respect for her, and there was no telling what they might try to do. Sailors are not angels, but usually, in fact, a lot of rogues, but they are highly respectable. They have a very fine code of honour, and a woman who is off the line is simply off the line to them. Certainly, I did not want them to know that the officer's wife was not the officer's wife.

One of my prisoners turned out to be an acquaintance of the officer of the . . . I told him that the officer of the . . . had his wife along, and introduced him to the girl. He laughed so hard he nearly fell over. He wanted to tell the joke all around. It was awkward for a moment, but I got the two men aside and talked earnestly to them.

"We must be gentlemen in this matter," I said. "She is a girl. We are men. We must protect her. The sailors must not know about it. You must both give me your word of honour that you will keep mum and tell nobody."

They both promised.

Everything went all right until this other prisoner took a shine to the girl, too. It was funny business. She kind of liked him. I kept an eye on the whole

affair and saw what was happening. Here was more worry and trouble. I took the two men aside and said to them:

"I don't care what arrangements you two fellows make with your fair playmate, but it has got to be kept quiet. The sailors must think that she is the wife of the officer of the . . . and that . . . is only a friend."

They made some kind of change, I believe. I never could figure just how it was. I never was much good at mathematics or at figuring out anything, for that matter. At any rate, they kept it quiet. The other prisoner was married, too, and he didn't want anything of the complicated romance to get around either.

I had come to expect my prisoners to be good company. Our former Captains' Club had been one of the most delightful social organizations ever formed. These two sentimental swains, however, were not much good for comradeship. It was difficult to get together with them for a pleasant chat or game of cards. They were always thinking about the girl, and, although they were acquaintances in captivity, their feelings toward each other had become slightly strained. There is something about the air down there in the South Seas, I guess.

One of the captains made up for the companionship that had been lacking. He was a fine fellow. He was jovial and intelligent, and a thorough seaman if there ever was one. We became fast friends and had many a long and sympathetic talk about the war.

Weeks passed, and we did not see another ship. The idle days became very boresome. It was broiling hot, and we had little exercise. Our water turned stale, and we had no fresh provisions. Our prisoners did not find their stay with us so pleasant now, but we could not find a vessel on which to ship them. One

decided that he could not stand it any longer. He wanted to put his feet on land at any price. He came to me with a strange idea. Would I not land him on a desert island and leave him there a castaway? Anything was better than shipboard. But the principal part of his plan was more subtle. He would be reckoned dead at home, and his people would collect his insurance money. Perhaps I would be so kind as to make it seem certain that he was lost. Yes, no? On the island he could live as a Robinson Crusoe, a kind of existence which he fancied would be quite agreeable. Unfortunately for him, I felt obliged to decline. I was not interested in swindling insurance companies.

XXIII

SHIPWRECKED IN SOUTHERN SEAS

WE AMUSED ourselves by playing with the sharks. The landlubber can scarcely imagine the hatred the sailor feels for those bloodthirsty monsters. We had a particular grievance against them. A swim now and then would have provided us with needed baths and would have been a pleasant and vigorous diversion from the endless monotony of cabin and deck, our wooden prison. Many a time I looked down into the cool, refreshing element, and a shark would idle beneath my gaze, as though waiting for me there. The sailors passed the time by angling for the voracious monsters. They would catch a couple, tie their tails together and throw them back into the water. The sharks, unable to agree on the direction of their mutual movement, would have a great tug of war. The sailors thought the plight of their loathed enemies quite comical.

Or they would take a large shark, tie an empty and watertight barrel to his tail, and heave him over. The fish would dart downward, but the barrel would stay relentless at the surface. Now would ensue a desperate struggle which we could follow by watching the gyrations of the barrel. The sharks displayed an excellent eye for chunks of bacon with hand grenades in them. When the bomb went off in the creature's stomach, pieces of shark would go flying in all directions.

We had been in the Pacific for five months now, and had sailed 35,000 miles. With our stale water and the lack of fresh food, scurvy was breaking out among our men, and then beri-beri, which "turns the blood to water." Limbs and joints were swelling. We imperatively needed fresh water and food and a rest on shore. But where could we go? All the islands of the Pacific were in the hands of the French, British, and Japanese. We certainly felt it keenly, now that the whole world was against us. There was no inhabited place that would welcome us. It made us feel very lonely.

"Well," I said to my boys, "we will pick out some nice deserted island where there will be no hand raised against us and no wireless to call the cruisers, and we will get water and some kind of vegetables and maybe shoot some game and have a fine shore leave. Then, after we have rested up, what ho, boys, and away for more adventure."

Buccaneering in the Pacific, with only three ships sunk in five months, seemed much too unprofitable. I planned that, after a brief sojourn on some peaceful South Sea Isle, we would sail for the Antipodes. Then we would destroy the English whaling station and oil tanks at South Georgia, sink a few ships, capture one on which to ship our prisoners, and, if we got away safely, continue our cruise in the prosperous waters of the Atlantic.

Our first plan was to sail direct to one of the larger Cook Islands. But we gave that up for fear of finding a wireless station there that might give us away. We did not want to move east of our present longitude, for that would have taken us against the trade wind and compelled us to use our motor. It was necessary to save the engine as much as possible and not have it wear out on us. We hoped we would need it for further

captures and escapes. Mopelia, one of the Society Islands (some geographies include it in the Scilly Isles), seemed about right for our purpose. It was a French possession, and, so far as we knew, uninhabited. It was one of those isles of the South Seas so fantastically beautiful and so awkward for the sailor to approach. Only seldom does he find one with a decent anchorage, and nowhere in the world are the winds and currents more treacherous.

On the morning of July 29th, we sighted Mopelia, and steered toward it. Words fail me when I try to describe its beauties. From the blue ocean rises a mass of green palms. The sunlight glows in the green. It somehow even seems to turn the sunlight green. Against the dark blue of the sea and the light blue of the sky, the sunlight seems to be drawing the green island out of the water, and the soft south wind carries the scent of flowers far out to sea. It is the greeting of the island, and we inhale it deeply.

Here was a typical coral atoll—the kind you dream about. A circular reef studded with waving palms and within the reef a lovely, placid lagoon. The coral shore was snow white, and, with the sun's rays reflecting from it, it looked like a sparkling jewel set in an alabaster ring, like emeralds set in ivory. There were coral terraces below the water. The shallower ones were white or pale green, and as you peered deeper into the water you saw every conceivable tint of green and blue, sea green, emerald green, blue green, azure blue, sapphire blue, navy blue, violet.

As we sailed nearer and nearer that alluring coral shore, we saw flowers among the palms, flowers of all colours, and immense numbers of orchids. The hues of the flowers were reflected in the water over the white coral that deepened and turned green. Within the circular reef the lagoon seemed fully as deep as

the sea outside, only at perfect peace and smooth like a mirror. It would have made a perfect anchorage for us, save that it had one entrance so narrow that only a small boat could pass through it.

A strong current ran through the opening. We cast our anchor on the coral and tethered our ship to it with a long cable. The pull of the current kept her far enough offshore. I was afraid, for a while, that a shift of the wind might blow her on the reef, but we saw, after a while, that she had dragged anchor. If the current were strong enough for that, why surely it would be strong enough to keep her from blowing ashore. Leaving several men aboard as a watch, we went on land for a glorious shore leave, sailors, officers, prisoners, and all.

What would we find? We wanted water and fresh food. When we got inside of the lagoon, we found to our astonishment that it was a breeding place for turtles. There were hundreds of them in the water and on the shore, huge fellows weighing two or three hundred pounds. The water was full of beautiful fish. I recognized the moray, a fish like the eel, which is a great delicacy and will provide you with a substantial meal, too. It weighs from fifteen to twenty pounds. They say the Romans used to feed their slaves to this fish. There were big lobsters without claws that promised to be the best of food. The atoll was alive with birds, hundreds of thousands of them, with nests and eggs everywhere. They were so tame that one of my boys whom I sent to collect enough eggs for an omelette returned, saying:

"I didn't get an egg. The birds were so tame and trusting that I hadn't the heart to disturb them and take their eggs."

Nor was the island without human inhabitants. We

found three Kanakas, Polynesians who had been left there by a French firm to catch turtles. They were greatly frightened when they found that we were Germans. The French had told them frightful tales about the *Boches*. We, however, quickly made friends with them. They were much relieved when they found that we did not intend to injure them, and when we made amicable overtures, they were only too glad to respond.

First, my boys ran hither and thither to satisfy their curiosity about this strange island. Then they quickly settled down to useful occupations. Some set about catching fish and lobsters. Others gathered birds' eggs. A few brought armfuls of cocoanuts. Three boys turned a big turtle on its back and pulled it along with a rope. There were wild pigs on the island. We shot a couple. Soon the boat put out to the ship loaded deeply with a huge collection of epicurean delicacies. That night the mess was fit for the table of a royal palace—turtle soup with turtle eggs, broiled lobster, omelettes of gull's eggs, roast pork, and, for dessert, fresh cocoanut.

For days we lived a delightful poetic life, dining in a way that millionaires could not afford. We smoked quantities of fish and pork and stowed it away. We found fresh water on the island and refilled our tanks. Our traces of scurvy and beri-beri disappeared, and we were rapidly getting ready to continue our cruise and work of havoc in Australian waters.

On the second of August, we made ready to leave the ship for another day ashore. At nine-thirty I noticed a strange bulge on the eastern rim of the sea. I called my officers' attention to it. At first we thought it a mirage. But it kept growing larger. It came toward us. Then we recognized it—a tidal wave

such as is caused by submarine earthquake and volcanic disturbances. The danger was only too clear. We lay between the island and the wave.

"Cut the anchor cable. Clear the motor. All hands on deck."

We dared not raise sail, for then the wind would drive us on the reef. So our only hope of getting clear of the island was our motor. The huge swell of the tidal wave was rushing toward us with breakneck speed.

The motor didn't stir. The mechanics were working frantically. They pumped compressed air into the engine. We waited in vain for the sound of the ignition. Now, right at the critical moment, our motor had failed us, just as it had so often failed us before. By this time, the tidal wave was only a few hundred yards away. We were lost. To our frightened eyes it looked like a whole mountain range of water. It must have been thirty or forty feet high. It came rushing with a roar that drowned out our voices.

A gigantic, violent hand seemed to grasp the ship. The wave swung her on high and threw her forward. It flung us crashing on the coral reef. Our masts and rigging went over, broken like matchsticks. The shattering impact of the ship smashed the coral, and pieces flew in all directions like shrapnel from an exploding shell. The swirling water seized great pieces of coral and whipped them around, beating them against the ship. The *Seeadler* had heeled over until her deck was almost perpendicular. The water swept over the deck, and the swirling eddies bombarded us with chunks of coral. I clung to an iron post near the lower rail. The rail saved me from the tons of shattered coral that were hurled up by the blow of the falling ship. In a moment, the wave had ebbed away, leaving us high and dry. It had passed

over the circling reef and the lagoon, though not over the main part of the island. And on its way it had swept hundreds of thousands of birds' nests into the lagoon.

I arose, scarcely knowing whether I was alive or dead, and stood alone with one foot on my slanting deck and the other on the rail. For a moment, I thought I was the only one saved.

"Boys, where are you?" I shouted weakly.

"Here," came the reply, "still standing like an oak."

My men and the prisoners had taken refuge in the bow, and had been sheltered by the rail, as I had been. Not a one was injured. For that at least we could be thankful. For that and not much else. The *Seeadler* was a total wreck. The jagged coral was rammed deep into our hull.

We stand like an oak! I adopted the reply of my sailors as our motto henceforth. We were castaways on this coral atoll in one of the loneliest and least-visited reaches of the South Pacific. Everything lost, but "we stand like an oak."

XXIV

CASTAWAYS ON A CORAL ATOLL

THE last German colony! We founded it on this beautiful, isolated coral atoll in the middle of the Pacific. The Imperial German flag of war flew from the top of the tallest palm. I was the viceroy, by chance and not by desire, of course, and my sailors and our prisoners were my subjects. The only visiting nationals from elsewhere were the three Kanakas, the turtle catchers. "The White King of the Society Isle of Mopelia," my mate facetiously called me. One of the Yankee captains put it differently. He called me "the Sea Devil King of the South Seas." And he caustically described our lovely isle as "a poisoned paradise." Everybody was good-humoured, despite our hard luck.

But our little South Sea colony passed its first nights uneasily. For sleeping places, we slung hammocks between the palms. At intervals, a cocoanut would fall from a height of fifty or sixty feet and go whizzing close by a man's head. While our fellow countrymen back in the cities along the Rhine were complaining about the night raids of the French and British bombing squadrons, we had our bombing problem also. It didn't make much difference whether you were bumped off with a falling cocoanut or a falling bomb. The result was all the same. After one whizzed by your ear, you would very likely go down to the open beach to quiet your nerves. Then if you tried to sleep there, the land crabs would soon con-

vince you that the beach was no place for a weary
war veteran either. Patrols of fighting marine crabs
would raid that beach every night. After being
chased out by the crabs, you would go back to your
hammock and lie awake wondering when the next
aërial cocoanut bombardment would commence.
So life during those first days on our tropic isle was
not all skittles and beer or orchids and cocoanut
milk. You can bet we worked hard getting up huts!
Luckily, there were no casualties from either crabs
or cocoanuts. We cleared a large space for our village, and built huts out of timbers, sailcloth, and
palm leaves. The first one up was a queer-looking
thing, but our architecture improved with practice.
Our prisoners, who were all Americans, helped us a
great deal. They understood the art of pitching tents.
They built a special town for themselves, and gave
the streets such names as Broadway, State Street,
Pennsylvania Avenue, and the Bowery. In time we
contrived to arrange quite decent dwelling places.
We had plenty of furnishings. From the wrecked
Seeadler, which remained perched forlornly on the
coral reef, we took everything we could carry. We
even built a chapel, took the Bible from the *Seeadler,*
and from parts of the wreck we built a fine altar and
crucifix. Of course, we also installed our wireless set
ashore in order to keep in touch with passing ships
and events happening out on this side of the world.
Nor did we neglect to take ashore a heavy arsenal of
arms and ammunition, including rifles, Luger pistols,
hand grenades, and dynamite. In short, we had a
perfect little town with everything except a calaboose. Some of our men who had romantic tendencies
constructed "country homes" for themselves a few
hundred yards away in the jungle. Then we named
the place Seeadlerburg, Sea Eagle Town.

There were gull's eggs everywhere along the shore, but the birds were brooding now, and most of the eggs we collected had half-formed little gulls in them. We got around this by clearing a large section of beach and throwing the old eggs into the lagoon. Then the gulls flocked back and laid more eggs, and thus a supply of fresh eggs was assured.

Our American prisoners were nearly all cheery fellows. Some of them fitted in with the new life better than my men. They seemed to know all about the art of fishing, and taught us Germans things we had never dreamed of. They were accustomed to what in the States, along the Gulf of Mexico, is called spearing eels. They fastened iron barbs to shafts of wood and with these speared big fish in the coral lagoon. They also showed us a clever way of catching fish on a grand scale. They took some forty men and boys and, just as high tide was turning, formed in a line about fifty yards offshore. Then the line came splashing in, driving the fish before it toward shore, just as the natives round up tigers for a rajah in India. Many of the fish floundered into shallow water, and a few minutes later were left stranded by the receding tide. You see, the water, as it backed offshore, left large pools on top of the irregular coral reef, and there the fish were trapped. Sometimes we caught five or six hundred pounds a day, and it was exciting sport.

One night, while we were sitting around our fire, we heard a scratching sound. It seemed to come from everywhere. We looked and found a lot of crabs with big claws. They were hermit crabs. We caught several and put them in boiling water to cook. Meanwhile, the crab invasion continued, and more from behind kept pushing the rest forward. We tried the

ones we had cooked, and they were delicious. They were as good as the best lobster.

"By Joe," I said, "boys, let's get busy."

We spread out a large sail and filled it up with crabs, like a sack. We must have had several thousand of them. For days we lived on them, until most of us couldn't look a crab in the face. We had 'em boiled, broiled, and in soup. Then that invasion of these hermits passed as mysteriously as it had come, and we never saw them again. But the turtles were always with us. We caught a number of them and kept them in a coral basin at one end of the lagoon.

The wild pigs on the island provided us with more fun and more food. They fed on cocoanuts, which is the best kind of fodder to make good pork. These animals were said to be the descendants of swine brought to the South Seas by early explorers long ago. They are found on many islands, and New Zealand is a regular paradise for them and for the hunter who likes to chase wild pigs. After generations of living on cocoanuts, they had changed a lot and had developed a special kind of tusk and jaw.

There were snipe on our island, too, and we hunted them with great success, thereby varying our sea food and pork diet. Using cocoanut shells for fuel, we smoked what flesh and fish we could.

By way of vegetables, we had cocoanuts, and bread made of cocoanut flour, which the Kanakas taught us to prepare, and hearts of palms. This latter is one of the rarest of delicacies, and outside the tropics only multimillionaires can afford it. The price, when you get palm hearts in Europe, is higher than that of Russian caviar. For the most part, it is reserved for castaway sailors and buccaneers like ourselves. It is the core taken from the very tip of

the cocoanut palm, right where the new leaves form. For each heart, weighing about ten pounds, a noble palm has to be sacrificed. The taste is between that of hazel nuts and asparagus, only finer and sweeter than either.

But I must tell you more about that invasion of hermit crabs. It caused the first and only fatality in the course of all our adventures. My dog Schnaeuzchen had all of the prying, curious nature of the dachshund. The island, with its teeming life, was an endless source of wonder to her. She investigated everything, forever had her nose sniffing somewhere or other. The swarming hermit crabs, which covered the ground almost like a carpet, sent her into a perfect spasm of astonishment. She jumped and barked and yelped. She cocked one eye and studied the strange creatures, and quite obviously did not like their looks. They crawled on all sides of her, and she was filled with bewilderment and fright. She was furious with them, but kept nimbly out of their way. Finally, however, the pugnacity of her dachs nature got the better of her, and she felt she must attack something. A particularly large and villainous-looking crab excited her ire. She leaped upon it to devour it. The crab raised its great, ferocious claws to strike at her. Schnaeuzchen gave a strange yelp of fright, and rolled over in a spasm. She kicked convulsively for a few moments, and then was still— dead. Poor little Schnaeuzchen! The exotic life of the South Seas had been too much for her. She was only two years old, and on the island she had for the first time found an opportunity to give vent to her passion for hunting. We gave her a fine grave, and planted a cocoa palm on it. Her comrade, Piperle, looked around disconsolately for her and was sad for a long time.

Piperle had an adventure with the birds. He undertook one day to invade one of the densely populated rookeries. Somehow or other, he contrived to antagonize the birds. I suppose he tried to raid a nest. The angry gulls swarmed above him. One seized one ear. Another seized the other. Several struck at his eyes. One hung on to his tail. Piperle howled and struggled. It was at this point that one of our men saw him execute an intelligent bit of strategy. There was a clump of underbrush near by. He struggled toward it, taking the birds with him. He dragged himself into the brush and thereby shook off the birds. He returned to camp a sadly mishandled dog, and never went near any of the rookeries again. From then on he confined his courage and daring to chasing the wild pigs at night, which he did with a prodigious barking and yelping. The pet opossum that our prisoners had carefully rescued from the wreck picked up an excellent living on the island, and came into the messroom every night, asking for water.

If our new home teemed with useful, edible creatures, it was not lacking in pestilential forms of life, either, these both of native origin and imported from ships. A thousand kinds of insects were everywhere. If you awakened thirsty at night and reached for your glass of water, you were likely to find that it contained more cockroaches than water. You had to reconcile yourself to getting up in the morning and finding your toothbrush alive with ants. The ants were particularly pervasive. We could only guard against them by putting the legs of tables, chairs, and other articles of furniture in cups of water. We slept at night to the ceaseless shuffle of rats, huge insolent fellows, running about on the tops of our tents. Piperle waged war against them, but the

odds were too great. It would have taken a whole regiment of terriers to end that plague.

Flashing birds of paradise flew from palm to palm. Gorgeous humming birds with green and yellow breasts darted among the branches. With every flower there seemed to be a great butterfly. The whole island was aglow with butterflies. They floated on wide, beating wings of greens, violets, and reds.

Once, in the middle of the night, I was awakened by a small, sharp, repeated sound—knick, knick, knack. It was the opening of tropical flowers. I went outside and there I saw the lovely Queen of Night, which blossoms by the light of the tropical stars. It is a great, gorgeous bloom, eight or ten inches across. There were thousands of them. Scores of glowworms, far brighter than any we know, hovered above each, eager to catch the magnificent perfume that the opening Queen of Night gives forth. In the darkness I could see the flowers only by the light of the glowworms. On every side were these eerie nocturnal lights, a dancing lamp of gathered glowworms illuminating each flower. In that unearthly gleaming, like a kind of moonlight only stranger, the odorous petals shone with the ghostly nuances of their naturally flaming colours, white, crimson, sapphire blue, violet blue. In the South Seas, the flowers have little scent by day, while the sun shines on them. At night, when the dew falls, perfume awakens. It is truly a perfumed night. And the nostrils of man are excited by the rich and almost oppressive blending of odours. The Queen of Night gives off the perfume of vanilla. Mingled with it comes the scent of hyacinth, orchid, mayflower, and heliotrope. Sweet-smelling breezes blow, and above is the tropical sky with its clustered flashing stars and gorgeous Milky Way. Hanging above the horizon is the far-famed Southern Cross.

XXV

LET'S GO RAIDING AGAIN

My "subjects" somehow managed to get along on terms of general amity. Our American prisoners took no exception to my mandates handed on to them by Leudemann, my prime minister. They said that, since they had been treated so well aboard the *Seeadler*, they wanted no other command over our colony. The two captains and their lady had made mutually satisfactory arrangements among themselves, and, so far as we knew, there was no unpleasant incident, although, for the purposes of my tale, it would have helped a lot if they had fought a duel with swords or cocoanuts or chunks of jagged coral on the shore of our tropic lagoon.

The three Kanakas proved to be thoroughly good fellows and helped us in many ways. We got along with them in pidgin English at first until one of them picked up a little German.

In the middle of the camp we made a sort of plaza. The *Seeadler's* batteries furnished electric light for it, and there we gathered every night. We still had plenty of champagne and cognac left from the capture of the champagne ship. So, in the cool of the evening, we sat out there on the edge of this equatorial Potsdammer Platz sipping drinks out of wine and brandy glasses, just as we might have at the Adlon in Berlin. There was plenty of pipe tobacco, and Dr. Pietsch had taken care to rescue from the wreck a store of his endless cigars. The wind blew.

the stars shone, and the orchestra alternately played German classics from the operas and American ragtime melodies. Ah, yes, this last bit of the once glorious overseas German Empire wasn't such a bad little paradise at all. We castaways out there in the solitude of the South Seas felt as though we were the only people left in the world, like Noah and his family on Mount Ararat.

But after about three weeks of this Garden-of-Eden-without-an-Eve existence, the monotony of it began to get on our nerves. Of course, there was the "wife" of the officer of the . . . but she was far too busy to be interested in the rest of us. We hadn't been sent out to colonize the South Seas and take life easy. So we cast about for a way to go buccaneering again. Our first need was for a ship to take the place of our unfortunate three-master impaled out there on the coral reef. The Kanakas told us that a French sailing vessel visited the island every year to take away turtle meat. The best guess that they could make was that it would be another six months or so before she arrived. Well, after six months, we would have a ship. We could always fall back on that. But, by Joe, six months was a long time to wait. The war might be won or lost by then. And it was highly unlikely that any other ship would stray into those waters for Heaven knows how long. We all grew impatient. Few sailors are keen about remaining cast away on a tropical isle for long, and especially on an atoll as small as Mopelia. We felt the itch to get out to sea again. I was particularly anxious to set something stirring. Before long the tropical sun and lazy life would sap my men's vitality, and all they would be good for would be to loll around.

We still had our lifeboats, and the hurricane season

was not on. So why not put to sea in one of them? We devised rigging and sails for our best lifeboat, mast, jib boom, main boom, gaff, stays, and back stays. We scraped, caulked, and painted her. She was not in any too good condition, and despite our labour she continued to leak a bit and needed constant bailing. Even in calm weather, we had to bail forty pails a day. We loaded her with provisions for half a dozen men over a long voyage. She was eighteen feet in length and only about fourteen inches above water amidship. Into this small space we stored water, hardtack, machine guns, rifles, hand grenades, and pistols. The only luxuries we allowed ourselves were a few tins of pemmican, a side of bacon, and an accordion. The music of the squealer was to be our solace during a cruise the length of which none could foretell. The great question was, could our tiny craft survive a storm? At any rate, she could sail, and that was something. We christened her the *Kronprinzessin Cecilie*—without, however, painting her name on the stern.

Of course, everybody wanted to go, but there could be only six of us at the most. So I picked the men who seemed to be in the most vigorous health at the time, Mate Leudemann, Lieutenant Kircheiss, Engineer Krauss, Boatswain Parmien, and Yeoman Erdmann. This left the colony on the atoll in the hands of Lieutenant Kling.

Our overloaded cockleshell with a crew of six was the smallest auxiliary cruiser in the war. For cruiser we were, and we were setting out to capture a ship, sail back to Mopelia, pick up our comrades there, and continue our raid. To find and take a ship on the high sea was a doubtful proposition, but we might get to some of the other islands, not too well populated and guarded, and find a vessel at anchor.

We could board her at night, overpower the captain and crew, and sail off with her. We planned first of all to visit the Cook Islands, some eight hundred miles distant, and if we found no ship there, continue on another thousand miles farther to the Fiji Islands, where there were sure to be ships loading with copra for the ammunition factories of Europe. We figured on making around sixty nautical miles a day, so that, if we had to go all the way to the Fijis, it would take us approximately thirty days. Thus we should be back with a ship in three months at most.

We discussed our tactics thoroughly for the expected capture. We would steal aboard. Half-past three in the morning was the best hour. Men sleep their soundest then. A couple of us would go to the officers' cabins, the rest to the forecastle. We would show our pistols, disarm them, and herd them below. It would be good to sneak to their clothing first and take away their belts and snip the buttons off their trousers. Then, when you have them put on their clothes they stand, without belts, suspenders, or buttons, holding up their trousers. Thus they are helpless. We had a few bombs loaded only with powder, harmless, but capable of making a terrific noise. If there is any trouble, you throw one. It hurts nobody, but the terrible explosion creates a general panic. A couple of men with their heads about them can do wonders with dozens in a panic. Another good thing is to have a couple of fellows outside shout suddenly and make a great disturbance. That creates excitement and throws people off their guard. I said to my bo's'n:

"Don't hurt anybody unless you have to. We don't want to spoil our clean record by killing anybody. But, by Joe, if a captain or a watchman raises a rifle or a pistol, don't wait till he shoots. Get him first."

On a bright summer morning—August 23, 1917, to be exact—we all shook hands. There was no cheering, merely quiet, earnest words of friendship and good luck. It was the first time that we sixty-four seamen had parted since the *Seeadler* had set sail to run the blockade eight months before, and it was only now, at the moment of saying good-bye, that we realized how closely attached to one another we had become. We who were going could see a brooding question in the eyes of those who were staying behind:

"How will that overloaded cockleshell stand heavy weather?"

Never mind, we would probably find out soon enough. The understanding was that, if we did not return in three months, something had happened to us. They should wait for us until then. Afterward, Kling and his men were to get away from the atoll as best they could.

We sailed out of the lagoon, through the coral entrance, into the open sea. The hulk of the *Seeadler* lay there helpless on the reef. The tide was high, and the breakers swept over the coral. She was a red brown now from rust and weathering. Each flooding billow raised her a bit, and then she sank back hopelessly with loud groans and creaks of despair on the coral bed. As we passed her she seemed to call over to us:

"Come aboard, I want to take you on your voyage. Don't desert your old friend."

And as a wave raised her it seemed as though she were struggling to get on an even keel again and come to us, only to find that the coral held her in a relentless grasp. Tears filled our eyes.

"Good-bye, *Seeadler*," I called; "perhaps we shall never see you more. And even if we do, you can

never sail again. Nevermore will songs resound on your decks. Nevermore will you raise your sails and fly a flag from your masts."

A brisk wind carried us westward with a swelling of our sails. The happy island receded. The last German colony and the wreck of the *Seeadler* slowly dropped out of sight over the rim of the horizon.

To-day the *Seeadler* still remains on the reef at Mopelia. After we had gone, Lieutenant Kling, afraid that the stumps of her mast might attract a passing warship, blew them out with dynamite. The explosion set a fire that burned away part of the woodwork. A quantity of ammunition still aboard blew up and cracked the forepart of the hulk. Afterward, when the *Seeadler's* history became generally known, the Harris-Irby Cotton Company of New York, which had originally owned the ship as the *Pass of Balmaha,* investigated the possibilities of salvaging the ship. A party of engineers was sent to Mopelia. They reported that the ship was unsalvageable. In my cruise around the world aboard the *Vaterland* I shall stop at the island and survey what once was my tropical domain. And again I shall board the old *Seeadler* on which we sailed and raided. So, until then, old ship! *Auf wiedersehen!*

XXVI

FROM THE SOCIETY ISLANDS TO THE COOK ISLANDS IN AN OPEN BOAT

It has been something of a sport of recent years to cross the Atlantic and even the Pacific in a small boat, sometimes under sail and sometimes under motor power. Tiny craft have done it, and at best it is not a comfortable kind of voyage. In sporting events, your ocean-going small boat always had a cabin, or an imitation of one. That is what we should have had, but we were not so lucky, and, besides, the load we carried made existence aboard our lifeboat that had been converted into a cruiser a cramped affair indeed.

There was only one place we could trust to be dry, the buoyant air tanks at the sides of the boat. In these we packed our hardtack, a few pieces of clothing, photographic apparatus, and the all-important tobacco. It affected the buoyancy of our craft, but we had to keep some things away from the sea water. In the body of the boat were placed the water tanks, our large supply of weapons and ammunition, cordage for the rigging, and several spare sails. Canvas shields at the side, which could be drawn over at the top and be made to form some kind of tent, sheltered us somewhat from waves and dirty weather. Without these we should have been practically drowned. Four mattresses could be stretched on the bottom, where four men could sleep while two kept

watch. As a concession to civilization, we had six pairs of knives and forks, six mugs, a coffee pot, and $5,000 in silver, gold, and paper, much of it in pounds sterling.

At six in the morning, the two men on watch filled the coffee pot and applied fire to it from a soldering lamp. With the slightest breeze and a rocking of the boat, it was impossible to bring the water to a boil. Then we were glad to get tepid coffee-bean soup instead of coffee. After toilets had been made with salty sea water, we squatted in the cockpit for breakfast of coffee and hardtack. Navigation was difficult in so small a boat. It was impossible to spread the charts out properly, and with the slightest carelessness the wind might take our priceless navigation papers overboard. We had to use the sextant and other navigation instruments in a boat that often pitched so much we could scarcely stand. The papers, charts, tables, logarithms, and so on, got sopping wet, and when we dried them in the sun they grew swollen and difficult to handle.

It was cool at night, but not unpleasant so long as our clothes were dry. The weather was fair, but an occasional whale would come alongside and douse us with the spray of his spout. Then, in our damp clothing, we felt the chill of the night. The days were broiling hot, but even while taking advantage of what little shade we had, we grew heavy and torpid. We had, above all things, to be careful of our water supply. We never dared drink enough to quench our thirst completely, and were, in fact, continually thirsty.

By way of amusement, we had readings aloud from the one book we had brought along, Fritz Reuter's comic story, *A Trip to Constantinople*, and at night the squealer wheezed and blared, and we whiled

away the tedious hours singing old German folk songs.

After three days we sighted Atiu, the first island of the Cook group and a British possession. There was no ship in sight. Too bad, but perhaps a ship might be expected soon. Anyway, we had to make port and get fresh food. Aside from the danger of storm, if our voyage continued for any length, we feared most of all beri-beri and scurvy, which our diet of hardtack would inevitably bring upon us unless we varied it with fresh vegetables.

A crowd of natives, fine-looking Polynesians, watched curiously as our little craft drew up to the dock. Kircheiss and I went ashore and straight to the house of the British resident. He lay stretched out in his shirt and trousers on a Borneo long chair on his porch, and didn't even get up when we approached. He was a good-looking fellow, but lazy as the devil. The lassitude of the South Seas had certainly got him.

"My name is Van Houten," I began, "and this is my chief officer Southart."

The resident looked at me suspiciously. It was a true British mistrust. Ordinarily, your Englishman is the best of fellows, a pleasant chap to meet, a perfect host. But in wartime you had to admire them. They were on the lookout for everything. Their brains seemed made only of suspicions. Kircheiss, who spoke English better than I did, continued:

"We are Americans of Dutch birth. A few months ago we made a bet at the Holland Club in San Francisco that we would sail from Honolulu in an open boat via the Cook Islands to Tahiti and back to Honolulu. The wager is for twenty-five thousand dollars. Would you, my dear sir, kindly give me a certificate that we have been here in accordance with the terms of our bet? Also, we should like to lay in

a supply of fresh water, canned goods, and fresh fruit."

The resident yawned, looked us over with a watery eye and replied:

"Well, a man must be a hell of a fool to go in for that kind of sport."

"Sure," Kircheiss said politely, "but, just the same, we should like to have the certificate. Won't you give it to us or tell us who will?"

"Oh, to hell with you, don't bother me. I've just had dinner and want to take my nap."

Even his British mistrust, with which he first regarded us, subsided into the indescribable something that comes over a white man who yields to the soft enervation of the tropics. He now looked at us merely as mad fellows who wanted him to do something too crazy to merit his consideration.

"Any news from the bloody war?" he asked. "Why are they so stupid as to carry on with this fighting business? In the end, it will only help these yellow races."

He continued like this and spoke highly of the Germans. Naturally, we did not express any pro-German sentiments.

"We simply must get this old bird to give us that certificate," I said to my comrade in Low German, pretending that it was Dutch.

"Yes," he replied in the same dialect, "it may come in mighty useful later on."

The resident, as he told us, had served in the Boer War, and should have known better, but he took our Plattdeutsch for the language of Holland. Presently he scribbled a note saying that we had called on him in the course of our sporting cruise.

"Any ships expected in port soon?" Kircheiss asked quite casually.

"How in hell do I know?" the resident responded

wearily. "Everything goes to the bloody war, and we don't see anything around here but these Kanakas." He continued in this strain and cursed his boredom on the island.

The resident was still rambling on in his lazy monotone when along came a man who wore a cassock and had a beard down to his waist. He was a French missionary priest who was overjoyed when we saluted him with a few words of French. The resident and an English trader were the only two white men on the island besides himself, and neither talked any French.

"*Allons, allons,*" he shouted, "by Joe, boys, you must pay me a visit."

And straightway he seized our arms and took us over to his mission house. There he poured out glasses of excellent wine.

"You are Americans," he cried, "you fight for la France? You are Hollanders? Ah, it is too bad that your country is not in the war with France. But I can see that you love la belle France."

With that he put on the gramophone a record of *La Marseillaise*, and had us sing it along with him, which we did with all our lungs. Since it had been written and dedicated to my great-grandfather, I didn't mind a bit. He chattered in French incessantly, in an ecstasy over having someone with whom he could talk his native tongue. He embraced us a dozen times and made us sit down to dinner. It was an excellent meal. The wine was particularly good. The conversation made us squirm a little. The good father was the best fellow possible, but patriotic to the very finger tips. He treated us to some choice denunciations of the Germans.

After another rendition of the *Marseillaise,* we took our leave.

"What will be your next stop?" asked the jovial missionary in parting.

"I think we will put in at Aitutaki," I replied. That was the nearest island and the next field of action in our hunt for a ship.

"Fine," exclaimed the priest cordially. "I have a friend there. You must call on him. Just mention my name. He will be delighted to see you. He is a Hollander, too."

A Hollander, too? And our knowledge of the Dutch language was so strongly salted with a German accent! In that case, when we got to Aitutaki we certainly would be anything but Hollanders, probably Norwegians.

Everywhere on the island were trees and fruits, cocoanuts, bananas, mangoes, and oranges. On the streets of the village, with its thatched huts, were South Sea beauties who wore wreaths of flowers and had dark, flashing eyes. They gazed with interest on the foreign sportsmen, the story of whose cruise on a bet had spread among the natives. We took aboard what provisions we needed and set sail for Aitutaki.

The weather turned miserable, by Joe. It rained every day, those drenching tropical downpours. Our sailcloth covering was not tight enough to hold the water out. The sea was heavy and continually washed into the boat. Often we bailed as many as two hundred and fifty pails an hour. Everything not stowed in the side tanks got wet. When the rain stopped for a while, the waves and spray kept things from drying. We were soaked to the skin and never did get dry. Our blankets and mattresses were dripping wet. When we lay in the sodden bedding, we were freezing cold, and could sleep scarcely at all. Often it was a relief to be called to go on watch. Then at least we could thresh our arms about and get warm. Cook-

ing was almost impossible now, and we seldom ever got coffee anything like hot.

Once we saw a waterspout forming right before our eyes. A fine, whirling drizzle close to the water attracted our eyes. It revolved ever more rapidly, seizing wider masses of water. In the sky was a little black thundercloud extending downward in the shape of a funnel. The whirl of spray on the water ran up swiftly. The cone of the thundercloud stretched down to meet it. They came together and united. A roaring and sound of bursting, a tremendous suction of water, and sky and sea were connected by a whirling column. Gyrating and swaying, it moved in our direction. Our boat lay in a calm. Not a breath of air around us. Will this wandering giant strike us and break upon us, deluge and swamp us? Automatically Leudemann at the rudder tries to steer us. Without wind our boat cannot move, much less steer. But the roaring monster collapses with a deafening clap. Its mass of water falls upon the sea, and from it a circular swell spreads out. We rock uncomfortably and thank heaven. During our voyages among the islands we narrowly escaped several similar spouts.

After three days we found ourselves steering our way through the maze of reefs, very beautiful but perilous, that extend out in front of the landing place at Aitutaki. Again there was no ship in sight, but again one might be scheduled to arrive within some reasonable time. That was our hope. A crowd of natives gathered to watch us come in, also half a dozen white men, among whom was the British resident. He was a tall, lanky fellow who wore glasses, and looked a perfect picture of President Wilson. We found this resident to be full of the same British suspicion. Unlike his colleague at Atiu, he was in no

wise lost in tropical indolence, but was active and shrewd. We saw that he entertained the liveliest doubts about us. Might we not be wandering Germans? Of course, he could not venture any forcible measures to investigate our case, such as searching our boat, for if we really were Germans we would doubtless be armed to the teeth, and in that case where would he be? He had no force to match ours. We tried our level best to quiet his suspicions by our offhand, natural behaviour. We thought our sporting voyage explanation and our request for a certificate, such as we had got from the resident at Atiu, plausible enough. It was too bad that we could not use the other resident's certificate, but in it were written our supposed Dutch names, and now we were Norwegians.

The resident began by saying to us that we would no doubt be delighted to meet a fellow countryman of ours. This "countryman" turned out to be a Norwegian carpenter. We surmised at once that he had been instructed by the resident to talk with us and see whether we were really Norwegians. My Norwegian was bad, but Kircheiss spoke the language like a native. I kept severely out of the way, and let Kircheiss have a long, friendly talk with the carpenter. Kircheiss convinced his man that he was as Norse as the Vikings. The carpenter was delighted to meet a fellow countryman so jovial and, as Kircheiss represented, so wealthy. He promptly reported to the resident that we were the truest Norsemen alive and could in no wise be Germans.

The resident, with his inscrutable President Wilson face, invited me to his house for dinner. I accepted. A British merchant named Low invited my lieutenant to his house. We suspected it was a dodge to separate us. Seemingly, the Norwegian's assur-

Alfred Kling, second officer of the *Seeadler*, was left in command at Mopelia. A passing French schooner, the *Lutece*, saw the wreck, came near to investigate, and was captured. Then Kling and his companions re-named the schooner the *Fortuna* and set sail for Easter Island.

German prisoners in the internment camp on the little island in Hauraki Gulf.

The New Zealand prison camp motor launch in which the Count made his getaway.

ance had not fully allayed the mistrust of these uneasy Britons. Kircheiss and I made every excuse we could to keep together, but the hospitality was so pressing that we could not refuse any longer without practically giving ourselves away.

"Even if we are apart," I said to Kircheiss on the side, "we have our pistols and hand grenades, by Joe. We will keep our eyes open, and we can take care of ourselves single-handed. If anything looks wrong, we will fight our way to the boat."

At the resident's house, a fine stone structure, I had a much-needed bath and shave. When I rejoined him, the resident studied my smooth jaws.

"Why," he exclaimed, "you are shaved."

"Yes, thanks to you, and I feel a hundred per cent. better."

"But one doesn't shave on a sporting trip, does one?"

He did not believe in anything, that Englishman. He was a true sceptic.

We dined pleasantly enough. The resident talked a lot, although he did not seem to be naturally a talkative kind. He asked me many questions, which I answered cautiously. A native servant brought him a note, and he scribbled a note in return. After a few minutes, the servant brought him another message, and again he answered it. This happened several times.

"Important messages?" I asked.

"Oh, no," he replied hastily, "they are from my friend Low. He wants to arrange to have us all take coffee at his bungalow."

It was very queer. I was prepared, though, and thanked my stars for the pistol and hand grenade in my pockets. I learned later that their scheme was, in fact, to question Kircheiss and me separately. The

purpose of the notes was to arrange questions to be asked of us, so that they might check up our separate answers to the same questions. These answers, it happened, had jibed fairly well, although not well enough to disarm suspicion altogether.

I thought it an imprudent time to ask when a ship might be expected, and hoped that some voluntary information on the subject might be vouchsafed. None was, however. I resolved to let the subject wait. People suspected of being a boatload of armed Germans might too readily be suspected of being interested in the arrival of ships.

When the time for leaving came, the resident told me that, if we would return on the following day, he would give us the certificate we desired, certifying that in the course of our sporting voyage we had called at the island of Aitutaki. The delay about the certificate was, of course, to detain us a day longer.

Away from this unsatisfactory interview, we encountered the Norwegian carpenter who informed Kircheiss that the natives believed we were Germans. The British had been recruiting soldiery among them for service in France, and for the purpose of getting recruits had stirred them up with a bit of war fever. The islanders therefore hoped that we were enemies so they could seize us. They planned to get our boat ashore and capture it. Upon hearing of this, I ordered that two men be on watch all the time, ready to repel any attack.

"Any ships expected in port?" Kircheiss asked the carpenter.

"There may be one to-morrow," was the reply, "or it may not be here for a month."

We held a council of war that night. Should we sail straight on? That would make them certain that we were Germans, but there was no wireless station on

the island, and they could not warn the other islands until a ship arrived to take away the news. Or should we capture the island, which we could easily do with our extensive armament, and then wait for a ship? Or should we still try to convince the resident that we were the Norwegian sportsmen we pretended? This latter temporizing measure we adopted, and decided to call on the resident the following day and try to get our certificate from him. In preparation for the visit, I instructed the men who remained behind to be ready for trouble ashore. If we needed them, they would hear a pistol shot. They should immediately open fire with machine guns and hand grenades. They should shoot into the air and throw the grenades into the water, where they would make the most noise. The row would create a diversion, and then they should hurry ashore with machine guns, rifles, and grenades to rescue us if need be.

The following day provided us with plenty of thrills. When Kircheiss and I went to the resident's house, crowds of natives followed us. The resident greeted us with a worried expression but came straight to the point.

"I shall have to examine your boat and papers," he said sternly.

"How so?" said I.

"The natives think you are Germans. I know you are not, but I must inspect your boat to satisfy them."

He vacillated between the desire of not letting us get away and the fear of a fight.

Outside, the Polynesians were gathering from all quarters. They made a menacing, ugly-looking mob. Left hand in pocket, I attached a carbine hook to the fuse of the grenade. With that mob of heathens

on the rampage, there was no use in trying to carry
the deception any further.

"It is true," I said to the resident, "we are Germans. But don't you think it would be better if we
remained friends? We are white men. I am with you
in front of these natives. Act the part that will impress them. Come and examine our boat."

"Very well," he replied, growing pale, "but you
won't take me with you?"

"No, upon my word, no."

When we stepped out on the porch, the islanders
raised a howl. I never thought there were so many
Polynesians in the world. I had never before stood in
the face of a mob. Sailors or soldiers would not have
made me so afraid.

"Don't be a coward," I said to myself. "On, by
Joe, on."

Kircheiss and I stayed close together. The resident
led us through the mob, which was overawed by his
presence. We were halfway to the boat when a native in Colonial uniform stepped up. He had seen
service with the British in France, we were afterward
told.

"Shall I arrest them, sir?" he asked.

"Arrest what?" I shouted. "Shut your trap. Why
should a fool like you try to arrest Norwegians?"
Then I muttered to the resident: "If that fellow
makes any fuss, I'll shoot him dead."

"Don't talk that way," he replied nervously,
and waved the native soldier away.

The crowd followed us to the landing. A small rowboat picked us up.

"You won't keep me with you?" the resident
asked again.

I assured him that we would not. So we rowed over

and climbed into my boat, impelled less by his own desire than by the attitude of the natives.

"Here is the log," Kircheiss, with an impassive face, handed him a log we had taken from one of our captured ships. He perfunctorily turned the pages and came upon a chronometric diary we kept in the book. Above was stamped in fat type: KAISERLICHE MARINE.

"What is that?" he stammered.

"Something in Norwegian," Kircheiss grinned sardonically. "I don't understand it."

The resident saw: GAND UND STAND.

"What language is that?" This time he was a trifle ironical.

"Oh, Norwegian, of course," said Kircheiss.

The resident raised a tarpaulin, but dropped it quickly. He had seen rifles. He raised another. There were neat rows of hand grenades, as easy to pick up as apples.

"Keep those covered," he exclaimed, as pale as ashes.

"Well," I asked, "how do you find everything?"

"Quite all right—quite all right." He smiled a very acid smile.

"Won't you tell your people here that everything is all right?" I suggested.

He turned to the crowd on the pier.

"Everything is in order," he called. "These gentlemen are Norwegian sportsmen, as they say."

"And now the certificate," I reminded him.

He wrote a note just as the resident at Aitu had done.

"You don't intend to take me with you?" he repeated.

"No," I responded, "but I should like to have

your company until we can get some fruit and tobacco."

I stood chatting with him on the pier while Kircheiss went to procure the fruit and tobacco. Hadn't we better take the island and wait for a ship instead of sailing off? I debated the question with myself, and then decided we had better go.

The last scene of this little drama was played as the resident and I shook hands and bade each other an apparently cordial farewell. He was a decent fellow, even if he had been suspicious, and I had eaten an excellent dinner at his house. I was glad that we didn't have to humiliate him before the natives, a dreadful fate for an Englishman.

As we hoisted anchor and raised sail, a cheer went up from the natives lined along the shore. They were trying to make amends for having treated us so shabbily and for having taken us for Germans!

But there at Aitutaki I had made the great mistake of our cruise. We should have captured that island. Three days later a schooner arrived. We could have taken it, rejoined our comrades, and continued our raids. Instead, the resident told the officers the story of our visit. The schooner sailed the next day and in a little while met a steamer to which it transferred the news about us. The steamer in turn radioed a warning to the whole South Seas. So we were now in for a warm welcome.

XXVII

THROUGH A SEA OF FLOATING BRIMSTONE TO FIJI

AT RAROTONGA, another island of the Cook group, we had a fright. By Joe, we were scared. It was night. We suddenly saw, right before us, in the shadow of the shore, a big steamer. She had no lights. She must be an auxiliary cruiser. Hard on the helm and every stitch of canvas up. We turned and sailed the other way as fast as the wind would carry us. We expected every moment to be spotted by their lookout and then see the ghostlike searchlight beam fingering toward us through the dark.

"Our luck is with us," I said to Leudemann, when finally we were far enough out at sea to consider ourselves past danger.

Months later, while discussing our adventures with a group of ship's officers, I was told by one of them that the supposed auxiliary cruiser that had frightened us at Rarotonga was really nothing more than a wreck. Several months before our approach to the island, a steamer had gone aground on a reef just offshore, and had been abandoned. The position of the wreck was such that at night it might readily be taken for a ship lying at anchor.

But we had decided when we got well away from Rarotonga that the Cook group of islands was no place for us. At Atiu we had found no ship to capture. At Aitutaki no ship either, only a lot of trouble, including the misfortune of being recognized as Ger-

mans. And now at Rarotonga we had nearly sailed into what we supposed to be an auxiliary cruiser in the dark.

"By Joe," I said to the boys, "we'd better clear out of here and try our luck in other waters."

"Aye, but where? The Fijis?"

"The Fijis," I responded. "We'll find plenty of ships there."

We had all along figured that we might have to go to the Fiji Islands, where a constant stream of sailing ships was always taking aboard copra for the munition factories in the United States. But we also were fully aware that sailing in a little open boat from the Cook Islands to the Fijis might easily be a perilous venture. Our voyage so far had gone fairly smoothly. There had been no hurricanes, and we thanked God for that. Our itinerary from our starting point at Mopelia in the Society group to the adjoining Cook group and among the islands of the latter represented jumps of several hundred miles each and quite a few days at sea. On to the Fijis, however, meant a sail across twenty degrees of longitude. The first half of the jaunt, or about a thousand miles, was over a vast open space of sea where there were no islands on which to find fresh food or on which to take refuge in case of need. In fact, we were to sail for thirteen days out of sight of land. We had expected, when we left Mopelia, that the leg to the Fijis would be a hard one, even if we had fair weather all the way. But now the weather turned against us for a whole week, and we began to think we had run across St. Swithin's day. We had forgotten—if we had ever known it—that this was the time when the equinoctial storms broke in those waters. Had we known it, we never would have headed for the Fijis.

For ten days we sailed through a drenching down-pour, the rainy season. The sea was choppy. The wind whipped the spray and the crests of waves over us in driving sheets. In our cockleshell, things were afloat, and it was bitter cold o' nights. We threw our mattresses overboard. In their soaked condition they were far worse to sleep on than the wet planks, and there was no use keeping them any longer. When the sun occasionally shone, our drenched clothes would dry quickly and stiffen like boards of salt. They rubbed and scratched the skin off our bodies. When they got wet again, which they promptly did, the salt would soak into the raw flesh and inflame it. Our bodies felt as though they were on fire. We had no regular sleep. Instead, a man would doze away suddenly at almost any time. Even the helmsman would drowse off like that, and, with a free rudder, the boat would veer around crazily.

One morning, when dawn came, we could hardly believe our eyes. The sea had turned from its normal blue to yellow. On scooping up a pail of it we found a scum that we concluded must be brimstone and ash. We were sailing through a field of brimstone. For three days we saw from horizon to horizon this yellowish expanse of volcanic dust. It no doubt came from some submarine eruption, perhaps the one we could thank for the tidal wave that had wrecked the *Seeadler*. The waves carried the gritty dust into the boat. It penetrated everything. Every surface became like sandpaper. Our skin grew rough and caked with it. Our blankets were like sandpaper, and so were our clothes.

As the voyage grew longer, we had to be more and more sparing with our drinking water. The supply began to run low. We could no longer collect rain water in our sails. They were coated with salt. We

tried to wash them out in the rain, but then the spray and the waves kept washing in and kept the sails salty and added a further salting to any water we collected. Our supply of fruit that we had picked up in the Cook Islands ran out now, and about all we had left was hardtack, not in itself a thirst-quenching kind of food. We also had a side of delicious bacon, but of course we dared not touch it for fear of increasing our thirst. You have often heard of the torments of thirst at sea? Well, they are not exaggerated, for exaggeration is impossible. When the rains stopped and the blazing tropical sun beat down on us all day and we still had days to sail on and on, then the torments of the damned, the torments of thirst smote us with a fiery agony. Our gums dried out and were like rough iron. We sucked our fingers and gnawed at our knuckles to bring a flow of saliva and refresh our burning mouths.

And then came the sailor's worst enemy, scurvy. Our diet of hardtack, lack of exercise, and general hardships brought it on. Our knees swelled up so badly that we had to cut our trousers. The rocking of the boat knocked them together or against the wooden sides, and then the pain was almost unendurable. Our lips were black and broken. Our tongues were swollen and hard. It was as if you had a stone in your mouth. Our gums became snow white and seemed to recede. Our teeth felt as though they were sticking far out of our jaws. They hurt constantly and were loose and felt as if they were going to drop out. With these shaking teeth we ate our hardtack. I never before knew how hard hardtack was. We had unending headaches, and it seemed as if something were pressing our eyes right out of their sockets. We got water in our legs, and could

hardly stand any more. We had to slide around the seats to do what had to be done in navigating the boat. In scurvy, the blood turns to water, first in the legs and then upward. When it reaches the heart you die. Where the blood is water the flesh is white, and you can see the line of the white creep slowly up. We wondered who would be the first—the first to have the line of white rise to the heart. My boys made marks to show the line clearly and mark its daily progress upward. It was a kind of sport. It was keeping a daily log, a log of death. Parmien was the youngest of us, but he seemed to be on his way to win the race. The line was higher on him than on the others. He joked about it. There was nothing terrible in it. We were all in a deep apathy. Our brains were like balls of cotton. Nothing mattered, certainly not death. Death would come, we thought, as a relief from these sufferings. The prospect of its arrival became more and more attractive.

"Boys," I said, "let us take pieces of ballast iron and tie them around our necks. One plunge and in a few seconds all of our pains will be gone."

"Yes. All right." There were mutterings of assent.

But Parmien, the youngest, the one who was nearest death, picked up the comic volume, Fritz Reuter's *Trip to Constantinople*, and began to read a funny story. We all laughed. That book had eased many a hard hour before, on this ghastly voyage, and now, perhaps, it saved our lives.

And so we continued on with but one instinct left in us, the sailor's instinct to navigate his craft. Mechanically, without any particular hope, without any particular thought, we trimmed the sails, guided the helm, and calculated our position as best we could. Nautical science was at a low ebb among us now. We were too far gone to reckon exactly where

we were, and were only vague in our steering. All we knew was that we should steer to the west where the island groups were.

You have read in many a sea story about the delight, the almost insane ecstasy, of castaway men adrift in open boats who are dying of hunger, thirst, and disease, when, at last, a rescuing ship approaches or they see land. No matter how the writers describe it, even the greatest of writers, they can tell you only a tiny bit, only a grain of sand. So, I won't try to say how we felt when we saw a speck on the horizon and the speck grew bigger and turned into the familiar green of a tropical island. We had been so much like dead men, who had thought that nothing could ever make us glad again. By Joe, that sight gladdened our hearts, though. We grew even weaker, but it was the weakness of happiness. As we drew near, we thought of nothing but land, fresh water, and soft food, a soft banana, for our loose, shaky teeth. Never mind ships or capturing ships. Never mind being taken prisoners. We headed straight toward a crude pier that stuck out into the water.

A crowd of a hundred natives, perhaps less, were gathered at the landing place watching our approach. They were ferocious-looking black warriors. We had now passed from the region of the brown, indolent Polynesians to those of the black, warlike Melanesians.

"What ugly customers," I said to Leudemann. "They look like cannibals."

The forbidding battle array on shore stirred a new strength in us. It certainly looked like a cannibal island, and miserable as we were, still we could not escape the thought of our skin and bones being fattened up in preparation for an old-time South Sea banquet.

"Clear the boat for action!" I ordered. Even in our present straits, we could still remember our old naval ways.

The German flag went jerking to our masthead, and rifles and machine guns were displayed.

A shout went up on shore and a babel of talk. Voices yelled in pidgin English.

"You Germans? How you get here from way off? Come on. Germans great warriors."

Still wary, we drew near the landing pier and talked with the natives. They were unmistakably friendly, very cordial. From what they told us they had, in the first place, grievances against their masters, the British. Then quite a number had been recruited and sent to the trenches in France. There some had been killed and some wounded, and most who survived had contracted tuberculosis from the unaccustomed climate and had been returned to the island worn-out shells of men. One of their most influential chiefs was particularly concerned about the war. He was on the pier, and he reasoned thus:

"White man send missionary. Missionary say we must not fight. Because all men children of God. All men brothers. They say we can have war no more. Then they say we must go fight. They have war. We no fight for ourselves, they say, we fight for them. How, if men are brothers? Our men killed. Our men come back sick with cough. Cough never goes away."

These people were of a warrior race. What the British had told them about how bad the Germans were had not made much impression. What stuck in their minds was the fighting power of the Germans. They had heard about it from the British, and those who had been in the trenches of Flanders knew about it first-hand. The sudden appearance of armed Germans at their remote island could but increase their

admiration. Morality among them had principally to do with a man's fighting spirit.

They said there were no white men on the island, and we longed to go ashore. With our scurvy-swollen legs we could hardly stand, however. It wouldn't do to be hauled ashore as cripples. It would not increase these warriors' respect for Germans as fighting men: Cripples do not fare well among savage peoples, and we thought it best not to reveal our impotence. So, we refused the natives' invitations to partake of their hospitality, told them we must hurry on to fight the British, and asked for fresh water and bananas. They brought great gourds full of water and bunches of bananas. We drew up to the dock and they handed these precious supplies down for us.

We had our fill of bananas and water, and, with shouts resounding from the shore, set sail again. This lucky spot was Niué, an outlying isle of the Fiji group. The sun blazed down upon us, but a fair wind carried us along briskly. The first day after leaving Niué we felt better. The second day we were on the road to high good health. It is amazing the curative effect of fresh fruit, especially bananas, when you are suffering from scurvy. They seem to put new life and blood into you and draw the sickness right out of the body as though some huge and marvellous poultice had been applied.

Our cure was completed at the isle of Katafanga. It is quite a large isle and inhabited by more natives. But we hit upon a stretch of shore that seemed permanently deserted. At any rate, we remained there for five days and saw not a soul. When we went ashore, we all walked with a comical staggering gait. You know the characteristic rolling gait of the sailor accustomed to having a deck under his feet? Ours was

an exaggeration of it. After two weeks in our constantly pitching boat and never a foot on land, we could not get our legs used to solid, unmoving earth. Even after five days of extensive pedestrianism on the beach we rolled along rather than walked. There was plenty of fruit around, and many streams ran down to the sea. We ate enough fruit to expel all the scurvy in the world and bathed luxuriously in the clear water.

On the island was a deserted house. We inspected it and saw that it had been owned by a German planter. We afterward learned that, at the outbreak of the war, the planter fled to the interior of the island, and an Englishman had taken possession of his house, then, not liking the island, had left it pretty much to itself. Among the rubbish in the house was a German mercantile magazine, and on the first page that I turned to I saw an advertisement of the paint firm of Erdmann and Kircheiss. One of our sailors was named Erdmann and my lieutenant was named Kircheiss. No relations of the paint firm, but we took it as a good omen. At any rate, coming upon the planter's house was certainly good luck. It had gone to seed a bit, but there still were Christian beds in it. For the first time since sailing away from Mopelia, we slept comfortably, and between sheets, too.

We were now getting near the larger islands of the Fiji group, where the sailing ships loaded with copra would be encountered. If we did not succeed in capturing a ship here, we never could hope to capture one. We found a handsome little sailboat belonging to the Englishman who had taken over the German's house, but we left her where she lay. She was more comfortable than our battered old lifeboat—

but the latter was a last relic of our old *Seeadler*. She had brought us this far, so we wanted to keep her until we had captured a ship. We raised sail, knowing that, for better or for worse, we were on the last leg of our voyage in the lifeboat.

We came to the main body of the Fijis, and sailed into a large gulf surrounded by distant islands. It was night, and we decided to wait till morning to see how many ships were passing and what island they were bound for. We reefed our sails and threw out our sea anchor, that sacklike drag of canvas that keeps a boat from turning broadside to the wind and waves and from drifting too fast. We lay down for a decent night's sleep. We would need all our energies for the morrow.

A sudden shout. I awakened. It was just daybreak. Straight ahead was a wild white line of surf. It broke over a long, low coral reef, and just behind it was a high cliff. We had run into a strong current during the night. Krauss had awakened just in time to see that it had carried us perilously near the reef. The wind was sweeping us toward the breakers.

"Raise sail," I shouted.

We scrambled frantically and raised the canvas. The wind was inshore. We could not head into it. We were being blown slowly, inexorably on to the reef.

People accustomed to the surfs along ordinary coasts have no idea of what breakers are like off the islands of the South Pacific. The surf all over the Pacific is particularly strong. But when it breaks over a mid-oceanic coral reef nothing can live in it. The strongest swimmer is sure to be dashed to pieces against the jagged coral.

And there wasn't the slightest hope of our moving against the wind and backing away from the reef.

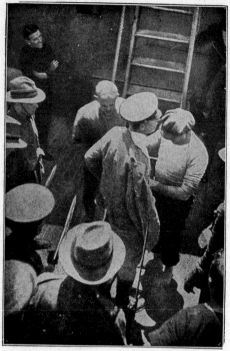

The Sea Devil is caught again. With bayonets
at his back they strip him of his weapons.

The New Zealand colonel in whose uniform Von Luckner made his sensational escape.

The Sea Devil and Kircheiss as prisoners on the New Zealand isle of Motuihi.

Slowly, slowly we were nearing it. The breakers roared like thunder. In a few moments, we would be flung into that death trap of water and coral.

Pistol in hand, I shouted something to the effect that I didn't intend to be ground to death by the breakers on that jagged coral.

The others looked for their pistols. One could not find his. Between the pull of the current and the power of our sails, we were drifting along the reef, edging toward it. The wind gave us an extra push. We were in the backwash, only a few yards away from the breakers. And still one man could not find his pistol. Instinctively, we all waited. And that was what saved our lives. Suddenly we saw the reef drop away, slanting back at a sharp angle, and a moment later we were drifting parallel to the coral.

It was then that I discovered there were two kinds of breathing. In times of terrible danger, the breath comes in short, quick puffs. The danger gone, you breathe deeply. By Joe, when we got clear of that reef I breathed such a breath that it seemed to go right down to my heels. I sat looking at my boys' faces. When we got our pistols ready, their faces had set tense, as if cast from bronze. With the danger past, their faces held the same set expression. It was an hour before their old expressions came back again. Two of my fellows found patches of gray in their hair afterward. (Maybe they had been there for years only to be discovered now!) Another's leg was absolutely blue in spots. In those frightful moments he had, without knowing it, grasped his thigh in a clutch like a drowning man. I tell you, by Joe, it was the hand of God that put the curve in that reef! When one of the boys, I don't know which, said in surprise, "We are clear!" I knew it was the hand of God.

XXVIII

CAUGHT BY THE BRITISH AT WAKAYA

THE island was Wakaya. Several old sailing ships were in the harbour. We gazed at them with hungry eyes, and eager plans of capturing one ran through our minds. Natives on shore spied us, took us for shipwrecked sailors, and put a boat out to meet us. It suited our plans to let them go right on thinking we had been shipwrecked. That might make it much easier for us to get some information about the vessels at anchor. Leaving a couple of my boys in the boat, the other four of us accompanied the natives to their huts, where they treated us hospitably. They were a simple, trusting people. Several half-breeds and a couple of white men, however, looked at us suspiciously. One half-breed was particularly offensive and insisted on asking us many questions. We did not like his behaviour at all.

Kircheiss and I took a walk along a path in the woods to talk over what seemed another menacing situation. A white man came galloping by on horseback. He was pale with excitement. He slowed down for a moment, gazed at us, responded curtly to our greeting, and went on. Thoroughly alarmed, we hurried back to the village. Some curious business was afoot, and we were determined to find out what it was.

"Our last half gallon of rum," Kircheiss murmured regretfully.

"Yes," I responded, "it is too bad, but it will go to a useful purpose."

We got hold of the half-caste who had been so inquisitive. The white man we had seen on horseback was with him. Something, indeed, was afoot. We talked casually with them and then suggested drinking. They were interested, and became enthusiastic when we produced our half gallon of rum. In the half-breed's hut we staged a drinking bout, which lasted half through the night. Nothing like rum to make men friendly and conversational. The half-breed got so conversational that he blurted out.

"Why, you're all right. But at first we thought you were Germans. We could get fifty pounds if you were Germans."

Now, as an American sailor would say, you've got to "hand it" to the English. They know how to spend money when it is useful. We Germans are usually more niggardly, or "careful" some might call it. We will try to save a mark and then lose thousands. Having received the wireless warning from the resident at Aitutaki of mysterious armed Germans in the South Seas, the authorities in the Fijis had passed word among the natives to be on the lookout for us, and had offered a two-hundred-and-fifty-dollar reward to anyone who turned in definite information about a party of Germans posing as neutrals.

It was clear enough that the half-breed and the white man had been plotting to hand us over to the authorities, but how far they had gone we did not know. We didn't find out that night. It was not until later that we learned the white man's horseback ride had been to give a warning about us to the captain of a cutter in the harbour, and that the cutter had at once shoved off to carry the message to the

officials on one of the larger islands a day's sail away. Not knowing this, we used a good deal of persuasion to put the idea firmly into the heads of the two men that we could not possibly be Germans. It may have been our eloquence, or, more likely, the genial influence of the rum, but, at any rate, they seemed to lose all of their suspicions and became convinced that we were the truest Norwegians from Scandinavia. Kircheiss and I, somewhat the worse from our session at detective work, slept at the Englishman's house.

The four others were offered quarters ashore for the night, but two of my boys remained in the boat as a precaution. It was well they did, too. During the night, native swimmers went out to her and cut the anchor rope. They were put up to it by a Malay police officer who was suspicious of us. Not knowing any of my men would remain on board her, since she was only an open lifeboat, he planned to search her. So he sent his swimmers out to pull her ashore and beach her. The wind was inshore. The anchor rope cut, the boat drifted in. Our two men were asleep, and only awakened when keel jarred against bottom. Dark figures were around in the water, trying to pull the boat on the beach. Our men, pistol in hand, drove them away and then pushed out into open water.

On the following day, we made our final costly error. The ships in the harbour weighed anchor and raised sail. We picked the one that seemed the newest and arranged with the skipper to take us along with him to Suva, on the main island Viti Levu. Of course, our plan was simply to sail a few miles out to sea with him and then take the ship ourselves after donning our uniforms and getting out all of our weapons. A sudden squall blew up and forced the vessels back

to port. We returned with her. And now we should have taken her while she lay at anchor. The people ashore would have seen what was going on, but we could have held up the island and then put to sea, storm or no storm. That was our first impulse. We should have followed it. Always trust your first impulse—at any rate, if you go into the pirate business. It is the boldest and best. Instead, we chose a more cautious course. Prudence ceases to be a virtue when you are on an adventure like ours. We had been bold enough heretofore, and I have no satisfactory explanation for our caution now. It may have been that we were not quite ourselves. Our voyage down from the Societies and the Cooks to Fiji, with those days of hunger, thirst, and scurvy, had sapped our strength and vitality. Perhaps, although we felt quite well, we had not yet got back our full vigour of body and mind. Perhaps we were low on red corpuscles. At any rate, we resolved to wait until the following day and capture our ship when it had got out to sea. While we waited, another vessel arrived.

She was a beauty, too, and would have delighted any seaman's eye as she came sailing into the harbour. She had just arrived, we were told, from Suva. She ran regularly among the islands, carrying merchandise to the traders. She was a handsome three-masted schooner with auxiliary motor power, new, clean, and trim, just the kind of ship we wanted.

"By Joe," I said to my boys, "there's our ship."

We immediately dismissed all idea of the old windjammer we had intended to capture, and devoted ourselves to this new beauty. A council of war was held, after which Kircheiss went to the captain of the vessel, which now had docked, and told him that we were Norwegians who, while making a cruise

in a lifeboat, had missed our ship, which was taking coal from Australia to Suva. Could we not take passage with him to Suva instead of on the other slower old craft, so that we could get back to our own ship? We would pay regular rates for the passage.

"All right," replied the captain, a jovial, unsuspecting fellow. "Come aboard at eight o'clock this evening. We sail in the morning."

It was our plan again that, once aboard this lovely ship and out at sea, we would suddenly appear in our uniforms and hoist the German flag.

We made ready to abandon the lifeboat. Our belongings required careful packing. We put rifles, machine guns, cartridges, and grenades in our canvas bags, wrapped our naval uniforms around these, and then rolled each bundle in a couple of blankets and tied it securely. A casual handling would not reveal the armament inside. Each of us took a pistol in one pocket and a hand grenade in the other. At eight o'clock we went aboard the schooner. Our manœuvres had been made carefully, and we had attracted no undue notice of the people who were suspicious of us.

Aboard, the captain received us hospitably, and we went around looking over what we expected to make our next prize of war. And a prize she was, just a year out of the shipyard and beautifully finished in every detail.

"Look at the saloon," I muttered to Leudemann as we wandered around, "think of what meals we will have here. No more hardtack with loose teeth to bite it. And look at those cabins. Won't those bunks be comfortable when it blows and rains? And what a fine big level deck to walk on, so different from the bottom of our lifeboat."

The schooner had two new motors capable of driving her along at a lively clip. They would enable us

to cover a lot of the wide Pacific and run down many a copra-laden clipper.

The captain told us he had aboard a miscellaneous cargo of cloth, white shoes, helmets, silk underwear for the wives of planters and traders, silk stockings, and so on. He was provisioned for a cruise of six months, and had aboard large stores of preserved fruits and vegetables and six thousand pounds of fresh meat. I said to myself:

"Just what we want, by Joe."

Here was the perfect prize. What would our comrades marooned back there on Mopelia say when we turned up with this beautiful schooner in tip-top shape, with powerful motors, well-provisioned and all? Already we could hear the lusty cheers, as, with the German flag at our mast, we drew up and cast anchor off the coral reef. I looked up at the trim masts and spars and around at the freshly scrubbed woodwork of the deck and spoke silently to the schooner, calling her by a new name.

"Ho, there, *Seeadler-the-Second!* You'll like it as an auxiliary cruiser. We'll have a lot of fun together, by Joe."

I could hardly wait for her to raise anchor and set sail. But we had counted that brood of mental chickens before they had hatched, by Joe.

A steamer slid into port!

The skipper of our clipper who was standing next to me said he supposed she had brought over the proprietor of the island. The new arrival lowered a boat. In it were a military officer and four Indian soldiers. The boat rowed straight toward our ship. We surmised at once that they were coming for us. Having received the message sent by the suspicious half-breed and the white man that there were six Germans on the island, the authorities had sent a

force of military police to arrest us. There had been some delay in this, as the only available boat on which to send the police was a cattle steamer, the *Amra*, and she could not raise anchor for some hours. She had arrived now right in the nick of time, had communicated with the shore, and been informed that we were aboard the schooner.

The storm had cleared during the early morning. The palm trees ashore were ablaze with the tropical sunshine. The water under us was of the deep blue that you see only in the South Seas. A brisk, refreshing wind blew from the west. The boat with the officer and four soldiers came rowing with long, powerful strokes. The Indians wore puttees and those funny little pants that leave the knees bare. They carried no arms other than bayonets. The officer had a sword and a revolver. We could easily have shot them down with our pistols, or thrown a hand grenade in their boat, or held them up at pistol point when they came aboard. Then we could have captured the ship and sailed away. The steamer would have been powerless in the face of our machine guns. There were mutterings among my men. They were full of fight. We should, they urged, make the capture and get away.

I passed an uncomfortable moment of indecision. Our uniforms were packed in our bundles, stowed below. We would have to fight off arrest and take the ship in the guise, not of naval soldiers but of civilians, and as civilians we would have to raise our weapons against soldiers. That not only went against the grain, but it went against the unwritten laws of the game. There are many sporting traditions that are carefully inculcated in every German naval officer. If we could have fought in our uniforms, it would have been as honourable naval men. In the

end, the odds would be all against us and the chances were at least a hundred to one that we would be captured before getting back home. If we fought as naval men and were later captured, we would be entitled to the treatment due honourable prisoners of war. If we fought in citizen's clothes, we were nothing more than international bandits and as such almost sure to hang finally from a yardarm. They say that all is fair in love and war, but this does not alter the fact that there are things you can do that are not playing the game. Of course, each side has its spies, and a spy, if caught, expects no quarter and gets none.

But during the War of 1870, and during the late war, too, we Germans were most severe with franc-tireurs, civilians who sniped at soldiers. It has been one of our cardinal principles that war must be waged by uniformed soldiers. In the World War, both sides were charged with introducing new methods of warfare that were not in accordance with the ethics of the game. But you will recall that even Allied cargo and passenger ships armed with guns to fire on submarines made it a general rule to carry gun crews of uniformed marines to handle the guns.

"No," I said to my men, "in the uniforms of our country we can fight. As civilians we cannot. At any rate, we are not going to drop a bomb down there and kill that poor defenseless police officer and his men in those short pants! There would be neither fun nor glory in that."

My officers were with me, and the men also saw the point, but agreed with much reluctance. Certainly, none of us wanted to go to a British prison camp. But there seemed no help for it.

It was the twenty-first of September, just two days short of a month since our departure from Mopelia.

The lieutenant and his four men in those short pants and bare knees came aboard. Followed by his men, he stepped up to me.

"I've got to arrest you," he began decently enough. "Who are you?"

"Allow me," I responded, "to introduce myself. I am Count Luckner, commander of the *Seeadler*. These men here are part of my crew."

"Are you Count von Luckner?"

"Yes."

He gazed around bewildered, frightened, and certainly nonplussed. I imagined I could see his legs shake. Apparently, he was digesting the fact that he and his men were practically unarmed and the certainty that we must be armed to the teeth.

"We have," I continued, "hand grenades and firearms enough to send you and your knee-pants army here to Kingdom Come, and if we were in uniform, you would be our prisoners. However, be that as it may, you have caught us in civilian clothes—but look here."

We took our weapons out of our pockets. I had had two of our men bring up our bundles. We cut them open and displayed the grenades, pistols, and machine guns. The lieutenant stared, still aghast in spite of my reassuring speech. The soldiers were funny. You could see the goose pimples on the skin below the lower edge of those short pants. They edged to the rail, evidently ready to tumble overboard. The captain of the schooner and his crew now knew what kind of guests they had welcomed aboard. They stood gaping.

"I must ask you to stand back a moment, Lieutenant," I exclaimed, "while I destroy my war material. Overboard with it all!" I called to my men.

Pistols, grenades, and machine guns dropped splashing into the water.

"And now, Lieutenant," I saluted, "at your service!"

"Right ho, Count," he replied, "you men have made a great name for yourselves on your cruise, and now you have played cricket with me. You will receive decent treatment. You have my word as a Briton for that." He emphasized the word "Briton."

Aboard the *Amra* we heard a different tune piped. They had an old black stewardess aboard, a particularly bad-tempered scold. The moment she saw us her shrewish tongue began to wag

"Just look at those Huns, and look at their muddy boots, soiling our clean deck. And then the black men are supposed to scrub it after them. These Huns should be painted black, and with tar. I'd rather be black than one of those Germans. Sinking ships with women and children is all they can do. I'd like to get a gun and shoot every one of them."

She certainly had been filled right up to her ear lobes with this war of frightfulness propaganda, and that old Jezebel knew how to do her bit of spiteful tongue-lashing. A ducking in cold water would have done her no harm. But we were prisoners now, and the berating of an ill-tempered old Melanesian woman was likely to be the smallest of our troubles.

I had no doubt as to what our first ordeal was to be. Unless the British had more recent news than we concerning our comrades whom we had left at Mopelia, which was not probable, we would be questioned as to the whereabouts of the *Seeadler* and the remainder of her crew. I told my men that they should give the same reply to all interrogations, namely that I had bidden them to keep silent and that I would answer

for all. That would prevent us from tripping one an-other up. We had taken care to throw away any notes or papers we had that gave any hint as to where we had gone ashore in the Society Islands. They could search us as much as they liked, but they would find nothing. One mischance, though, befell us. I was to learn in a few days that one of my com-rades had dropped a notebook, which presently was found. In it he had a brief diary of the *Seeadler's* voyage. I questioned the diarist who had kept the unfortunate record, and he told me that his notes about Mopelia were very sketchy. He remembered clearly that he had written we had captured the sailing ship *Manila*. After that was a single entry.

"Landed stores at Mopelia."

There his diary broke off. There was no mention of our having sunk the *Manila* or of our having lost the *Seeadler* at Mopelia or taken refuge on the island.

"And now," I said to my men as we came in sight of Suva, "you keep your mouths shut, by Joe. Let me do the lying. They've got us, but they must not get the boys back at Mopelia."

XXIX

JAILED IN FIJI WHILE THE OTHERS ESCAPE TO EASTER ISLAND

Our arrival as prisoners was the event of the year at Suva, the capital city of the Fiji Islands. Our capture was the only warlike happening that had come along in those parts to break the monotony of life in the dreary South Seas. The newspaper got out a lurid special edition filled with a harrowing account of the capture of the captain and a part of the crew of the desperate raider, the *Seeadler*. It gave the hour when we were expected to reach Suva. So a huge crowd, that is, a huge one as crowds go in Fiji, had gathered at the pier to look us over. A company of infantry lined both sides of the approach to the pier with bayonets fixed. They certainly were a comic-opera-looking lot in their hot-weather knee pants.

During our march down the street between the gauntlet of bayonets and the crowd behind them, a half-caste fellow, seeing us unarmed and helpless, stepped forward and spat in the face of one of my boys. I jumped out of line and gave him a blow straight from the shoulder that sent him down in a heap. His friends had to carry him away. I had acted on the impulse of the moment and expected to be run through with a bayonet, but the officer in command of the soldiers shouted:

"Serves him right! Good for you, Count!" Then addressing himself to the crowd he added: "These men have done nothing to deserve such treatment."

He said it as though he meant it, too. That English-man was a real fellow, I tell you.

＇ We were promptly questioned. Where were the *Seeadler* and the remainder of its crew? Of course, my boys kept mum. I, on the other hand, invented a story about accidentally getting separated from the rest, who were still aboard the *Seeadler*—where, we didn't know. The story, of course, was not believed.

At first they kept us at the Governor's Rest House, a fine place with a garden, where visiting white people often stopped. Our meals were borne to us by coolies from the local hotel. The temporary commandant of the Rest House was a Lieutenant Wodehouse, a fine fellow. After a day or so he was replaced by a Lieu-tenant Whitehouse, whom we didn't like so well. He was what the British themselves would call "a bit of an ass, y'know." Whenever he talked with me he kept his hand on his pistol. He apparently thought me a sort of ogre, a bad man sent to frighten nice young lieutenants. Presently he came, hand on pis-tol, and announced:

"General Mackenzie wants to see you, all of you."

"More questions, by Joe," I thought.

Appearing before a general was an event of some moment. We felt we had to look worthy of the Ger-man Navy. We had our uniforms, which were some-what faded after the long trip at sea. But we slicked them up as best we could and generally made our-selves as presentable as possible. They loaded us into stinking cattle cars. For a visit to a general? *Qurre!* we thought. They led us to a stone building and ushered us in. It was a jail!

"Is this your General Mackenzie?" I sneered at Whitehouse. "You're a fine British officer."

He walked away, ashamed, himself, of the dodge he had used to get us to the jail without the desperate

attempts he, in his stupid timidity, expected us to make.

But the jail was not so bad. We got our meals from a restaurant. They separated me from my men, which I did not like. Nor was it exactly military ethics to confine prisoners of war in a common calaboose. But the authorities were nervous. They believed the *Seeadler* was lurking somewhere near by, and they expected our comrades to come raiding ashore and try to rescue us. Of course, they kept on trying to get us to tell them where the *Seeadler* was, but they learned nothing.

Lieutenant Whitehouse was still our jailer. Keeping a good hold of his pistol, he came up to me again. He spoke very politely this time:

"A Japanese admiral wants to see you, sir."

I laughed at him.

"First it was General Mackenzie, and now it is the Japanese admiral. Ho! Ho! What tricks are you up to this time?"

"No, really, upon my word, really, Count, the Japanese admiral wants to see you."

"By Joe, Lieutenant, I was fool enough to get all slicked up to see your General Mackenzie. But I'll be hanged if I'll budge an inch to see your old Japanese admiral."

I didn't know what kind of foolishness it was this time, and intended to protest and stall as long as I could. He went away rather sheepishly. In a few minutes another lieutenant showed up.

"There is a Japanese admiral who really does want to see you, Count Luckner, you know," he said.

"Oh, since you say so, Lieutenant, it must be so," I replied.

I brushed up my uniform and accompanied him through the courtyard to a pier. A splendid cruiser,

the *Ysuma*, lay out there at anchor in the harbour.
A boat manned by Japanese sailors was waiting there
for me at the landing. Aboard the cruiser, the magnificent deck contrasting with the dingy jail that now
was my home, I felt like a man who, long confined in
darkness, suddenly walks into sunlight.

My feelings changed to those of discomfort as the
Admiral welcomed me. He was a grave, courteous
little man, clad in an immaculate white uniform. My
own uniform had once been white, but in spite of all
the washing I had given it, it was now a dingy gray.
The gold braid had turned green from the corrosion
of the sea water. So I tried to make up in dignity of
bearing what I lacked in perfection of dress. He introduced me to his officers:

"Here is the man we have chased for three
months." And then turning to me:

"I am sorry, sir, to meet you in this situation. I
would rather it had been in a good, square fight."

"I should far rather be your prisoner, Admiral,"
I answered, "than the ignominy of living in this
beastly Fiji Island jail."

The Japanese had not known of the jail part of it.
The officers looked in cold astonishment at the British lieutenant, who was much embarrassed.

In the luxurious saloon I was extended gracious,
indeed ceremonious hospitality, the hospitality of
Japan. The admiral offered me cigars and cigarettes
and poured out the champagne for me. I took a
cigar, but refused the wine.

"I am a teetotaller," I said, "a prohibitionist, as
the Americans would say."

I suspected that I would be questioned about the
Seeadler, and didn't want my tongue lubricated with
champagne!

The admiral placed three books before me. The

frontispiece of one was the picture of the *Emden;* of the other, a picture of the *Moewe.* He turned the pages. Both were filled with Japanese writing. The third book was empty. The admiral placed this book before me and presented me with a pen.

"Write something about your cruise," he asked. "In our country we write about the deeds of the enemies we have met. We tell what they did for their countries, so that it may fill our youth with enthusiasm to do as much for our country. Write down one or two things that I can use."

"Gladly," I replied, and began to write briefly of our experiences while rounding Cape Horn.

"Just a question first," interrupted the admiral. "Did you put to sea from a neutral port, the United States, Argentine, or Chile?"

"We sailed from Hamburg," I responded. "We flew the Norwegian flag and were searched for an hour and a half by a British cruiser."

"Examined by the British?"

"Yes."

Those grave Japanese faces lighted up with smiles of exquisite amusement.

After I had written my short piece, the admiral spoke again.

"And now, Count, tell me where you have been."

"Admiral," I responded, "that is a question I should prefer not to answer right away. First tell me where you looked for me."

He brought out a big chart. A quick glance, and I saw the island of Mopelia. Around it was a faint line in pencil. That told me what I wanted to know. Undoubtedly, they had found the diary my boy had lost, the last entry of which mentioned Mopelia.

The admiral pointed to the Tasman Sea, between Australia and New Zealand.

"I was on your trail here, Count, but I lost you near New Zealand."

"I am sorry to say, Admiral, that my ship was never within six thousand miles of those waters."

"But," he responded, "the ships you sank in the Pacific were all to or from Australia."

"I know, but——" A little judicious hesitation.

"But where were you, Count? Tell me."

"I cruised back and forth south of the Hawaiian Islands over the waters where the Australia-San Francisco ships, the eastbound and westbound, pass." There is nothing like the truth.

"You are right, Count. I should have thought of it."

"I am glad you didn't," I replied, "or you would have captured me."

He dropped the questioning for a while and asked me about the Battle of Jutland, which always seems to interest Japanese naval men tremendously. When I said I had been through the battle, they made me tell them every detail I could remember. They were interested in everything. The admiral's comment on what I told him was interesting.

"Another proof," he exclaimed, "that the smaller fleet was superior per ship to the larger."

And now the admiral came square to the point.

"Tell me, Count, where your *Seeadler* is."

I was in a tight hole. I must strike a blow for my comrades out there on Mopelia. The elements I had to work upon lay in the fact that the diary which had been found mentioned merely that we had put stores aboard at Mopelia and told of the capture of the *Manila* and said nothing of the fact that we had sunk that ship. Then, also, the truth is rarely believed. I proceeded to skate very near the truth.

"The *Seeadler*," I replied, "was lost."

"How was it lost?"

"We got on the coral reef at Mopelia. We tried our best to get off, put our stores ashore to lighten the ship. But it was no use."

"What did you do then?"

"We went aboard the *Manila*."

"The four-masted schooner, *Manila?*"

"Yes, we captured her and took her along with us."

"Where is the *Manila* now?"

"She is waiting for me off Mopelia. My men are having a good vacation on the island until I come back."

"I say, Count, we Japanese are not such fools. You had the four-master *Manila*, and you sailed from Mopelia to the Fijis in a small boat."

"Yes," I replied. "There was not room enough for all of us aboard the *Manila*."

The admiral looked at me with a sly Oriental smile.

Fine, I thought. I had figured out their minds correctly. They had not set straight out for Mopelia, in spite of their knowing that we had landed stores there, because it seemed wildly impossible that I with my five men had sailed from Mopelia to the Fijis in an open boat.

"Count," exclaimed the admiral, "I will tell you where your crew is. You did not leave a four-masted schooner and sail twenty-three hundred miles in a lifeboat. You sailed here in the *Manila*, and, having got here, you put out in your lifeboat to capture another ship in a near-by harbour. You tell me your crew is at Mopelia, hoping I will get up steam immediately, go hurrying away for a few thousand miles on a wild-goose chase, and leave them in peace. The *Manila* is in these waters. In four days, your crew will be my prisoners."

He respected me too much to think that I would

ever give my crew away. He knew I would try to throw him off the scent. His object was to outwit me, to get my story and read between the lines.

"Very good, Admiral," I thought, "let us see how it will work out."

We parted the best of friends. He was an excellent fellow. Our meeting had been one of mutual deceit with lies that no gentleman would tell in ordinary times. Now they were quite respectable, as ruses of war.

The ironical thing was that my men, who under the command of Lieutenant Kling were still living like lords at Mopelia, were destined to have much better luck in getting a ship than my little party had had through all our terrible hardships.

They caught a wireless message one day telling of our capture. So, fearing that their own whereabouts might soon be discovered, they hastily began to build a boat to sail away in, but, with the materials at their disposal, they were unable to construct anything like a seaworthy craft, capable of carrying that whole crowd. Then Dame Fortune smiled on them.

A French square-rigged schooner sighted the island and the wreck of the *Seeadler*.

"By Joe," exclaimed the captain, "we passed here six months ago and there was no wreck here! We may find castaways on the island. It looks as though we may find a good profit, too."

You see, a captain gets a third of the value of any wreck, ship, or cargo, that he saves. The schooner quickly veered toward the island.

It was a Sunday morning. On the island the men were sitting around, washing clothes, writing diaries, and so on. The chef was shooting snipe for dinner. Then the cry:

"Ship ahoy."

Kling took out a lifeboat with a boarding party, the strongest men he had, some of them the champion wrestlers. As they approached the schooner, the captain leaned over the rail and shouted down to them:

"Don't row so hard, boys. We will come for you."

Our sailors swarmed aboard. Pistols out.

"Hands up!"

The Frenchmen recognized the German uniform.

"*Mon Dieu—des Allemands.* I turn off my course to save castaways and I am captured by the *Boches! Mon Dieu!*"

The schooner was not big enough, nor had aboard provisions enough, for both the Germans and the prisoners. Kling decided to leave the prisoners, including the crew of the schooner, on the island, where they would be comfortable enough. When he was a week or so out, he would send a wireless that would bring ships to their rescue. So, the whole of Seeadler-town was given over to the prisoners, and the schooner sailed away. She was named the *Lutece*, but my men discovered that she had been the German ship, the *Fortuna*. She had been seized by the French during the war. So she got her old name back. She was German again—a German auxiliary cruiser. For Kling fully intended to go right on buccaneering.

Three days after the *Fortuna* sailed, our former prisoners saw a cloud of smoke on the horizon. Steaming at full speed, her funnels belching smoke, the Japanese cruiser, *Usuma*, steered to the island. On her bridge the admiral swore in Japanese.

"By Joe, the Count fooled me all right. He told me the truth. There is the wreck, and there are his men. Everything except the *Manila*. He tricked me with the tale about the *Manila*."

The Japanese found only men of the Allied nations. "Where are the Germans?"

"I'm sorry," replied the French captain, "but they sailed away three days ago in my ship, the *Lutece*."

The Japanese admiral was thoroughly disgusted at that, but of course he took the whole crowd aboard and took them back to the Fijis. It was of no use to go racing about the immense spaces of the Pacific looking for a solitary sailing square-rigged schooner.

Kling's plan was to sail around Horn into the Atlantic, sink a few ships there, and then try to steal through the blockade and get back home. His course took him to Easter Island, a small, remote possession of Chile where there was no wireless station. There he intended to overhaul the ship, which was in bad condition, and take aboard supplies and fresh water. On October 4th, they sighted the island, but while sailing into the harbour struck an uncharted, sunken rock. The *Fortuna* was old and worm-eaten. The rock crashed right through her planks. The ship pounded and quickly broke up. The men had to swim for it.

The lives of some of them, at least, were saved in a curious way—by two pigs. These animals we had brought from Germany aboard the *Seeadler* to serve as fresh pork. They soon became pets, however, and we kept them. They were quite companionable and romped around the decks with the men. Kling had them aboard the *Fortuna*. When the ship sank, the swimmers, including the two pigs, found themselves among sharks. These seemed to prefer pork to human flesh. They seized the two pigs and began to fight over them among themselves. You bet the men in the water swam as hard as they could. They were quickly picked up by native canoes that

had put out as soon as the wrecking of the ship had been seen from shore.

The cargo of the *Fortuna* consisted of Parisian fineries, silk stockings and underclothing, handkerchiefs, parasols, tennis shoes, brilliantine, scented soaps, perfumes, and such. It had been destined for the natives of the South Seas, to whom the French bring a truly Parisian elegance. In the breaking up of the ship, many cases filled with these swanky trappings of civilization remained afloat. The natives salvaged them, and pretty soon it seemed as if the whole island had been on a shopping tour through Paris and had visited the women's shops chiefly, or the Galeries Lafayette. Men and women alike arrayed their dusky selves in all manner of silk and lingerie! The population was delighted. Kling and his men were the bringers of this treasure. They graciously told the natives they could have anything they found, and in return they were granted all the hospitality the island could muster. The Chilean governor, an excellent fellow, placed a house at the disposal of the officers, while the sailors were sought after by the natives as guests in their huts.

They remained on the island for nearly two months enjoying life and surveying the strange monuments there, huge monoliths that tell of an ancient, forgotten civilization of people who long since have passed into oblivion. On November 25th, a Chilean steamer that made regular trips to the island hove in sight. When it raised steam for its return voyage, our men were aboard. The Chilean authorities on the mainland received them with friendly hospitality, regarding them as shipwrecked sailors and therefore not interning them. They lived as guests of German colonists in Chile from then on until the end of the war.

XXX

THE ESCAPE FROM NEW ZEALAND TO THE SMOKING ISLE

THE thought of every prisoner is—escape! That was what we thought about, by Joe, and what we dreamed about. Occasionally, I'd wake up with a start, dreaming we were still in our small boat and about to be dashed against that coral reef. Usually my sleep was not troubled with such nightmares. But I often dreamed of getting away, capturing another ship, and continuing our cruise. This did finally come about, but not for many months.

No opportunity of escape presented itself during our stay at Suva, which was not long. Kircheiss and I were shipped from the Fijis to a little isle off the coast of the north island of New Zealand, right near the entrance to Auckland harbour. The other four went to the island of Somes, where they had a hard time under a bad camp commander, a Major Matthis. No chance to escape came their way, but with Kircheiss and me it was different. We had a highly exciting time, and thus were spared the mental and physical stagnation that is the lot of the average prisoner of war.

The public of New Zealand was inflamed against us. When we arrived there was a great outcry and demand that we be shot. This amazed us, but we discovered the reason a few days later. You see the inhabitants of these islands thought that we had sunk

the big New Zealand passenger steamer *Wairuna*, with all on board. As a matter of fact, we knew nothing of the *Wairuna* and hadn't even heard of her. Later, it developed that she had been captured by our fast auxiliary cruiser *Wolf*, sister ship of the *Moewe*, and her crew taken aboard as prisoners. But so far as the New Zealanders were concerned, their ship and all on board her had vanished as though swallowed up by the sea. So they were frantic about it, and my boys and myself nearly lost our lives as a result. After carrying out her raid, the *Wolf* slipped through the blockade again and back into Germany. At the time of our arrival in New Zealand from Fiji, nothing was known of the *Wolf*, and it was supposed that we had sunk the *Wairuna* with her passengers and crew. The rage of the public was such that the authorities had to hide us away in their naval barracks at the Devonport Torpedo Yard, and then transfer us secretly to a prison camp on the island of Motuihi, near by. Meanwhile, the populace clamored for us to be turned over to them so they could lynch us.

The little island of Motuihi, a beautiful strip of land, had long been the internment place of many Germans who had been captured when the British seized our possessions in Samoa and in other parts of the South Seas. They were all civilians, from ten to seventy years of age, traders, plantation owners, and officials. They greeted us with pride and affection, but more particularly with anxiety. They said we were sure to be shot. I laughed at this. "By Joe, who wants to kill us? On what grounds could mere prisoners of war be shot down in captivity?" I asked.

But things looked a little less rosy when, forty-eight hours later, we were taken by boat to Auckland and then whisked by automobile, under cover of night, through valley and forest to a freight train

pulled up in a wild, remote place. They locked us up in a freight car, where there were two beds. They told us it was to protect us against the public. The train pulled out and, after an all-night journey, stopped near the outskirts of the city of Wellington, the capital of the islands that comprise New Zealand. Here they put us into another automobile and rushed us to the Danish Barracks in Wellington, an old jail, an almost prehistoric relic of more primitive days in New Zealand. A native keeper who led us along a corridor tugged at my coat and pointed into a cell. There were my boys, Leudemann, Krauss, Parmien, and Erdmann. They were in chains. We were all to stand trial together. We spoke to one another for a minute, and then Kircheiss and I were led to our cells.

On the following day, Kircheiss and I were taken aboard an old cruiser in the harbour and ushered into the saloon, where there were about a dozen men who wore black coats and four-cornered caps with tassels. Our four boys were standing in a corner. I was boiling mad.

"What's this?" I said. "Is justice becoming ridiculous? Why are we put in jail like this and some of my boys in chains? Is that for prisoners of war? And what man of you is able to judge of our warfare? You are civilians. Are we to be judged by civilians? I will answer only to naval men."

Just then Sir Hall Thompson, British naval commander in New Zealand waters, came down the stairway. I turned to him.

"I am glad to see you, sir. Why are we treated like this? And are prisoners of war to be tried by civilians?"

"Count," he replied, "public opinion forces it.

The public has demanded that within three days of your arrival in this country you must reveal where you sank the *Wairuna* and why you sank her without saving a single life, and also where your ship *Seeadler* is."

"But I know nothing about the *Wairuna*," I replied. "I did not sink her. In every single capture that we made, I took the crews aboard my ship, kept them there until we were overcrowded, and then sent them home."

"You say you didn't sink the *Wairuna?*"

"No! Nor ever even heard of her!"

"Will you give me your word of honour on this?"

"I give it to you now."

"Very well, Count, that is good."

"But why do you keep my men in chains?"

"We want to know where the *Seeadler* is."

"I want to tell you, sir, that my men will die before they will say anything. They have orders from me not to talk. If anyone is to tell anything about the *Seeadler*, it is I. You would give your men the same command under the same circumstances, and you would want them to obey as my men are obeying."

"You are the one to ask, Count, about information of the *Seeadler?*"

"Yes."

"Then tell me where she is."

"Captain, may I sink deep in the earth if I ever betray my crew. I respect you. I would not put such a question to you if you were my prisoner."

"Count," he replied, "your men have set an example to our sailors. I understand and appreciate your attitude. So long as your men show themselves to be disciplined sailors, they will have excellent treatment. And I hope that you, yourself, will have a

pleasant stay with us and find nothing of which to complain. Gentlemen," he addressed the judges, "the court martial is over."

My four men were taken back to their island, and Kircheiss and I to ours.

At Motuihi things were not so bad. The food was good and discipline was not too strict. The camp commander, Turner by name, seemed very proud to have a couple of real war prisoners in his charge. He had really excellent cause to be pleased. Now that he had enemy naval officers in his camp, he was raised to the rank of Lieutenant Colonel, and his force of guards was increased to eighty men. It likewise seemed to add to his dignity that he had among his captives someone whom he could call Count. The principal annoyance now was the strict watch they felt obliged to keep over us to prevent our escape. Headquarters at Auckland had to be telephoned every other hour and told that everything was all right. Colonel Turner was also provided with a fine new motor boat, so that, if anything went wrong with the telephone wire, he would still have a means of swift communication with the mainland.

"By Joe, what a fine motor boat," I exclaimed when I saw it.

"Maybe we could use it," commented Kircheiss.

You couldn't blame the authorities for being a bit nervous. They still did not know where the remainder of the *Seeadler's* crew was, and were worried about a possible raid to liberate us. Likewise, Kircheiss and I had the idea of escape buzzing furiously in our heads. In fact, the prisoners on Motuihi before we arrived had already thought of a jail break. They had formed no definite plan, but had gathered materials that might be useful. One had contrived to filch and hide away a number of tools. Another had

found a derelict floating mine and taken the fuses from it and also a large quantity of guncotton, which he stowed in his mattress. He slept on the guncotton every night. Another had succeeded in "finding" charts of the harbour with the location of the mine fields. In any plan of flight, I could, by including the men who had collected them, have these materials at my disposal.

The motor boat was, of course, the centre of all scheming. The idea was to sail away in it with an able-bodied company of prison camp comrades, capture a sailing ship, and go buccaneering again. One of the prisoners, a young fellow, was a motor expert. The camp commander had assigned him to look after the engine of his motor boat. So he was one man whom we would have to have with us. I didn't think there would be much trouble in getting away with the boat. Although there were sentries all over the island, we were sure we could invent some way of outwitting them. We would have to stow the boat with a large amount of supplies. This, our motor expert could do while pretending to tinker with the engine. He could hide the material away in the air chambers of the boat. Much more difficult was the job of collecting all the food, weapons, and other equipment. This took a long time, and all the patient manœuvring that is traditional of prisoners and their schemes of escape.

First it was necessary to quiet the uneasiness of the camp commander. He apparently expected me to go breaking out of his camp breathing fire from my nostrils. The camp doctor was a German Pole, quite intelligent, but of degenerated spirit, who was used by the commandant to spy on the prisoners. He made the friendliest sort of overtures to me, and I, having been told that he was an informer, made it

seem as though I were being completely taken in by his smooth ways.

Nearly everybody in the camp suffered severely from rheumatism. I was one of the few who had the good luck to escape the malady. But I pretended to get it badly, so badly that I was only able to walk with crutches. The commandant was pleased when he found that I was almost helpless. For how could a cripple attempt an escape? The doctor pretended to try his best to cure my supposed ailment, but gave me a kind of treatment that was designed to make it worse. His hoodwinking was complete when I asked him to help me to get word to my people in Germany to send me five thousand pounds, and promised him part of this in return for his aid. I kept the hypothetical five thousand pounds dangling before his nose, and his avarice blinded him so much that I was able to make a ready tool of him.

My crew for the projected flight consisted of nine men, seven of whom were North German Lloyd merchant-ship cadets captured by the British in Samoa. When war broke out, they happened to be at the American South Sea port of Pagopago. Slipping away in a small boat, they got to German Samoa, only to find it in the hands of the New Zealanders.

I did my recruiting secretly. The plan of escape was kept from the other prisoners. Always to keep your secret among as few as possible is a good rule even among prisoners. You never know who is a spy. The fellows I chose were all lively lads, ready for anything.

One day a couple of the prisoners said to me:

"Count, let's get up a show for Christmas, a play."

Show, play, theatre—that was an idea for me.

"Certainly I will," I replied. "I often got up shows in the navy. We will have a theatre here at Motuihi that will beat the best in Berlin. But you,

must leave everything to me. I will direct everything."

"All right," they said.

I got permission from the commandant to produce the show. In fact, he waxed quite enthusiastic about it. Not only would it give the prisoners something to do, but it would also provide amusement for the jailers. Life on the island was mighty boresome to all of them.

In a little while, the prison camp was humming with preparations for the grand spectacle I was going to stage. This was the cover under which my fellows and I prepared all of our equipment for our escape. It deluded the guards, and also fooled the prisoners whom we couldn't take with us. When we wanted material, always apparently innocent things, we asked for it and said it was for the show. When we built anything, it was for the show.

We even built a wireless set out of things supposed to be for our *grosses shauspielhaus*. We made bombs out of tin cans and the guncotton that had already been procured. The bombs had fuses that could be lighted from a cigarette. One of my men worked on a farm in the interior of the island, and got a lot of dynamite and blasting powder used in blowing up stumps. We stole a couple of pistols from the camp arsenal. We made a fake contrivance which looked like a perfect Lewis or Maxim machine gun, but it worked well enough and it looked even more formidable. Cadet von Zartowsky took odds and ends and made a sextant that afterward took us fifty nautical miles off our course, pretty fair, considering the circumstances.

We had no great trouble in hiding away a considerable supply of food in the air chambers of the motor boat. Of course, I not only had talked of elaborate

plans for the supposed theatrical events that I was directing, but I also had the prisoners prepare a lot of bona-fide stage props, more even than could be used. These were made up by the rest of the fellows who were not in our plot. Most of the actual material needed for our escape and subsequent raiding cruise had to be fixed up stealthily by the boys who were to make the dash for freedom with me.

One midnight, a guard happened to notice three of my men busily at work. One was painting a large German flag. Another was making a red pistol holster. The third was sewing a sail out of bed sheets. We intended hoisting a sail on the motor boat in order to conserve fuel if we had to cruise about in that little boat for a long time. The guard reported what he had seen to the commandant.

"Oh, it's all right," said Colonel Turner," it's stuff for the theatre."

But next day he came and questioned me:

"Look here, Count, I can understand how you might need a flag and a pistol holster for your show, but what about the sail?"

"Oh, that's the curtain!" I replied.

Of all the people I met in New Zealand, there was but one for whom I had a complete contempt. He was a fellow named Hansen, a German by birth and a naturalized New Zealander. In spite of his naturalization, he had been interned. He happened to notice that the motor expert, while supposedly working on the engine of the *Pearl*, the colonel's boat, had carried something suspicious aboard. Anxious to curry favour with the commandant, he reported that we were acting suspiciously. The commandant was contemptuous of a rat like that in the first place, and then he was utterly infatuated with our theatre. He said that whatever we were doing could only be

in preparation for our show. Nevertheless, he tried to investigate, but found nothing to confirm what the squealer had told him.

After weeks of hard labour, we were ready. At night we cut the wires connecting the island with the mainland and set a barracks afire. That created the diversion we needed. Everybody, guards and all, flocked to put the blaze out. I was among the foremost, and attracted all attention to myself. I seemed to have a passion for fighting fires. My boys were with me. When the excitement was at its highest, we stole away singly and boarded the motor boat. The engine purred, and we were away in the darkness.

We were safe from pursuit for a while, anyway. There was no other boat at the island, and Motuihi could not communicate with the mainland. It was only when the wires were repaired or when the mainland was due to get its next report that the chase after us could begin. When our escape did become known on the mainland on that night of December 13, 1917, every kind of craft available went out to look for us. Private owners took up scouting for us as a sport. Boats chased one another and shot at one another, and one steamer went on the rocks. Finally, a false rumour spread that we had capsized and drowned, and the weary pursuers were glad to accept it as true and return home.

We had our difficulties in finding our way in the night through the Hauraki Gulf on which Auckland lies, but at an hour or so past midnight we saw sweeping shafts of light. The authorities at Auckland were looking for us with a searchlight, a ridiculous procedure, but one calculated to impress the population. We steered by the searchlight beams now, and picked our way along easily enough.

Of course, it would take a separate volume to re-

cord all of the details of our work of preparation and
our final escape. I am only giving you a description
of the high spots. But, by the way, I almost forgot
to tell you how we were dressed. We all had New
Zealand uniforms. Mine was the most interesting
of the lot and provided material for Australian hu-
morists and cartoonists for many weeks. As the commander of a man-o'-war, even of a twelve-foot
wooden one, with the unwarlike name of *Pearl*, I
absolutely had to have a sword. One of my boys, just
an hour before our escape, slipped into the wardrobe
of the prison camp commandant. Not only did he
take Colonel Turner's best dress uniform, but he also
swiped his sword and scabbard.

We lay off an isolated bay of Red Mercury Island,
northwest of the Bay of Plenty, for two days, during
which we had a couple of narrow escapes from searching boats. A government cutter had almost sighted
us when she damaged her propeller on the rocks and
had to limp back home. The third day we put out to
sea, and as we bounced about on the waves I swore
in the cadets as regular midshipmen of the Imperial
Navy and promoted Vice Corporal von Egidy to the
rank of naval junior lieutenant. As commander of a
war vessel, even though she was only the colonel's
motor boat, I had the authority to do this. Then each
helped the other cut his hair short in naval fashion.

Two sailing vessels came by. We decided to seize
them both, sink one, and keep the other. We went
after the first one, but a sudden puff of wind carried
her along at a great rate, and we could not catch
her. This was very unfortunate, for she reported our
capture of the second boat, which she witnessed.
Bombs poised, machine gun pointing, and German
flag raised, we swiftly approached the *Moa*. She hove
to. My boys and I clambered on deck. With Colonel

Turner's sword in my hand, I ordered the captain and crew herded below, the captain, an excellent old salt, growling:

"You're escaped prisoners, eh? Our boys are doing their bit in France, and at home they can't even guard prisoners."

The *Moa* was a fine craft but as flat as a match box. Intended for coastwise trade, she had no keel and drew only three feet of water, but she had huge masts. A storm blew up, and we scudded before the wind. The *Moa's* captain rushed up bristling with excitement. His boat, he protested, was not adapted for sailing on the high sea, much less through a storm. We were risking our lives, he expostulated. We should take down sail.

"We are sailing for our lives, by Joe," I responded, and kept all canvas up.

The skipper stayed on deck all night and poured out oil to quiet the waves. We went on our watches, undisturbed. Ordinarily, we would have been somewhat worried, but the storm was taking us along swiftly—away from pursuit. The waves began to break over our stern, and the *Moa* bobbed up and down. She had a deckload of lumber. Overboard with it. We started to work and were ably assisted by a breaker that crashed over us and in an instant swept most of the lumber into the sea. We were towing the motor boat we had taken from the commandant at Motuihi. A wave swamped her, and she tore loose from the towline and sank.

We steered to the Kermadec Islands, an uninhabited group where the New Zealand government keeps a cache of provisions for castaway sailors. Curtis Island, one of the group, came in sight on December 21st. It appeared in a cloud of smoke, a land of volcanoes and geysers. Presently we spied the

sheet-iron shed where the provisions were stored.
Kircheiss and four men landed on the inferno-like
coast and in due time returned, their boat loaded
deep with provisions. The New Zealand government
was kind enough to provide many useful things for
shipwrecked sailors and sometimes for escaped
prisoners of war. There were tools, oars, sails, fishing
tackle, blankets, bacon, butter, lard, canned beef—
in short, everything. We had intended to leave our
prisoners on Curtis Island, but that den of steam and
sulphur fumes seemed unfit for anyone. So we decided to take them on to near-by Macauley Island,
there put them ashore with a supply of provisions,
and send a wireless message to summon aid for them.

"Smoke to the north, behind island," sang the
lookout.

Two men were still on the island. I sent hastily
for them. The *Moa* raised sail and ran before the
wind. The steamer was in sight now. She sailed toward
us. We changed our course. She, too, changed her
course. The skipper of the *Moa* recognized her as the
New Zealand government's cable steamer, *Iris*, an
auxiliary cruiser. She had cannon, and we had none.
Our goose was cooked.

We still tried hopelessly to run away. She gained
on us, and signalled us to stop. We kept on. A flash,
a distant roar, a hissing in the air, a splash in front
of us. She was firing on us.

"Heave to," I commanded, and we were prisoners
once again.

The *Iris* was manned, not by naval men, but by
a nondescript crowd that put pistols to our backs as
we came aboard, and searched us to the soles of our
shoes. Then these gentry robbed us of our personal
possessions. They were wildly jubilant over their
victory. I gathered from them that the ship that

had escaped us having brought the news of our capture of the *Moa* to Auckland, the authorities there had surmised that we must be headed for the cache of supplies at Curtis Island. When we arrived at Auckland, the New Zealanders had their own little victory celebration. Sightseers in all sorts of boats came out to have a look as the *Iris* with the *Moa* in tow steamed into harbour, the victor of the Battle of the Kermadecs.

We were jailed at Mount Eden, the local prison of Auckland, as a punishment for our flight. For a calaboose, it was not bad. After twenty-one days there, we were distributed among various prison camps. Kircheiss and I went to River Island near Lyttelton on the south island of New Zealand. Even the yard of our prison in Fort Jervois was a veritable cage. It was screened not only around but also across the top with lines of barbed wire. The commander of the camp, Major Leeming of Tasmania, was one of the best fellows I have ever met. He, too, felt himself a prisoner here on this lonely island and soon became our third man at cards, which we played to while away the hours during the long evenings.

A drawbridge that had been smashed by a hurricane was being repaired, and we prisoners had access to the waterside for a while. In the yard stood a row of empty tar barrels. One of the barrels fell over, and I happened to notice that it was picked up by a small coastwise schooner that often lay at dock farther down the shore. I threw in another barrel. It floated. The boat picked it up. My plan was made. I could arrange one of those barrels so that I could float out in it. I would pick the time when the little schooner was at shore. Then I would get into the barrel and roll myself off the dock. The boat would pick the barrel up. It might seem a bit heavy, but they would

think it had tar in it. The barrel once aboard, its lid would open and a man armed with a knife would step out, like a jack-in-the-box. Thus I would have a boat. I would pick up Kircheiss, who would be waiting, and we would go sailing and perhaps get to some neutral island.

I had everything, and waited. Major Leeming had been so kind to me that I did not want to embarrass him by escaping under his command. He, expecting an addition to his family, was to take a furlough. I would do my jail-breaking while he was away. But soon after Major Leeming went on his furlough, Kircheiss and I were ordered back to the prison camp at Motuihi. Of course, there was a new commandant at Motuihi now, a Major Schofield. Most of the prisoners there received us with enthusiasm. Even the treacherous Polish doctor brought me a bottle of champagne, hoping that I would not mention our former little business transaction in which he was to get a percentage of that $25,000.

Some of our own countrymen who had spent so many hours learning parts for that theatrical show seemed to hold it against us. But, after all, had I not treated them to a far better melodrama from the life of a sailor?

Presently, several fellows came to me and asked if I did not think something could be undertaken. They had already contrived to get a few pistols and build a folding canvas boat. We could not very well go to sea in that. But if we could contrive to station ourselves at some other part of the island, we could wait until a sailing ship came along, put out in our flimsy little craft, and attack her. We consulted with the former governor of German Samoa, Dr. Schultz-Ewarth by name, who was a prisoner at Motuihi. He with his personal servant, a giant fellow, formerly

a German baker, was allowed to wander where he pleased on the island. It was his man who hit upon the idea of hiding in the interior of the island by building a cave in the side of a dry river bed that he had discovered, the cave to be so disguised that searchers would not notice it. We could easily get out of the camp and into the other parts of the island, and, at the same time, give the impression that we had escaped over a cliff to the shore and been picked up by a boat. We could keep to our retreat until the search had died down, and then we could watch for a passing sailship and attack it. The plan seemed an excellent one.

We gathered more weapons, while Dr. Schultz-Ewarth and his man, on their long rambles, began the construction of the cave. Things progressed rapidly. Then the Armistice came. If it had been delayed a week, there would have been another escape at Motuihi.

After the Armistice, we were prisoners for four more months on the north island near Auckland, but were allowed visitors. One day, a Maori chieftain's wife from the tribe of the Waikotas, a people who made a name for themselves as warriors against the English in their heroic struggle for freedom in 1860–61, called with her retinue. This lady, whose name was Kaihau, handed me a letter. It was written in Maori, and translated read as follows:

I come to you, O illustrious chieftain, and pass on to you for the future preservation of an old tradition the mat of the great chieftain Wai-Tete.

As she handed me the letter, she brought forth from under her dress a mat that she had hidden there while passing the prison guard.

My surprise was great, and I nudged Kircheiss, but he was as mystified as I. Fortunately, there was a German lady present who had been living in New Zealand for some time. She understood the customs of the handsome aborigines who once ruled in New Zealand, and explained to me that I was about to receive the highest honour that the Maoris can bestow upon anyone.

The chieftain's wife began to dance around me with great rapidity and wild abandon. The name of this dance was the Haka-Haka, or something like that, and at the conclusion of it she presented me with a green stone found only in New Zealand. Again she spoke.

"O great warrior from across the seas, we greet you as a chieftain of the Waikatos, and among my people you shall be known henceforth as 'Ai-Tete,' meaning 'Holy Water.' We believe that the spirit of our Maori hero Ai-Tete has returned to us in you."

I accepted the stone and pressed the Maori woman's hand to express my gratitude. As she was about to take her departure, she requested that I hide the mat and stone and carry them to Germany with me, which I did. But before concealing them, I had my picture taken wearing nothing but the garb of a Maori chieftain, this simple mat. Except for the absence of full war paint and the usual tattooing, my friends said I made a perfect aborigine. Perhaps so. Even in Germany there are those who look upon me as more of an aborigine than a civilized being.

When the day on which we were to sail drew near, the president of the Soldiers' Mothers' League visited me and wished me a pleasant trip on behalf of the mothers of 80,000 soldiers. She said she came because New Zealand's sons who had been war prisoners in Germany had returned home in good health to their mothers. Therefore, she considered it

her duty to pray God that I, too, might soon be restored to my mother's arms.

So at last we sailed away from New Zealand, "the land down under," where we had had the last of our adventures, enjoyed a few hardships, spent many weary and delightful hours, and met many hospitable and kindly people. On the whole, I have happy memories of the Antipodes.

In July of 1919, I stepped on German soil again and hurried home, just in time to pass a few more weeks with my father, who died on September 3d. The old warrior held steadfast to his faith in the Fatherland to the last. But to his dying hour he was filled with regret because his government would not let him take an active part in the Great War.

On January 3, 1920, all my men returned—that is, all save one. Their clothes were faded from the tropical sun and corroded by the sea water, but they returned without a stain upon either their honour or their loyalty.

The only gap in our ranks after those long adventures was the excellent Dr. Pietsch, our ship surgeon. The news of Germany's collapse reached the remote part of Chile where he was living. When he heard it, he fell dead of heart failure.

Returned to my beloved Fatherland, I found so many things changed and different from what I had hoped. In this connection, there is one memory always before me. It is of my mother. I was sitting at her sick bed when even the doctors had given up hope. Only then did I realize how much I loved her, but I also realized with sorrow and regret how much more I should have done for her. Exactly the same feeling I have to-day when I find my country lying low. Never have I loved my homeland so much as now.

To the youth of America I would like to send a message: Europe is one continent attached to still another even greater land mass. That other is the continent of Asia, filled with many strange races, all speaking different languages. Even Europe itself is split up into many nations speaking more than thirty different tongues. This I believe is largely responsible for the constant wars that are the curse of Europe. As an old sailor who has sailed before the mast around this world many times, I want to tell you Americans how lucky you are to live in a great country occupying a large part of this continent, with the wide Atlantic for a barrier on one side and the Pacific on the other. Yours is a great inheritance. You should be proud of it. You should make yourselves worthy of it.

As a sailor who has sailed under many flags and whose friends and pals are the citizens of many countries and many climes, it is my dream that one day we shall all speak the same language and have so many common interests that terrible wars will no longer occur. But keep your bodies fit, and if your country needs you, just remember the motto of the sea:

"Don't jump overboard! Stay with the ship!"

To all my countrymen, wherever they may be, I would like to say: Look up to the bright sun and not into mouse holes where it is dark. Take my lads for your example. When their ship was wrecked on the coral reef of that atoll in the South Seas there was one thing that was not wrecked—their courage. Even when the *Seeadler* met her fate, from stem to stern went up the cry, taken from an old refrain, "The German oak still stands."

AUF WIEDERSEHEN!

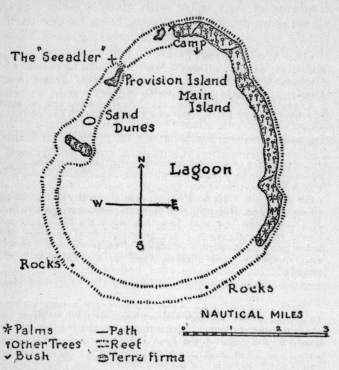

Mopelia

x Observation Point   Long. 16°46' S. Lat. 153°54' W.

The "Seeadler" +

Camp

Provision Island

Main Island

Sand Dunes

Lagoon

N
W — E
S

Rocks

Rocks

NAUTICAL MILES

0   1   2   3

* Palms   — Path
9 Other Trees ···· Reef
✓ Bush   ◎ Terra firma

Mopelia, a coral atoll of the Society Islands, where the Sea Devil planned a brief sojourn, and where the *Seeadler* was wrecked by a tidal wave. "A circular reef studded with waving palms and within the reef a lovely, placid lagoon. The coral shore was snow white and, with the sun's rays reflecting from it, it looked like a sparkling jewel set in an alabaster ring, like emeralds set in ivory."

APPENDIX

(Note A, see page 107.) Lloyd's Register of 1917–18 describes the *Pass of Balmaha* as follows: Steel ship (captured and taken to Cuxhaven), built 1888 by R. Duncan & Co., Port Glasgow, gross tonnage 1571, length 245.4, breadth 38.8, depth 22.5.

Until the World War, she was British-owned, and up until her fatal voyage her master was Capt. "Dick" Lee of Nova Scotia.

* * *

(Note B, see page 209.) Author's note: Since the War, it has developed that the Count was mistaken regarding the identity of this cruiser. Instead of the *Kent*, she was the *Lancaster*, and her commander was Captain Phillips, now of the British battleship *Queen Elizabeth*. Recently an American newspaper man, Robert H. Davis of the New York *Sun*, met him in the Mediterranean, loaned him a copy of one of the early editions of this book, and asked him: "Is it romance or truth?" "Quite accurate, I should say," replied Captain Phillips, "and in accordance with the records."

* * *

(Note C, see page 216.) "Count Luckner is to be congratulated on getting his ship through without being seen. Every effort was made to intercept him. . . . Those messages came from the cruiser *Lancaster* and not from the *Kent*. I was commander of the *Lancaster*. The raider must have passed within 200 miles of us on the inside waters as we lay off the west coast of Chile," said Captain Phillips of the British Navy.—New York *Sun*, May 24, 1928.

MAY WE HELP?

THE PUBLISHERS of Star books have tried to maintain a high standard in the selection of titles for their list, and to offer a consistent quality of workmanship and material. They trust that the book you have just read has, in part at least, earned your esteem for other titles in their list.

They are trying to make the Star Library comprehend the best in the literary fields of biography, science, history, true adventure, travel, art, philosophy, psychology, etc.

Believing that you will be interested in other books of a nature similar to that which you have just finished reading, the publishers have reproduced on the following pages a few extracts from other Star books. These are pages picked at random. Although there is no continuity, we hope that they will give you some idea of the style in which the books are written and perhaps the character of the subject from which you may form an opinion as to its place on your personal book shelf.

CHAPTER XI

VON SCHWIEGER'S ACCOUNT OF HOW HE SANK THE *LUSITANIA*

Thirteen years have rolled by since that tragic day in May, 1915, when 1,152 non-combatants, nearly half of them women and children, many of them neutral Americans, went down on the big Cunarder. No single deed in our time ever came so near to transforming a civilized state into an outlaw among the nations.

I had often wondered just what the truth was about the sinking of the *Lusitania*. The accounts had been rather conflicting. At the time of the disaster, and even years later, when the United States Federal Court conducted its final inquiry, we had only one side of the story, fragments pieced together from the accounts of dazed survivors. The tale they had to relate was of the usual war-time Atlantic crossing interrupted by a sudden explosion; of the listing of the ship; of vain attempts to get away in lifeboats; of the rapid sinking of the liner; of nightmare hours in the water; and then of bodies piled in the morgues at Queenstown. Only 764 of the 1,916 who had sailed on the *Lusitania* lived to tell that tale; 1,152 innocent travellers had been sent to their death by the hand of man—and that man a German.

From the day when the tragedy of the *Lusitania* cast its shadow over the world, and in the opinion of most of us made Germany the common enemy of mankind, many have wondered what the German version of the affair could be. No tale of the U-boat war

Reprinted from Lowell Thomas' RAIDERS OF THE DEEP *by Permission*

could be complete without it. So, from time to time during these thirteen years, I had picked up bits of information concerning the sinking of the *Lusitania*. Pieced together, they provide us with a fairly complete story. Not that it is likely to change our opinions regarding the savageness of the deed; but there is a certain amount of satisfaction in clearing up points that have long been so great a mystery.

Zentner was not on board the *U-20* when she sank the *Lusitania*. During that cruise he remained behind on leave, taking a course in wireless telegraphy. But he was able to tell me about the disastrous event, and I gathered accounts of it from other men to whom Commander Schwieger had told the story. The sum of it all makes a swift, calamitous tale.

The *U-20* stood out to sea on April 30, 1915. Her orders were to patrol the waters to the southwest of Ireland and to enforce the submarine blockade that Germany had declared against England. She was to torpedo any boat she encountered in the zone of the blockade. Apparently it is untrue—in spite of what has often been said, and what most of us thought— that she was sent out with special orders to sink the *Lusitania*. On May 5th the U-boat sank an English sailing ship, and on the next morning sank an English steamer. At noon of the same day she sighted a passenger steamer of the White Star Line, but the ship was too far away to be torpedoed. Later in the afternoon she torpedoed and sank an English steamer. For two days more the *U-20* continued its patrolling cruise off the southwest coast of Ireland. The fog was so dense as to make operations almost useless. No ships were sunk. The oil supply was running low, and only two torpedoes were left. On the morning of the 7th the fog was as dense as ever. The *U-20* turned its nose homeward for Wilhelmshaven and kept its course

until two twenty in the afternoon. The fog by now had lifted a bit.

The following is translated from Commander Schwieger's official log kept aboard the *U-20*. It was given to me by Commander ————, a former companion-in-arms of Schwieger:

2.20 P. M. Directly in front of us I sighted four funnels and masts of steamer at right angles to our course, coming from south-southwest and going toward Galley Head. It is recognized as a passenger steamer.

2.25 Have advanced eleven meters toward steamer, in hope it will change its course along the Irish coast.

2.35 Steamer turns, takes direction to Queenstown, and thereby makes it possible for us to approach it for shot. We proceed at high speed in order to reach correct position.

3.10. Torpedo shot at distance of 700 metres, going 3 meters below the surface. Hits steering centre behind bridge. Unusually great detonation with large cloud of smoke and debris shot above the funnels. In addition to torpedo, a second explosion must have taken place. (Boiler, coal, or powder?) Bridge and part of the ship where the torpedo hit are torn apart, and fire follows.

The ship stops and very quickly leans over to starboard, at the same time sinking at the bow. It looks as though it would capsize in a short time. There is great confusion on board. Boats are cleared and many of them lowered into the water. Many boats, fully loaded, drop down into the water bow- or stern-first and capsize. The boats on the port side cannot be made clear because of the slanting position. At the front of the ship the name *Lusitania* in gold letters can be seen. The chimneys are painted black. The stern flag is not hoisted. The ship was going about twenty miles an hour.

The log, as far as it pertains to the event, closes with an entry that states that the steamer seemed badly hit and sure to sink—which seems to refer to a possible supposition that two torpedoes might be needed to sink so large a ship—and then goes on: "I could not have sent a second torpedo into the crowd.

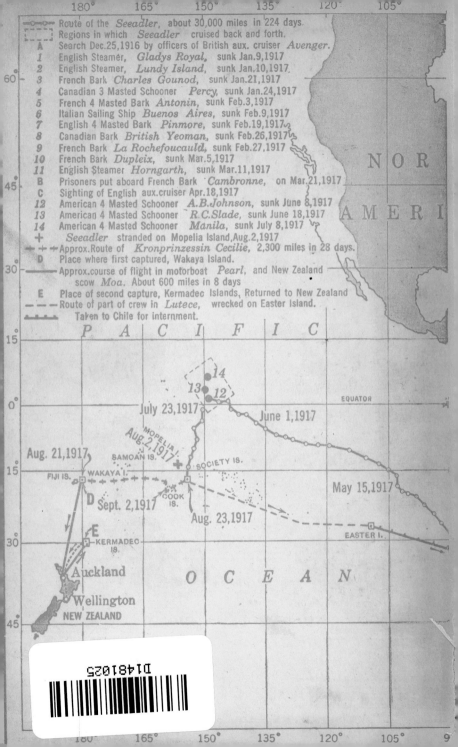

Route of the *Seeadler*, about 30,000 miles in 224 days.
Regions in which *Seeadler* cruised back and forth.
A Search Dec.25,1916 by officers of British aux. cruiser *Avenger.*
1 English Steamer, *Gladys Royal,* sunk Jan.9,1917
2 English Steamer, *Lundy Island,* sunk Jan.10,1917.
3 French Bark *Charles Gounod,* sunk Jan.21,1917
4 Canadian 3 Masted Schooner *Percy,* sunk Jan.24,1917
5 French 4 Masted Bark *Antonin,* sunk Feb.3,1917
6 Italian Sailing Ship *Buenos Aires,* sunk Feb.9,1917
7 English 4 Masted Bark *Pinmore,* sunk Feb.19,1917.
8 Canadian Bark *British Yeoman,* sunk Feb.26,1917.
9 French Bark *La Rochefoucauld,* sunk Feb.27,1917
10 French Bark *Dupleix,* sunk Mar.5,1917
11 English Steamer *Horngarth,* sunk Mar.11,1917
B Prisoners put aboard French Bark *Cambronne,* on Mar.21,1917.
C Sighting of English aux.cruiser Apr.18,1917
12 American 4 Masted Schooner *A.B.Johnson,* sunk June 8,1917
13 American 4 Masted Schooner *R.C.Slade,* sunk June 18,1917
14 American 4 Masted Schooner *Manila,* sunk July 8,1917
+ *Seeadler* stranded on Mopelia Island,Aug.2,1917
+ + +Approx.Route of *Kronprinzessin Cecilie,* 2,300 miles in 28 days.
D Place where first captured, Wakaya Island.
———Approx.course of flight in motorboat *Pearl,* and New Zealand
　　　scow *Moa.* About 600 miles in 8 days
E Place of second capture, Kermadec Islands, Returned to New Zealand
— — —Route of part of crew in *Lutece,* wrecked on Easter Island.
▪▪▪▪▪Taken to Chile for internment.

P A C I F I C

N O R

A M E R I

14
13 *12*
July 23,1917
June 1,1917
EQUATOR

MOPELIA I.
Aug.2,1917
SAMOAN IS.
SOCIETY IS.
May 15,1917

Aug. 21,1917
WAKAYA I.
FIJI IS.
D Sept. 2,1917
COOK IS.
Aug. 23,1917
EASTER I.

E
KERMADEC IS.

Auckland
O C E A N
Wellington
NEW ZEALAND